MW00711603

IDENTITY-FOCUSED ELA TEACHING

Countering the increased standardization of English language arts instruction requires recognizing and fostering students' unique identity construction across different social and cultural contexts. Drawing on current sociocultural theories of identity construction, this book posits that students construct multiple identities through the use of five identity practices: adopting alternative perspectives, exploring connections across people and texts, negotiating identities across social worlds, developing agency through critical analysis, and reflecting on long-term identity trajectories.

Identity-Focused ELA Teaching features classroom activities teachers can use to put these practices into action in ways that re-center implementing the Common Core State Standards; case-study profiles of students and classrooms from urban, suburban, and rural schools adopting these practices; and descriptions of how teachers both support students with this instructional approach and share their own identity-construction experiences with their students. It demonstrates how, as students acquire identity-focused practices through engagements with literature, writing, drama, and digital texts, they gain awareness of the ways exposure to different narratives, beliefs, and perspectives serves to mediate their own and others' identities, leading to different ways of being and becoming over time.

Richard Beach is Professor Emeritus of English Education at the University of Minnesota, USA.

Anthony Johnston is Assistant Professor of Education at the University of Saint Joseph, USA.

Amanda Haertling Thein is Associate Professor of Language, Literacy, and Culture at the University of Iowa, USA.

IDENTITY-FOCUSED ELA TEACHING

A Curriculum Framework for Diverse Learners and Contexts

Richard Beach
Anthony Johnston
Amanda Haertling Thein

NEW YORK AND LONDON

First published 2015
by Routledge
711 Third Avenue, New York, NY 10017

and by Routledge
2 Park Square, Milton Park, Abingdon, Oxon OX14 4RN

Routledge is an imprint of the Taylor & Francis Group, an informa business

© 2015 Taylor & Francis

The right of Richard Beach, Anthony Johnston, and Amanda Haertling
Thein to be identified as authors of this work has been asserted by them
in accordance with sections 77 and 78 of the Copyright, Designs and
Patents Act 1988.

All rights reserved. No part of this book may be reprinted or reproduced
or utilized in any form or by any electronic, mechanical, or other
means, now known or hereafter invented, including photocopying and
recording, or in any information storage or retrieval system, without
permission in writing from the publishers.

Trademark notice: Product or corporate names may be trademarks
or registered trademarks, and are used only for identification and
explanation without intent to infringe.

Library of Congress Cataloging-in-Publication Data
Library of Congress Cataloging in Publication Control Number: 2014037383

ISBN: 978-1-138-81202-4 (hbk)
ISBN: 978-1-138-81203-1 (pbk)
ISBN: 978-1-315-74904-4 (ebk)

Typeset in Bembo
by Apex CoVantage, LLC

Printed and bound in the United States of America by Publishers Graphics,
LLC on sustainably sourced paper.

CONTENTS

PREFACE

The Origins of This Book

This book focuses on fostering students' identity construction and development in English language arts classrooms. Our interest in writing about adopting an identity-focused approach for teaching English language arts originates from several different sources. Given his interest in this issue, Richard taught a graduate research course at the University of Minnesota and UCLA in which students conducted case studies of how individuals' identities influenced their literary or media responses, writing, language use, and social relationships.

Amanda, one of Richard's former students, took this course and later completed her dissertation on students' gender identities in a low-income neighborhood high school. She then teamed up with Richard to conduct a study in the same school of 12th-grade students' responses to multicultural literature. This study found that students' responses to literature reflect their own identity experiences in constructing race, class, and gender difference (Beach, Thein, & Parks, 2008). Anthony, then a doctoral student at the University of California, Berkeley, drew on this study to conduct his dissertation research on 11th-grade students' responses to literature in a low-income school, finding that these students' identities, as shaped by lived-world experiences, influenced their literary responses, writing, and classroom interactions. Amanda continued to conduct research in Pittsburgh and, later, Iowa schools, on the influence of students' identities on their literary responses.

Drawing on this research, in 2012, Richard began working with four teachers at Jefferson High School, a largely White, suburban Minneapolis high school in Bloomington, Minnesota, brainstorming ways to implement an identity-focused curriculum, a project that lasted for two years. To determine how students in these teachers' classes would respond to a curriculum based on an identity-focused approach, he began observing and talking to students in these teachers' classes, as well as analyzing their writing.

Our research and observations of students' positive reactions to an identity-focused curriculum led us to write this book, which includes suggested activities for implementing this curriculum. Rather than focus primarily on these activities, we believe it is important to demonstrate how this curriculum was implemented through descriptions of concrete classroom activities as well as through case-study profiles that include perceptions of participants' engagement with these activities.

The Goal of This Book

This book argues that a primary goal of secondary English language arts (ELA) is to provide a language and a road map for considering how and why identities are constructed. Ideally, students who carry a narrow or limiting identity narrative can, through ELA instruction, re-author the self. To help teachers achieve this goal, we demonstrate how identity construction itself is a curriculum resource for reflexive and reflective purposes.

For the purposes of this book, we go beyond individualistic notions of identity consisting of a single, autonomous self, to define it in terms of adopting and enacting alternative identities in different social worlds. We describe how students in ELA classes in two quite different settings—a Bay Area urban high school, South Bay High, and a suburban Minnesota high school, Jefferson High School—construct their identities through uses of different identity practices constituting their identities in the different social worlds they inhabit. In participating in these social worlds, students develop certain identity practices to address certain challenges. For example, when students recognize that their family and their peer groups have different expectations for their actions, they learn to vary their actions across these different worlds, acquiring the identity practice of negotiating differences between these social worlds, or what we're defining as "figured worlds" (Holland et al., 1998).

This focus on students' identities as constituted by uses of identity practices leads to recommended activities for responding to literature, engaging in drama, writing, language study, and media analysis designed to foster use of these practices constituting what we're defining as an *identity-focused approach* to teaching ELA.

Chapter Overviews

Chapter 1 elaborates our conceptions of identity associated with adopting different identity practices, focusing on five identity practices that serve as the basis of Chapters 3–7:

- Adopting alternative perspectives
- Making connections across people and texts

- Negotiating identities across different social worlds
- Engaging in critical analysis of texts and the world
- Reflecting on one's experiences based on long-term identity trajectories

Through use of these identity practices in interpreting and constructing texts, students generate artifacts that serve to display competence to peers and teachers. For example, through responding to literature or participating in drama activities, students can move into and through alternative worlds, adopting different perspectives and ways of knowing that contribute to their identity experimentation.

Chapter 2 focuses on ways to plan activities for fostering uses of these five practices through interpreting and constructing texts to generate artifacts. We include examples of teachers' planning activities to demonstrate how teachers plan their activities based in their students' particular identities, as well as their school and community contexts. We also cite connections between the activities they are employing and the English Language Arts Common Core State Standards (CCSS) (Council of Chief State School Officers and the National Governors Association, 2010), explaining that by adopting an identity-focused approach, teachers will have a host of opportunities to meet and exceed the CCSS.

Chapters 3–7 each address one of these five identity practices, featuring examples of classroom activities and case-study profiles from South Bay High and Jefferson High School.

Chapter 3 describes how students construct their identities through adopting alternative perspectives or ways of knowing to address the questions: "Who am I?" "Who are you?" and "When and where am I?" by both responding to characters' alternative perspectives and also constructing texts requiring them to adopt alternative perspectives/ways of knowing. We cite examples of students experiencing alternative cultural and historical perspectives through their responses to literature, leading them to recognize the value of different ways of knowing and believing.

In Chapter 4, we describe how students learn to make connections with and across people and texts. This includes descriptions of how urban school students made connections between *The Absolutely True Diary of a Part-Time Indian* (Alexie, 2007) and "partner texts," for example, historical documents about the relationships between Native Americans and Whites, to explore identity issues in their own lives and the characters' in the novel. We also describe activities for making connections related to literary response, drama, writing, and language activities.

Chapter 5 describes activities related to negotiating identities across peer group, family, classroom, sports, workplace, digital, and media worlds according to differences in the practices and norms operating within each of these worlds. We illustrate how students cope with negotiating the competing demands of these worlds through a case-study profile of Alejandra, a student at South Bay High, an undocumented student who is continually negotiating differences between her traditional family world, school spaces, and the world of her more progressive peers. And we cite examples of students engaged in ethnographic writing projects in which they study the culture of a particular site or event to identify the cultural norms and roles operating in that site or event, leading to an understanding of how identities are constituted by adherence to these cultural norms and roles. We also focus on how students construct identities through participation in online worlds such as social networking sites.

In Chapter 6, we describe how students learn to adopt critical stances toward texts and their social worlds, leading them to seek to make changes in the world. Based on the importance of emotions fostering critique, we describe how students such as Jeffrey, an African American male, focused on the topic of racism in a novel, as well as how students engaged in critical analysis of how larger institutional systems shaped characters' identities in literary texts. We also describe a project in which a group of students at Primdale High School (pseudonym), located in Minnesota, wrote a script for a play about the influence of Whiteness on the culture of their school and community, resulting in students changing their perspectives on their own identities as well as, through producing the play, leading others to change their perspectives.

Chapter 7 describes activities for fostering students' reflection on their experiences based on long-term identity trajectories constituting identity development as they acquire certain identity practices over time. We include activities involving analysis of characters' long-term development, as well as ways of responding to and creating autobiographies and biographies portraying development. And we suggest use of e-portfolios to collect student texts to foster reflection on their growth in identity practices over time.

Chapter 8 summarizes key points in the book related to fostering students' identity construction. It also discusses use of formative assessment and feedback to foster students' metacognitive reflection on their development of identity practices over time, as well as the need for ELA teachers to engage in cross-disciplinary curriculum planning with other teachers to encourage school-wide implementation of an identity-focused approach.

In addition to the material in these chapters, we provide additional extensive resources, teacher units, and student work on the book's resource wiki, http://constructingidentities.pbworks.com, for each of the book chapters.

References

Alexie, S. (2007). *The absolutely true diary of a part-time Indian.* Boston: Little Brown.

Beach, R., Thein, A. H., & Parks, D. (2008). *High school students' competing social worlds: Negotiating identities and allegiances in response to multicultural literature.* New York: Routledge.

Council of Chief State School Officers and the National Governors Association. (2010). Common Core State Standards from English Language Arts. Authors. Retrieved from http://www.corestandards.org/ELA-Literacy

Holland, D., Lachicotte, W., Skinner, D., & Cain, C. (1998). *Identity and agency in cultural worlds.* Cambridge, MA: Harvard University Press.

ACKNOWLEDGMENTS

We would like to acknowledge the support provided for writing this book by our editor, Naomi Silverman. We also want to recognize the invaluable participation by our two focal teachers, Rose (pseudonym) of South Bay High and Elizabeth Erdmann of Jefferson High School, and their students; as well as contributions by Jefferson High School teachers Susan Bianchi, David Johnson, Jackie Van Geest, and Kristen Varpness, along with contributions by teachers Jay Ritterson, Steph (pseudonym), and Sam Tanner.

1

INTRODUCTION

What Is Identity-Focused ELA Teaching?

The Trouble With Tre

Tre, an African American, 17-year-old junior, is having a difficult day. Early in class, Tre lays down across two seats and loudly states, "Man, this is too much, I ain't doing this shit." Rose, his teacher, has just distributed a two-page document explaining the final essay assignment responding to *Bless Me, Ultima* (Anaya, 1995), a coming-of-age novel set in New Mexico about a young boy's crisis of faith between his Catholic upbringing and the indigenous beliefs his ancestors held. Tre pushes aside the directions and the outline template and does not look at them again. Later, he joins a circle of chairs for a Socratic Seminar along with nine other students. To prepare for the discussion, students were given a handout with quotes from the book. For each quote, students were asked to write both a comprehension and an analytical response. Tre promptly tosses his handout with the quotes, his journal, and the book on the floor in front of him with a loud smack. He then buries his head in his hands with his face directed toward the floor. The hood on his black North Face jacket is tightly closed with the string drawn. He stays very still like this; it is unclear if he is listening at all.

Six minutes into the Socratic Seminar, the student discussion leader sharply says, "Tre!" hoping to get his view on the quote under discussion. Tre jerks his head up as if he has been awoken, leading to some stifled laughter by the other students. The teacher steps in for the first time in the seminar and calmly asks Tre for his thoughts on a quote related to tensions between believing in a Catholic God while also believing in an indigenous god, the Golden Carp. After some prompting by the teacher, Tre asks a few questions that help him grasp the content of the quote—questions that are essential because he has not read the book. Tre hesitantly begins to provide analysis of the Golden Carp and the Catholic God as being "like the two fishies, the black and the white one, that like, need to be floating around each other?" A young woman named Cat, sitting next to him, says, "Yeah, like the yin-yang thing." Quickly, another African American male student named Amari interjects, saying, "That's just a joke. Tre is just joking." In that moment, Tre's face seems to quickly change twice—first to disappointment, then to resignation. With all eyes on him, Tre quickly elects to acquiesce, giving his "who me?" smile, then he laughs and the class laughs with him. Rose then moves on to get perspectives from other students.

But it was not a joke. It was Tre's one thoughtful, analytic connection he would attempt to make in the twenty-five-minute Socratic, and one of the few he would make that semester. The yin-yang concept could have been a promising line of inquiry, given that the main character finds balance in his life by learning to embrace both belief systems. Since students viewed Tre's comment as a joke, this idea was not pursued. Tre put his head back in his hands and, for the rest of the seminar, was silent.

Tre's story brings to light a number of pedagogical questions. For instance, teachers might wonder how they can convince students like Tre to engage in school reading. Teachers might also wonder how writing tasks like the essay assigned to Tre's class could be constructed in such a way that they excite students rather than create resistance. Finally, teachers might wonder how they can foster safe and generative discussion spaces in which a range of ideas and perspectives are taken seriously and explored. In this book we will suggest that explorations of and answers to of all of these questions—and others—begin with a pedagogical focus on identity work as central to ELA teaching and learning.

Returning to Tre's story, a focus on identity work allows a bigger picture of what was happening in the classroom to come into focus. Within the context of this classroom, Tre's repeated resistance to academic work and his use of jokes and laughter to distract from his lack of preparation positioned him as a "jokester." As Tre repeated this positioning, and as his peers came to recognize and reinforce this positioning, his identity as a "jokester" in this class became "sedimented" or stuck (Holland et al., 1998). The strength of this identity is what kept Tre from succeeding in trying on a new, more academic identity. Further, it kept Tre and his peers from fully exploring a new literary interpretation—one that might have generated rich discussion, engaged writing, and genuine excitement about reading and learning.

In this book we argue that a pedagogical focus on identity can both help students gain a conscious and critical awareness of how they and others are positioned in a range of social situations in the many diverse contexts of their lives and help them transform identities that limit and constrain their learning and their lives. And we argue that, because identities are constructed, performed, and negotiated through language, narrative, discourse, and text, identity work is at the heart of the teaching of ELA.

In the remainder of this chapter we a) define and explain the theory of identity that guides the pedagogical framework we forward in this book, b) provide a detailed discussion of why identity work is central to ELA pedagogy, and c) introduce the five key identity practices that provide the basis for our pedagogical framework.

What Is Identity and Why Does It Matter in Teaching Adolescents?
A Traditional "Individual" View of Identity

The very notion of identity is a relatively recent phenomenon beginning with Greek drama and reflected in Shakespearean characters such as Hamlet, pontificating on his role and purpose in life. From this period to the 20th century, identity was often defined in terms of the metaphor of the "inner" versus "outer" self. In this view, one has a true "inner" self that may or may not align with one's visible, public, "outer" self (Lawler, 2008). In the first part of the 20th century, the Modernist movement in art and literature also promoted an autonomous, stable, individual view of identity and a true inner self that was understood to be continually in opposition to the conforming forces of "outer" society. Remnants of this stable and individual view of identity are still evident in many self-help books as well as in literature units on the "individual versus society" that focus on the dangers of conformity and the search for the true self. This emphasis on individualism also reflects a Western rejection of Eastern values related to the collective, interdependent nature of society. Such differences are reflected in contrasts between the archetypes of the rugged individual found in Hollywood Westerns, for instance, and Japanese samurai film heroes who always operated as a collective group.

What is important to notice in this individual view of identity is that each person is understood as having one true, stable identity that does not shift or change even as one's life circumstances and experiences shift and change. In this view, the authenticity of the identity one projects to the outer world depends on how well one resists societal pressures and how closely that projection matches one's true inner self.

The notion of the autonomous, individual identity is problematic, especially as we consider how it positions adolescents in school contexts. If we imagine each of our students as having just one true, fixed identity, then we are unlikely to pay much attention to the ways in which classroom, school, community, and other sociocultural contexts shape who students are in our classrooms. We might conclude, for instance, that a student "lacks motivation" simply because of her own internal attitudes, applying deficit thinking to fail to notice how cultural expectations have shaped how that student came to see herself at school. Returning to our story of Tre, an individual view of identity might lead his teacher to think that he has always been and will always be an "unmotivated jokester" by nature.

Notions of identity as fixed and predetermined undergird problematic labeling and categorizing of students in schools. For instance, schools routinely label students as "struggling readers" and "behaviorally disabled." Once categorized this way, these labels are difficult to shake. The persistence of these labels reifies two assumptions—first, that students' labels represent intrinsic, permanent qualities; and second, that changing such qualities can only be accomplished through motivation—which students are perceived as lacking. If a student like Tre is not engaged in school or is violating school rules, these actions are attributed solely to the student himself as intrinsically flawed, deeply unmotivated, or both. In the section that follows, we explain how an alternative, sociocultural view of identity can provide a more nuanced view of adolescents' school experiences.

A Sociocultural View of Identity

In this book we draw on an alternative, sociocultural view of identity that emerged from the postmodern movement. The postmodern movement led to questions about a view of identity as individual, singular, and stable and to arguments that such a view ignores the ways in which people and their identities are shaped by social and cultural forces of society. Sociologists like Bourdieu (1984) posited that identities are sometimes collectively shaped by social and cultural constructs such as race, class, and gender. Similarly, Foucault (1994) saw identities as shaped by discourses, or institutionalized ways of knowing and thinking. For example, a person's identity as a lawyer is constructed in part through her ability to use legal discourses. Social psychologists focused on how allegiances to certain groups influenced identities. Sociolinguists examined how language uses and categories—themselves social constructions—shape identities. This phenomenon is evidenced in social class, racial, and regional identities that are marked by dialect difference.

In questioning identity as idiosyncratic and autonomous, and in coming to see identity as shaped by "outer" forces, this "sociocultural" view conceptualizes identity as fluid and multiple. In this view, the binary between "inner" and "outer" identity collapses. People are not born with one stable, findable, "inner" identity. Instead, people construct, perform, and "improvise" identities in light of their cultural histories and in response to current social situations (Holland et al., 1998). Ken Hyland (2012) explains this well. He perceived:

> Identity not as belonging *within* the individual person but *between* persons and *within* social relations; as constituted socially and historically (Vygotsky, 1978). Identity is not the *state* of being a particular person but a *process*, something which is assembled and changes over time throughout interactions with others . . . *who we are*, or rather *who we present ourselves to be*, is an outcome of how we routinely and repeatedly engage in interactions with others on an everyday basis.
>
> *(Hyland, 2012, pp. 2–3)*

People take up "artist," "jokester," "parent," or "teacher" identities through their social relationships with others. As Hull and Katz (2006) note:

> We enact the selves we want to become in relation to others—sometimes in concert with them, sometimes in opposition to them, but always in relation to them. Our sense of self-determination at any given moment is tempered by the constraints of specific social, cultural, and historical contexts, and especially for children and adults who are members of oppressed or disadvantaged groups, these constraints can seem, and can be, overpowering.
>
> *(p. 46)*

And, rather than the notion of the *single*, unitary self, Richard Precht (2011) describes how people may adopt different *states* of the self:

> My corporal self makes me aware that the body in which I am living is really my own body; my locational self tells me where I am at a given time; my perspectivist self tells me that I am the center of the world experienced by me; my "I" as experiential subject tells me that my sensory impressions and feelings are really my own and not those of others; my authorship and supervisory self makes it clear to me that I am the person who has to accept responsibility for my thoughts and actions; my autobiographical self makes sure that I do not step out of my own role and that I experience myself throughout as one and the same person; my self-reflexive self enables me to think about myself and play the psychological game of "I" and "me"; and my moral self works as conscience to tell me what is good and what is bad.
>
> *(pp. 38–39)*

He also notes that there are no clear, clean distinctions between these different selves, only that the fact that we shift between these states suggests that there is no single "self."

In sum, a sociocultural view suggests that identities shift and change as we move through our lives. Further, this view suggests that we perform different identities in response to different social situations. Drawing on this sociocultural view of identity, we define identity in this book as *the performance of practices grounded in a social and cultural history and improvised upon in particular social situations through the positioning of the self and others.*

Our definition highlights the fact that adolescents' identities cannot be defined solely by what we see of them in our classrooms on a day-to-day basis, but instead must be conceptualized as far more complex and nuanced. Viewing identities as performative, fluid, and shaped by previous social and cultural experiences requires us to question why a student may struggle with reading an esoteric poem in an ELA class but have no trouble reading a manual for a complicated video game. We might ask how the task of reading the poem is inaccessible to this student given his lack of knowledge of poetic conventions or the thematic issue at hand, or how the poem challenges his beliefs and assumptions given an unfamiliar cultural context. We might be less quick to assume that this student is simply a "struggling reader," and instead acknowledge that his performance of another equally literate identity outside of the classroom may provide insights into how this student might be more fully engaged in the ELA classroom.

Our definition of identity also poses a challenge related to some of the dominant means by which adolescents are identified and understood by adults and society at large. Although adolescence is commonly thought of as a developmental and biological phase that everyone must pass through on the way to adulthood, it is important to recognize that adolescence is in fact a culturally constructed category that was—in essence—coined by developmental psychologist G. Stanley Hall (1904/2012) in the early 20th century. Since that time, common assumptions about who adolescents are and what they experience have solidified into a set of monolithic and static beliefs about adolescents' identities. For instance, it is commonly assumed that adolescents must rebel against adults; rely upon peer networks; experience prototypical crises related to issues such as sex, drug and alcohol abuse, bullying, and suicide; and maintain a myopic and self-centered view of the world (Lesko, 2012). Further, adolescents are typically imagined to be highly impressionable, incomplete people, who will not become complete until they reach adulthood. A sociocultural view of identity, which rejects fixed identity categories, compels us to rethink this universal view of adolescent identity and asks us to imagine the many complex, socially, culturally, and historically driven ways that adolescents experience life and perform identities. Moreover, such a view asks us to view adolescents as complete human beings with experiences, beliefs, and opinions that matter.

In sum, a sociocultural view of identity requires a more complex and nuanced view of adolescents, their capabilities, and their interactions with texts than does an individual view of identity. Moreover, it provides a counter to a number of limitations that an individual view of identity poses. In this book we argue that taking up a sociocultural view of identity in approaching your students—and helping your students understand this view of identity—can open up new possibilities for understanding and critiquing language, narrative, discourse, and text as they position and shape our possibilities.

Why Is Identity Work Central to ELA Instruction?

From a sociocultural perspective, identities are performed, mediated, sedimented, and disrupted through language, narrative, discourse, embodied performances, and digital forms of communication. Therefore, we argue that the ELA classroom is always already a space for identity work. Bringing identity work to light opens up a host of possibilities for helping students become more conscious of the ways their identities and those of others are positioned by text, discourse, narrative, and so forth in their everyday lives. Such consciousness allows for imagining new ways of constructing, responding to, and critiquing texts that might reposition identities. Further, focusing on identity in the ELA classroom allows students to see how various uses of texts, language, discourse, and narrative matter in material ways to their own lives and the lives of those around them. When ELA matters to students, their engagement and motivation increases.

Identity work is central to reading and responding to literature. As students respond to literature, drama, and film, they adopt characters' and authors' perspectives as constructed through language, narratives, genres, and audio/images/videos. Bringing awareness to this process allows students to become conscious and critical of ways that language, narratives, genres, and images mediate characters' identities.

For instance, in research that coauthor Amanda and her colleagues (Thein, Oldakowski, & Sloan, 2010) conducted in a socioeconomically diverse school outside of Pittsburgh, they found that learning how identities are shaped through social, cultural, and institutional forces allowed students to better understand character development in *To Kill a Mockingbird* (Lee, 1988). Students noticed, for example, that Calpurnia, an African American housekeeper in a White household, performed different language variations, dispositions, and even seemed to hold different beliefs in her social worlds outside of her work in the Finch's White household. Students were able to link these differences to Calpurnia's different roles, responsibilities, and identities relative to the competing norms of her various social worlds. Understanding Calpurnia's socioculturally fluid identity, then, allowed students to develop a far more nuanced understanding not only of Calpurnia's character but also of some of the racial and social class tensions that are central to the questions and themes Lee poses in the novel.

Identity work is central to understanding the social and cultural ways that language is constructed and the various purposes it serves. Godley and Minnici (2008) found that by focusing on identity construction in a unit on vernacular language variation, the primarily African American students in the class they studied were not only able to locate and understand variation between African American Vernacular English and Standard English, but were also able to pinpoint grammatical and linguistic nuances between forms of African American Vernacular English spoken in different neighborhoods in their city. Students noticed that this variation marked identity performances that aligned people with particular groups and disaffiliated them with others.

Identity work is central to understanding how writing and speaking construct and shape experiences. Through their writing and speaking, students draw on the experiences of their "autobiographical self" to construct a "discoursal self" (Ivanič, 1998, p. 24) through language, narratives, genres, and audio/images/videos (Ringer, 2013, p. 273). For example, via their classroom discussions, students and teachers construct their identities through speech acts of questioning, requesting, challenging, inviting, doubting, and so forth (Zimmerman, 1998). By sharing oral and written narratives about their lives, students portray their past experiences from their present perspective in ways that enact their identities. As Raul Sanchez (2012) notes about written autobiographies:

> Identity is an event, and events are acts of writing. Identity is thus an act—the act of writing. And the writing subject is an act of identity formation, which is to say that it is an act of writing. Thus, identity lets us equate the writing-subject and the act of writing.
>
> *(p. 245)*

The potential for the ELA classroom to be a space where students can engage in ideas, identities, ideologies, and narratives that both reflect and challenge those of their everyday lives is worth exploring. The ELA classroom is one of the few spaces in which youth, particularly youth who are marginalized in most school spaces, have the opportunity to seriously experiment with different, alternative identities. Such experimentation involves exploring different ways of expressing and sharing both ideas and emotions, as well as grappling with the complexities and ambiguities of what it means to be human. In a sense, this has always been the purview of the ELA classroom; however, we argue that this benefit of engaging in identity practices is increasingly absent, particularly in schools with marginalized, underserved youth. In addition, we argue that students need a language to think about identity as a construct and practices to gain the skills and knowledge necessary to develop the sort of complex, multiple, improvisatory, and flexible identity necessary for both academic success in college and for the labor market they will soon enter.

How Can Identity Work Increase Engagement and Motivation?

When identity work is central to ELA teaching, students' engagement and motivation increases. Too many students are still disengaged with school, as reflected in relatively high dropout rates as well as the "achievement gap," particularly for students of color who will, by 2030, comprise the majority of students in schools (this is already the case in California as of 2014). Recognizing the diversity of students entails drawing on knowledge of differences in students' cultural backgrounds and communities that shape their identities. Recognizing how some Latino students' experiences with moving between their migrant family background and their school worlds is itself an identity competency that teachers can draw on to foster learning. Additionally, we encourage an individualized approach to thinking in terms of identity. Too often, teachers make assumptions about students based on gender, race, class, or sexual orientation in ways that undermine the very intent behind noticing the "diversity" each student brings to a classroom. By focusing on identity construction, ELA teachers can enhance students' sense of self-confidence, agency, and social skills—all of which contribute to improving students' engagement and motivation to learn.

One explanation for the lack of engagement in middle and high school is that, given the emphasis on the use of "teacher-proof curricula" linked to standards-based assessments and the push for preparing students for mandated testing, teachers have little autonomy in employing activities they believe will engage their students.

Moreover, this focus on teaching "content" to prepare for tests has shifted attention away from fostering competencies associated with engagement in learning. This shift ironically reduces engagement and student performance on tests. As a research review on the influence of a focus on social-emotional learning on students' academic achievement noted:

> If one could develop students' competencies in the areas of self-awareness, self-management, social awareness, relationship skills, and responsible decision-making, then students would engage in more positive social behaviors and have fewer problems with misconduct and less emotional distress, resulting in more engagement in the classroom and hence better test scores and grades.
>
> *(Farrington et al., 2012, p. 49)*

Teachers are more likely to give students whom they perceive to display positive social behaviors higher evaluations or grades than students without positive social behaviors (Cross & Frary, 1999).

Providing students with opportunities to display competence to their peers as having identities with expertise serves to enhance their engagement in school. For instance, students use digital video production as a resource to portray and represent themselves in different ways for different audiences within social worlds (Hull & Katz, 2006). By doing so, students are then recognized for their productions as a display of competence associated with positive uptake from audiences who perceive them as being effective video producers.

By developing metacognitive awareness of how narrative, writing, language, embodied performances, and digital communication work to construct identities, students can begin to perceive themselves not simply as autonomous entities, with fixed identities grounded in the developmental phase of adolescence, but as people who construct and perform various identities through language, narratives, genres, and images—in essence, they can begin to understand how they are constituting a "self as author" (Ivanič, 1998, p. 25). Further, such a metacognitive awareness can help students see how different disciplinary discourses construct different ways of knowing, thinking, and performing identities (Gee, 2011) across school subjects. For example, students might notice how, by adopting the language of psychology, they are also adopting particular attitudes and beliefs and performing particular identities in relationship to other people's behaviors. Finally, a metacognitive awareness of identity work allows students to acquire "academic mindsets" or "beliefs, attitudes, or ways of perceiving oneself in relation to learning and intellectual work that support academic performance" (Farrington et al., 2012, p. 28).

A review of research indicates that four of these mindsets—the belief that "I belong in this academic community; my ability and competence grow with my effort; I can succeed at this; and this work has value for me" (p. 28)—foster perseverance or grit in achieving academically. For example, students who experience a sense of belonging in a classroom community are more motivated and have a higher sense of being competent than students who lack this sense of belonging (Osterman, 2000). And students who assume that their abilities and competencies are fixed, and therefore assume that they can't succeed in certain activities, are less motivated and do less well in school than students who believe that they can succeed and improve in their ability (Farrington et al., 2012).

How Is Identity-Focused ELA Different From Other Models of ELA? How and Why Versus What One Teaches

Identity-focused ELA is a larger pedagogical focus or framework for approaching ELA. It does not preclude reader-response, critical literacy, inquiry-based approaches, or even some versions of formalism, for instance. Instead, an identity-focused approach to ELA reframes these common paradigms and instructional approaches, focusing these approaches on identity work and students' identity needs. In addition to reframing common approaches to ELA, our framework provides a new language and discourse for thinking about the work of ELA, which is leveraged by sociocultural theories of identity. For instance, while current approaches to ELA position the text as the central focus of learning, our framework centers learning recursively on both the student and the text.

Teaching and learning therefore starts with the student as she is positioned and positions herself in a specific community and school context, moves to her engagement with text, and then returns to the student. In sum, our framework is one that refocuses, bolsters, and builds upon other approaches to ELA. But, most importantly, it suggests a new stance toward students, one that makes clear that *how* and *why* a teacher teaches is at least as important as *what* she teaches.

How a teacher teaches refers to adopting certain identities associated with building supportive relationships with students or modeling identity practices, for example, demonstrating adoption of alternative perspectives. Because students acquire identity practices through use of those practices, how a teacher adopts and models the practices plays a key role in fostering their use.

And *how* a teacher teaches influences how students' see that teacher as a person with whom they have some attachment that motivates them to learn. As Geert Kelchtermans (2009) notes:

> Implicit in the claim "how I teach is the message" is the acknowledgement of teaching as a relational, social and public act. The teacher (educator) wants to be seen by the students in a particular way, but at the same time his/her ideas about him/herself as a teacher (educator) are influenced by what others—in this case their students—think about him/her. The way teachers understand themselves as teachers thus matters, yet this to a large extent is influenced by how others see him/her or what others say about him/her as a teacher (educator).
>
> *(p. 262)*

Why teachers teach refers to how teachers make decisions about their actions for interacting with or judging their students. Such decisions reflect teachers' beliefs about teaching and students—beliefs that play a significant role in teacher identity (Kelchtermans, 2009). For example, both of the teachers featured in this book, Rose (pseudonym), a teacher in an urban Bay Area school, South Bay High (SBH), and Elizabeth Erdmann, a teacher in a suburban school, Jefferson High School in Bloomington, Minnesota (JHS), avoided adopting an authoritative, rule-bound identity. This reflects their belief in the importance of establishing positive, supportive relationships with students. As Elizabeth noted:

> There are things as a teacher that I like to do and things that I don't like to do. Like, I really don't like saying to students, "take your hat off" or "put your phone away" or managing people's behaviors as much as having a conversation or having them do something. . . . I don't like being confrontational. I don't want to create a culture where I'm the enemy.

A Change in Stance: Helping Carlos Resist the Resistant Reader Label

To illustrate the importance of the how and why of teaching, we cite the example of Carlos, another student who, like Tre, had been positioned by himself and others as a struggling reader. Carlos's story illustrates how a change in Rose's *stance* toward his identity and how Carlos's perception of Rose's identity engaged him in ways that enhanced his literacy learning.[1]

At the start of the semester, during a unit on *Bless Me, Ultima* (Anaya, 1995), Carlos, a 16-year-old Latino male, was recognized as a happily resistant reader by his peers, positioning himself as someone who seemed to enjoy finding humorous ways to display his resistance to reading (such as making jokes during discussions of the book). This posture was rewarded socially by his peers, but it also meant he was failing the class. On a survey about his literacy experiences, Carlos expressed that he rarely reads books assigned in school and never reads outside of school for pleasure other than gaming manuals and magazines. In class, Carlos's position as a resistant reader facilitated his social relationships with his peers, who enjoyed his sense of humor and the way his very presence gave them a modicum of confidence about their own fragile academic identities.

Carlos had been absent for a week, and during that time the class was reading Sherman Alexie's (2007) young adult novel, *The Absolutely True Diary of a Part-Time Indian*. When Carlos returned to the class, he discreetly mentioned to the teacher that he had read the entire book in three days when he was home sick. Initially his teacher, Rose, did not believe Carlos, given his history as someone who liked to joke around and as someone who did little academic work. However, after answering a few questions about later sections in the novel, it was clear that Carlos had, in fact, read the entire book—and it was also evident that he had been deeply engaged in the reading, because he had read the book quickly and could recall specific details well.

Anthony, as a co-teacher with Rose, was giving a lecture that day on the importance of reading a novel in ways that allow for the sort of deep engagement with the text that Carlos experienced. So, during the lecture, he illustrated this sort of engaged reading by recognizing and celebrating Carlos as someone who had read the entire book in only a few days. The class reaction included incredulity and also applause. Carlos, however, quickly denied having read the book; he jumped up and stated, "No! I didn't read that book! I was just playing about that!" But his blushing and grin gave him away, and he was clearly pleased that he had been singled out for this academic achievement. His friends in the class jokingly teased him about trying to deny it.

Over the next few weeks, Carlos would become seen as someone whom other students could rely on to explain different parts of the book. When a student did not read, or could not remember a detail, Carlos was often approached for help before students asked the teacher. In an interview with Anthony a few weeks after this event, Carlos explained his initial resistance to being seen as an engaged reader, saying, "Because that's not me."

This statement, and Tre's acquiescence in the above example, suggests that students often need little coercion toward positioning themselves in limiting ways. However, it was pointed out to Carlos that he was, in fact, the one who had read the book in three days, so, in fact, *was* an engaged reader. He smiled and said he felt proud of that—and said that it was his first time he had read an entire book in such a short time and that he felt "lost in the book." This new feeling provided Carlos with not only a new discourse offered by Sherman Alexie, but the sense of accomplishment and the recognition he received gave Carlos a new discourse with which to "author" himself. Carlos actively challenged his resistant reader identity and, when given the chance to be reflexive about this move, saw his academic identity in a new light. As one might expect, Carlos continued to enact the identity of being a class clown and a resistant reader at times, but his new identity as an engaged reader whom others could rely on for information about the novel was often present as well. Carlos would earn a B in the class and, for the first time since entering high school, pass all of his classes that semester.

Carlos and Tre's stories highlight an all too familiar tendency of labeling, sorting, and ranking that leads to a type of in-class tracking (Oakes, 1985) even in schools like this one, where tracking was not part of the school's structure or value system. Faced with the teacher's apprenticeship of observation dilemma (Lortie, 1975) and the student's experiences of being labeled in both official ("below basic") and unofficial (resistant student) ways, the tendency to marginalize and limit adolescent identity seems inescapable. However, as Carlos's story shows us, given the right structures, activities, and supports, ELA *in particular* can be an opportune space for all participants to challenge these limiting identity narratives we bring to the classroom.

What Does a Change in Stance Look Like?

First and foremost, changing your stance toward your students and their identity work means creating a classroom space that supports students in experimenting with different identities. For most of her students, Rose's ELA class was a safe haven. Rose elected to handle issues of discipline through building relationships and using humor rather than doling out consequences, and students knew that they were cared for and had freedom to "be themselves." This established a relaxed atmosphere that was often funny, at times heated, usually loud, and rarely formal. The relaxed standards and absence of punishment and sanctions for unwanted behavior may have benefitted students like Carlos (and perhaps not Tre), but an unintended byproduct was a lack of rigor, discipline, and time on task found in a more structured academic setting. Aware that teaching is often a process of picking and choosing one's battles, Rose elected to apply culturally competent norms for behavior (often in ways that were at odds with school rules) so that students experienced a safe classroom space to display competence. Rose leveraged the students' sense of ownership of the classroom space to push students in individual ways to experience academic success.

The fact that Rose was willing to build supportive relationships with her students was critical to fostering their positive identity construction. Essential to students' success in schools is the degree to which they experience both a sense of belonging in a school through meaningful, caring relationships with teachers—a sense of belonging that has a strong influence on their self-perceptions of their identities—as well as how they assume others perceive them (Chhuon & Wallace, 2012; Nakkula & Toshalis, 2006).

When students experience a sense of belonging in a classroom, it serves as a "space of authoring" (Holland et al., 1998) in that they perceive themselves as serving as peer-teachers contributing to co-construction of knowledge in that classroom. Being perceived as valuable resources by their peers serves as a display of competence that can bolster self-confidence. For example, in playing video games, students may be constructed as novices or experts through displays of competence. At the same time, students can serve as resources for others in ways that define their identities as mentors or collaborative team members (Sjöblom & Aronsson, 2013). Constructing these identity positionings through game play therefore involves acquiring

> [p]ractices in which participants make themselves available to each other as skilled and knowledgeable players in a specific site and medium, but also how these negotiations of status and central positions within a community of players are essential for understanding young people's orientations towards learning and identity in relation to a specific field of practice.
>
> *(Sjöblom & Aronsson, 2013, p. 182)*

Giving students opportunities to collaboratively design their own learning experiences (selecting texts they want to read, designing a final exam that they want to take, choosing themes from books they care about, having freedom to select from a variety of modes of acquiring skills or online content) is important—it allows students to perceive school less as something that is being done to them and more as something that they feel ownership of and therefore care about enough to fully engage. Through such co-planning with students, students acquire a sense of ownership of their learning that builds on and allows them to display their unique identity competencies.

Shifting Your Identity as a Teacher

Your own identity as you position yourself in relation to your students will become important as you move toward an identity-focused approach. While teachers often position their identities in ways that reify them as adults who are separate from their adolescent students (Lewis & Finders, 2002), an identity-focused approach to ELA that views students as complex and complete people negotiating a range of identities will ask you to question such tidy binaries. When you view your students as more than just a universal group of adolescents, you raise their status. They become equal participants with you in the process of identity work. As such, you will also need to be open to sharing your own identity work with students. As Jane Danielewicz (2001) notes, "[W]hat makes someone a good teacher is not methodology, or even ideology. It requires engagement with identity, the way individuals conceive of themselves so that teaching is a state of being, not merely ways of acting or behaving" (quoted in Pardo, 2013, p. 2).

Tre and Carlos's teacher, Rose, modeled her own identity work—work that influenced her students' willingness to engage with her in identity-focused ELA. Rose was in her third year as a teacher at the time of the study, but she was deemed a veteran on the school's young teaching staff, in part because she came to the profession later in life than most new teachers do. Like many in her position, she was a White female, but she did not regard herself as such, nor did the students. Her identity as a lesbian who identified as gender queer, coupled with her imposing presence and many tattoos (including on her neck and hands), challenges the identity narrative many likely have of a prototypical White woman teacher.

She was also very warm, maternal, quick to smile, and had a bawdy sense of humor the students enjoyed—traits that influenced her students' own practices. While her appearance could be unsettling to some parents, it was quickly apparent that her identity and appearance lent themselves to building relationships across difference, since many students viewed her as marginalized from the dominant White culture in some of the same ways that they were. In one sense, Rose herself is representative of the thrust of this text. Calling her a "White woman teacher" completely obscures Rose's complex identity—a former truck driver, a poet, someone who was frustrated with the school's administration, a caretaker for at-risk LGBTQ youth, a master's student, someone who was raised working class with government assistance, and someone who requested she not be referred to as "Ms." in this book.

It's important to note that engaging in your own identity work with your students is not about exposing every aspect of your personal life. Instead it is about treating your students as equal human beings who deserve your full engagement in the work of ELA. That means that rather than coming to class with specific lessons that you want to teach students about identity, you will need to come to class with deeply felt questions that you genuinely hope to explore with students—questions about which you do not already have answers!

With this in mind, this book offers not a curriculum guide or methodological approach, but instead, a pedagogical framework focused on the incorporation of five key identity practices into the everyday work of the ELA classroom. In the next section we briefly explain each of these practices. Chapters 3–7 provide detailed descriptions, classroom examples, and instructional ideas related to each of these practices.

Definitions: Identity Practices and Competencies

This book advocates changing the talk about identity in schools and in classrooms. Given school's history of assessing, labeling, sorting, and streamlining students based on antiquated understandings of identity, there is much work to be done. However, in many segments of society, identity as a theoretical construct has changed immensely. Primarily, identity is not viewed as fixed, predetermined, or stable, but rather as something multiple, fluid, and "in process."

Ironically, the time in life when identities seem the most in flux is while young people are in schools—a space whose structures and routines impede this important developmental process. However, the thrust of this book is that literacy engagements can provide both a space to encourage new understandings of identity and practices to support identity exploration.

By *identity practices*, we mean those specific *actions* students employ to acquire *competencies*, defined as those abilities, knowledge, and skills constituting identity construction (Scollon, 2001). For example, students engage in the identity practice of establishing relationships with peers through social interaction with those peers. They acquire the competencies of supporting, sharing experiences or empathizing with, and commending peers in ways that constitute their identities as friends.

People therefore construct their identities through acquiring and employing these identity practices—as is the case with you as a teacher employing the practices of teaching to construct your teacher identity. These practices are mediated through uses of language, embodied performances, texts, images, and so on, practices whose meanings are understood by participants of certain "historically contingent, socially enacted, culturally constructed 'worlds'" (Holland et al., 1998, p. 7). As Norris (2011) notes:

> Identity is embedded and (co)produced in . . . the *social-time-place* of a particular social actor together with other social actors, together with and within historical time, together with cultural tools, and together with and within the environment.
>
> *(p. 30)*

Take, for example, the identity practice of negotiating identity across different social worlds. Students learn to adopt and enact different identities as they enter into new social worlds, leading to their being recognized by members of those social worlds as someone with the abilities, knowledge, and skills valued in that world (Wenger, 1998). For example, Carlos experienced an identity shift over the course of the semester that was spurred by a change in the identity practices he displayed in Rose's classroom. As a result, he was seen as a competent reader by his peers, and therefore a resource for knowledge about a particular book.

Because of his willingness to adopt the identity of an active reader consistent with academic expectations operating in the world of Rose's classroom, Carlos became recognized as not only someone who read the novel but also as someone who was competent in deeply engaging in a novel and in being able to recall and interpret events from that novel. Carlos was able to display competence because Rose created a classroom context that promoted open-ended discussion as well as supportive feedback so that his peers perceived him as someone who could share knowledge about the book. Carlos then had the support and safety necessary to embrace a new identity related to this display of competence.

At the same time, we recognize that acquiring competencies is a long-term developmental process and does not presuppose that once one is "competent," such development ends. Given his success in passing all of his classes for the first time in high school, it is likely that Carlos will continue to enact his identity as active reader consistent with the expectations of Rose's classroom world and future worlds, which will lead to development of competency as an engaged reader.

Definitions: Interpreting and Constructing Texts

In ELA classrooms, students engage in identity work through *interpreting and constructing texts*, texts that include language, events, performances, or print/digital/video texts. Through his interpretation of *The Absolutely True Diary of a Part-Time Indian* (Alexie, 2007), Carlos not only acquired information about the novel that he could then share with his peers, but he also learned to interpret some of the identity themes in the novel. Taking his cue from Alexie's use of cartoons in the novel, Carlos designed a comic book in which he explored the question, *What makes a healthy family?* This text then became an artifact that displayed his competency as both a cartoonist and also a critical thinker interested in the notion of what constitutes healthy families.

Definitions: Artifacts/Display of Competence

Students generate *artifacts*—such as texts, videos/images, objects, performances, or exhibitions—as *displays of competence* demonstrating use of certain identity practices (Pahl & Rowsell, 2010). Display of competence through sharing of artifacts is an important component of our curriculum framework outlined in this chapter. Central to experimenting with new identities is recognition of competence; students need to be recognized by their teachers and peers as people who are able to effectively employ certain actions or resources. As Laura VanDerPloeg (2012) notes, "[I]dentity relies on recognition. We say that someone 'has' a certain identity because the person is recognized by others as being 'that sort of person'" (p. 19). For example, a student who performs various alternative roles in a drama activity becomes known as "someone who can act."

When students are recognized for their competencies, they gain a sense of self-confidence and agency, as well as new beliefs about identities that might be possible. Displaying competence in the ELA classroom can then lead students to see themselves as people who are insightful readers, engaging writers, skillful discussion facilitators, versatile actors, and creative digital authors, to name a few.

To be recognized and identified as people with these identities, students need audiences—opportunities to actively display their competence to their teachers, their peers, and other adults (Czikszentmihalyi & Larson, 1984). Students are often already familiar with displaying competencies and being recognized for those competencies in other areas of life. For instance, students display physical competence on the soccer field and artistic competence in an art or music class. Opportunities to display competence are rare in academic classrooms, unfortunately, because students in these settings are typically asked to be passive participants in teacher-directed instruction (Czikszentmihalyi & Larson, 1984).

Identity-Focused ELA Instruction: Five Key Practices

Our identity-focused ELA framework revolves around five overlapping identity practices we consider to be the most relevant for constructing identities in the ELA classroom context, recognizing that there are a myriad of other identity practices involved in constructing identities:

- Adopting alternative perspectives
- Making connections across people and texts
- Negotiating identities across different social worlds
- Engaging in critical analysis of texts and the world
- Reflecting on identity development over time

In the sections that follow, we describe in greater detail the five identity practices we perceive to be most relevant to constructing identities in the context of ELA classrooms; we devote separate chapters to each of these practices.

Identity Practice 1: Adopting Alternative Perspectives (Chapter 3)

As students begin to recognize how their identities are shaped by participation in a certain world, they may also discover that being a member of that world entails adopting particular ways of perceiving and knowing valued in that world. Paula Moya (2005) posits that, since all knowledge is situated, identity serves as an epistemic resource for knowledge construction:

> Identities provide us with particular perspectives on shared social worlds . . . what we 'know' is intimately tied up with how we conceptualize that world and who we understand ourselves to be in it. Our conceptual frameworks are thus inseparable from how we comprehend ourselves in terms of gender, culture, race, sexuality, ability, religion, age, and profession—even when we are not consciously aware of how these aspects of ourselves affect our points of view. Our identities thus shape our interpretive perspectives and bear on how we understand both our everyday experiences and the more specialized and expert knowledge we encounter and produce through our research and teaching.
>
> *(p. 102)*

For example, when Kevin, a 10th-grade student in a school outside of Pittsburgh, began to interrogate the social world of his religious community through a blogging project related to social worlds, he learned that membership in that community involved adopting certain beliefs in order to acquire an identity as a member.

At the same time, as Kevin began to notice his own movement across different worlds, he recognized that there are different perspectives associated with being in different worlds. He noticed that his beliefs about science and faith differed as he identified as a member of his religious community and as a member of a secular, academic community. Noticing these alternative perspectives led Kevin to weigh the merits of each perspective for framing issues and problems and for entertaining various solutions.

The goal of experimenting with and "trying on" alternative perspectives and forms of knowledge is not to change students' beliefs per se, nor is it to move students toward necessarily "better" perspectives. Instead, the goal is to encourage students to be flexible in their thinking and to more thoroughly understand the array of perspectives that exist related to any issue. Experiencing these competing perspectives through their interactions with peers and teachers leads students to determine which beliefs about the self they wish to accept, creating tensions between beliefs about the self they subscribe to versus alternative beliefs that challenge these notions(Perry, 1970).

Becoming open to considering alternative beliefs, perspectives, and attitudes also allows students to see new possibilities for their identities. For example, a student who experiments with a feminist critical perspective might begin to interrogate the kinds of gender role assumptions that shape her self-perception and identity. She may then decide that she sees strength and agency in some of her gendered practices and subsequent positionings, and she may simultaneously choose to shift other practices to position herself in new identities that grant her different degrees of agency.

Identity Practice 2: Making Connections Across People and Texts (Chapter 4)

Another practice related to identity construction in the ELA classroom involves making connections across people, events, and texts (Beach et al., 2014). Given that students construct their identities through their social interactions with others, their ability to make connections with others is central to their identity construction. Based on his interviews with students in a high school in Austin, Texas, Robert Crosnoe (2011) found that the extent to which students had a lot of friends in the school was central to their sense of fitting in or not fitting in to the school culture. Students drew on their peer-group friends for judgments about their own and others' identities.

We also distinguish an identity-focused approach from other current approaches to teaching ELA. For example, we build on and extend a reader-response approach to emphasize the need to not only draw on students' own background experience and knowledge to apply to responding to literature, but to also have students describe how their experiences in responding to texts relate to their own identity construction (Sumara, 1998).

In the semester that Anthony spent in Rose's classroom, he witnessed two different pedagogical approaches to literacy instruction. When students read *Bless Me, Ultima* (Anaya, 1995), the students engaged in a relatively traditional approach to literature instruction, including weekly quizzes about the reading, guided questions to aid comprehension, vocabulary development, a New Criticism approach to literary analysis, and the highly scaffolded writing of a five-paragraph essay as a final assessment. However, in the second half of the semester, Rose employed a reader-response approach (Rosenblatt, 1995) to Sherman Alexie's (2007) young adult novel, *The Absolutely True Diary of a Part-Time Indian*, described above, coupled with a culturally relevant, student-centered and project-based pedagogy.

Anthony and Rose collaborated to develop this curriculum, which was intended to create conditions for adolescents to share reflections on their identity construction through literacy activities. Students came to Rose's class with a range of experiences in negotiating competing demands of their family, school, peer-group, neighborhood, and workplace worlds. Rose drew on these experiences in providing instruction focused on helping students understand the actions and resources that are involved as they negotiate their identities across these different worlds. These activities included sharing a reading artifact—a piece of text that students brought to the class that they saw as informing their development as individuals. Another activity involved guided writing on prompts that encouraged deep and personal responses (e.g., what were you scared of as a child? what keeps you awake at night? what makes you happiest?). These writings were treated as authentic, legitimate texts that could be placed in conversation with Alexie's novel.

Building on Sumara's (1998) approach to literacy instruction, the intention of these activities, writings, and discussions of the novel was to create a shared literacy experience wherein the narratives of the students, the classroom, and the novel could all be placed in conversation, allowing students to explore their authentic questions about identity construction related to the novel.

The final project was called the Touchstone Text and involved a presentation (in a format selected by the student) of a thoughtful, nuanced, and clear development of a line of thinking around a concept of great interest to the student. While the project was not intended to be the student's "final word" on his chosen concept, it was intended to present the audience with an advanced interpretive stance around a particular idea that struck the student as he read the novel or that he brought to the reading in advance. Carlos's comic book in which he described two families, one healthy and the other unhealthy, as he explored what were the indicators of each, was one example. The curriculum described was tailored to create ideal conditions for students to "try on" various ideologies and discourses and to display and sanction the narratives they carry as classroom texts.

Identity Practice 3: Negotiating Identities Across Different Social Worlds (Chapter 5)

Another identity practice involves students' ability to adopt different identities across the school, peer-group, home/family, community, workplace, or virtual spaces (Beach et al., 2014; Beach, Thein, & Parks, 2008). As they move across social worlds or spaces, students assume different identities that are shaped by the norms and expectations operating in each particular social world or space. As Lin (2008) notes: "Who I am or what I make out my identity to be (to myself and others) at a certain moment (which can be relatively transient or lengthened) seems to be always situated in a consideration of *where I am speaking from and to whom*" (p. 203). In interacting with her teachers in the classroom, for instance, a student takes up a different identity than when she's interacting with peers in the lunchroom.

These are often discussed as "figured worlds" (Holland et al., 1998), worlds that are not pre-established, static entities but rather are constructed by their members given their particular knowledge, interests, beliefs, goals, and practices in which they engage in the said world. These worlds are therefore continually shifting as membership changes across time and, subsequently, as the practices and values of that social world change. At the same time, elements of these worlds (roles, general activities, scripts) remain relatively static due to the historical role the "figured world" has played. The ways that an urban high school classroom is both similar and different from thirty years ago and today is a vivid example of this. For example, as described in Chapter 1, Rose's classroom is a "figured world" with its own unique norms and expectations that were constructed by Rose and her students as a relatively safe space for engaging in identity experimentation, and yet, who the teacher was, the general talk about teaching and learning, what the daily routines consisted of, and the positions that students took were informed by the historical and social understanding of the classroom space.

Identity Practice 4: Engaging in Critical Analysis of Texts and the World (Chapter 6)

Another key practice we discuss in this book involves adopting critical stances on text and lived worlds through challenging status quo, "commonsense" assumptions that shape people's or characters' beliefs and actions. For example, in the South Bay High AP English Literature class, students grappled with the ways literature explored universal questions. Eduardo, a male Latino student, posed the question: what does it mean to be a "man" so that you're not reifying a macho, sexist, or homophobic image in a Latino culture? The young man then read three books that dealt explicitly with male identity—Hemingway's *The Sun Also Rises*, Twain's *The Adventures of Huckleberry Finn*, and Marquez's *Chronicle of a Death Foretold*. Next, he wrote an extensive essay engaging all three authors in a dialogue with his own notions of being a man as articulated by the messages he carried from his own cultural and social context. When such questions become central to the curriculum, students begin to adopt a critical stance on how social and cultural forces shape and limit identities. Such an understanding can lead students to critical and complex understandings of identity construction.

Adopting a critical stance builds on our first identity practice of adopting cultural, historical, and institutional perspectives on how cultures and institutions shape identities. Adopting these perspectives leads to acquiring what Ladson-Billings (2010) defines as a "sociopolitical consciousness" that encourages students to critique some of the limitations of their own or others' cultural, historical, and institutional perspectives. For example, socioeconomically privileged White students might examine their own upbringing, noticing some of the limitations of "Whiteness" and middle-class cultural norms (Payne & Laugher, 2013).

Identity Practice 5: Reflecting on Identity Development Over Time (Chapter 7)

The final identity practice we focus on in this book involves reflecting on one's ability to employ certain identity practices associated with those competencies constituting identity construction. By engaging in reflection, students identify their successful acquisition of certain competencies as well as competencies requiring further work. Such reflection requires a metacognitive ability to step back and identify specific instances of their strengths and weaknesses, something that can be a challenge for students.

Adopting an Identity-Focused English Language Arts Curriculum

This book makes the case for the importance of a sociocultural view of identity in the ELA classroom and offers a model for organizing English language arts curriculum and instruction around students' social and cultural identity construction. As we will explain, viewing identity as social and cultural makes evident the need for curriculum and instruction that moves away from an inward, myopic focus on identity as a static, individual, intrinsic state to an outward focus on a fluid, shared, historical, generational, and cultural perspective on identity construction.

We therefore perceive an identity-focused approach for teaching ELA as emphasizing:

- students' unique experiences, interests, and needs for planning activities building on those experiences, interests, and needs; planning evident in the activities included in this book.
- building positive social relationships between yourself and students, as well as between students, to create a sense of a classroom community that supports

students' adopting alternative identities; positive relationships evident in the classrooms described in this book.

- adopting alternative perspectives challenging status quo perspectives, leading to students' entertaining alternative identities.
- making connections between texts and people so that students learn to perceive patterns constituting characters', their own, and others' actions constituting identities.
- negotiating alternative identities across different fictional and lived social worlds.
- critiquing how these social worlds support and limit identity construction.
- fostering students' reflection on their learning and identity development.

The degree to which students are willing to adopt these practices depends on their level of engagement in acquiring these practices. As Nasir and Hand (2008) note:

> The practice-linked identity one negotiates in relation to a practice is shaped by the nature of engagement that is afforded and constrained within the features of the practice. In other words, practices, by virtue of their organization, norms, conventions, and structures, afford different levels of engagement for participants, and thus differentially support the development of practice-linked identities. Because practice-linked identities are defined as a sense of connection between the self and the practice, it is likely that in practices in which an individual feels this sense of closeness, that he or she is more likely to be more engaged.
>
> *(p. 147)*

Fostering students' engagement in use of practices—for example, their willingness to adopt alternative perspectives—entails creating the kinds of activities illustrated in this book. Such activities have served to foster student engagement in constructing and reflecting on their identities.

Rather than focusing inwardly on identity in ways that reify myths of adolescent self-absorption and egocentricity, this instruction is based on study of history, culture, and institutions portrayed in literature and nonfiction texts that fosters an understanding of how identities are shaped and shift through changes in institutions, cultural values, and generational values. For example, to foster students' development of alternative identities, in this book, we describe activities for engaging students in challenging identity work related to language, literature, drama, and writing, in both traditional and digital literacy modes.

Summary

In this introductory chapter, we stipulated our definition of identity as going beyond autonomous conceptions of the self to recognize that students adopt alternative identities according to their participation in different social and cultural contexts, as evident in Tre's and Carlos's actions in Rose's class. We also posited the need for an identity-focused approach to foster students' identity development through organizing instruction around five identity practices related to instruction in English language arts classrooms. (For additional resources, activities, and further reading, see http://tinyurl.com/osvhkuk.)

Note

1. Both of their stories, and the stories of others in this book, as well as many of the examples of instruction and theoretical constructs, were initially explored in Anthony's (2014) qualitative and multi-case dissertation, *Finding Yourself in a Book: Literacy Engagements and Marginalized Adolescent Identity Development*, at University of California, Berkeley.

References

Alexie, S. (2007). *The absolutely true diary of a part-time Indian*. Boston: Little Brown.

Anaya, R. A. (1995). *Bless me, Ultima*. New York: Warner Books.

Beach, R., Anson, C., Kastman-Breuch, L-A., & Reynolds, T. (2014). *Understanding and creating digital texts: An activity-based approach*. Lanham, MD: Rowman & Littlefield.

Beach, R., Thein, A. H., & Parks, D. (2008). *High school students' competing social worlds: Negotiating identities and allegiances in response to multicultural literature*. New York: Routledge.

Bourdieu, P. (1984). *Distinction: A social critique of the judgment of taste*. Cambridge, MA: Harvard University Press.

Chhuon, V., & Wallace, T. L. (2012). Creating connectedness through being known: Fulfilling the need to belong in U.S. high schools. *Youth & Society, 46*(3), 1–23.

Crosnoe, R. (2011). *Fitting in, standing out: Navigating the social challenges of high school to get an education*. New York: Cambridge University Press.

Cross, L. H., & Frary, R. B. (1999). Hodgepodge grading: Endorsed by students and teachers alike. *Applied Measurement in Education, 12*(1), 53–72.

Czikszentmihalyi, M., & Larson, R. (1984). *Being adolescent: Conflict and growth in the teenage years*. New York: Basic Books.

Danielewicz, J. (2001). *Teaching selves: Identity, pedagogy, and teacher education*. Albany: State University of New York Press.

Farrington, C. A., Roderick, M., Allensworth, E., Nagaoka, J., Keyes, T. S., Johnson, D. W., & Beechum, N. O. (2012). *Teaching adolescents to become learners. The role of noncognitive factors in shaping school performance: A critical literature review*. Chicago: University of Chicago Consortium on Chicago School Research.

Foucault, M. (1994). *The order of things: An archaeology of the human sciences*. New York: Vintage Press.

Gee, J. P. (2011). *Sociolinguistics and literacies: Ideologies in discourses* (4th ed.). New York: Routledge.

Godley, A., & Minnici, A. (2008). Critical language pedagogy in an urban high school English class. *Urban Education, 43*(3), 319–346.

Hall, G. S. (1904/2012). *Adolescence: Its psychology and its relations to physiology, anthropology, sociology, sex, crime, religion and education*. Charleston, SC: Nabu Press.

Holland, D., Lachicotte, W., Skinner, D., & Cain, C. (1998). *Identity and agency in cultural worlds.* Cambridge, MA: Harvard University Press.

Hull, G., & Katz, M. L. (2006). Crafting an agentive self: Case studies of digital storytelling. *Research in the Teaching of English, 41*(1), 43–81.

Hyland, K. (2012). *Disciplinary identities: Individuality and community in academic discourse.* New York: Oxford University Press.

Ivanič, R. (1998). *Writing and identity: The discoursal construction of identity in academic writing.* Philadelphia: Benjamins.

Kelchtermans, G. (2009). Who I am in how I teach is the message: Self-understanding, vulnerability and reflection. *Teachers and Teaching: Theory and Practice, 15*(2), 257–272.

Ladson-Billings, G. (2010). Challenges to conceptualizing and actualizing culturally relevant pedagogy: How viable is the theory in classroom practice? *Journal of Teacher Education, 61*(3), 248–260.

Lawler, S. (2008). *Identity: Sociological perspectives.* Cambridge, UK: Polity Press.

Lee, H. (1988). *To kill a mockingbird.* New York: Warner.

Lesko, N. (2012). *Act your age!: A cultural construction of adolescence.* New York: Routledge.

Lewis, C., & Finders, M. (2002). Implied adolescents and implied teachers: A generation gap for new times. In D. E. Alvermann (Ed.), *Adolescents and literacies in a digital world* (pp. 101–113). New York: Peter Lang.

Lin, A.M.Y. (Ed.). (2008). *Problematizing identity: Everyday struggles in language, culture, and education.* New York: Erlbaum.

Lortie, D. C. (1975). *Schoolteacher: A sociological study.* Chicago: University of Chicago Press.

Moya, P.M.L. (2005). What's identity got to do with it: Mobilizing identity in the multicultural classroom. In P.M.L. Moya (Ed)., *Identity politics reconsidered* (pp. 96–117). New York: Palgrave Macmillan.

Nakkula, M. J., & Toshalis, E. (2006). *Understanding youth: Adolescent development for educators.* Cambridge, MA: Harvard Education Press.

Nasir, N.S., & Hand, V. (2008). From the court to the classroom: Opportunities for engagement, learning, and identity in basketball and classroom mathematics. *Journal of the Learning Sciences, 17*(2), 143–179.

Norris, A. (2011). Mobile literacies—academic achievement is the "new cool": Acquisition, learning, and practice of transnational urban American youth, ICERI2011 Proceedings, pp. 4520–4527.

Oakes, J. (1985). *Keeping track: How schools structure inequality.* New Haven, CT: Yale University Press.

Osterman, K. F. (2000). Students' need for belonging in the school community. *Review of Educational Research, 70*(3), 323–367.

Pahl, K., & Rowsell, J. (2010). *Artifactual literacies: Every object tells a story.* New York: Teachers College Press.

Pardo, L. (2013, December 4). Using literacy tools and critical thinking to challenge teacher candidates in identity construction. Paper presented at the Literary Research Association conference, Dallas.

Payne, E., & Laugher, J. (2013). Culturally relevant pedagogy. *English Leadership Quarterly, 35*(3), 2–5.

Perry, W. G. (1970). *Forms of intellectual and ethical development in the college years: A scheme.* New York: Holt, Rinehart, & Winston.

Precht, R. D. (2011). *Who am I?: And if so, how many?* New York: Spiegel & Grau.

Ringer, J. M. (2013). The consequences of integrating faith into academic writing: Casuistic stretching and Biblical citation. *College English, 75*(3), 270–297.

Rosenblatt, L. (1995). *Literature as exploration.* New York: Modern Language Association.

Sanchez, R. (2012). Outside the text: Retheorizing empiricism and identity. *College English,* 74(3), 234–246.

Scollon, R. (2001). *Mediated discourse: The nexus of practice.* New York: Routledge Press.

Sjöblom, B., & Aronsson, K. (2012). Participant categorizations of gaming competence: *Noob* and *imba* as learner identities. In O. Erstad & J. Sefton-Green (Eds.), *Identity, community and learning lives in the digital age* (pp. 181–197). Cambridge: Cambridge University Press.

Sumara, D. J. (1998). Fictionalizing acts: Reading and the making of identity. *Theory into Practice,* 37(3), 203–210.

Thein, A. H., Oldakowski, T., & Sloan, D. L. (2010). Using blogs to teach strategies for inquiry into the construction of lived and text worlds. *Journal of Media Literacy Education,* 2(1), 23–36.

VanDerPloeg, L. (2012). *Literacy for a better world: The promise of teaching in diverse classrooms.* New York: Teachers College Press.

Vygotsky, L. (1978). *Mind in society: The development of higher psychological processes.* Cambridge, MA: Harvard University Press.

Wenger, L. (1998). *Communities of practice: Learning, meaning, and identity.* New York: Cambridge University Press.

Zimmerman, D. H. (1998). Discourse identities and social identities. In C. Antaki & S. Widdicombe (Eds.), *Identities in talk* (pp. 87–106). London: Sage.

2

HOW CAN IDENTITY-FOCUSED ELA WORK IN MY CLASSROOM?

> Learning is, in part, about meaning making, about creating a story that involves self and world, purpose and benefit. It is also about developing a story of oneself as a learner, about learning to be and act as a learning self . . . as the learner changes, her capacity and inclination to contribute to the larger culture do as well.
>
> *Robert Halpern (2013, p. 20)*

Identity Construction as the Curriculum Focus for ELA Instruction

In the first chapter, we argued for the importance of focusing on students' identity construction as central to their learning in the English language arts classroom. We also argued that a focus on identity construction allows for students to find value, purpose, and engagement in ELA learning.

We therefore suggest that adopting an identity-focused approach provides a central curriculum focus for teaching English language arts. Such a focus goes beyond solipsistic, self-centered notions of identity as linked to the autonomous self—a notion often reflected in curriculum units on "the individual versus society." Instead, the approach we offer embraces the idea of identities as socially and culturally constructed by having you carefully consider the social and cultural contexts in which your students participate and engage for thinking about how these contexts influence identity construction.

Planning in Context: Situating Instruction With an Awareness of the Community, School, and Classroom Contexts; Students' Identity Practices; and Texts as Actions and Spaces

In Chapter 1, we described our identity-focused curriculum framework—a framework that requires teachers' knowledge of community, school, and classroom contexts; students' identity practices; and texts as actions and spaces that mediate students' identity practices. We also described five identity practices that can serve as the basis for devising activities to foster students' use of these practices.

In the approach we share, we advocate making displays of competence a key element of the ELA classroom. For example, in Elizabeth Erdmann's English classes at Jefferson High School in Bloomington, Minnesota, students continually share their work on a classroom website she created using Google Sites. Because Elizabeth has students view and respond to each other's work, students are then recognized by their peers for their competence. She notes,

> I'll let them do a creative project where they can bring in some sort of talent and they will do it and then they get noticed for something so that they—you're in a classroom with 36 kids, when they can get to be a person that's not just a student; you get to show what they know and be a different person.

In our interviews with her students, they noted that they were most engaged in activities associated with such displays of competence, perceptions consistent with previous research on students' shifting engagement during the school day (Csikszentmihalyi & Larson, 1986).

This suggests that it is important to create a safe classroom space in which students feel comfortable taking risks associated with displaying competence. Students are more likely to take risks when they feel that they will be supported by you and their peers for doing so. This includes setting guidelines that will help students provide descriptive, nonjudgmental feedback to one another. For example, in Rose's 11th-grade English class (described in the introduction), students participated in sharing a reading artifact involving a piece of text (such as a poem, novel, letter, ticket stub from a concert, or photograph) that both carried a story and played an essential role in shaping that student. Rose helped model the expectations for the activity by sharing poetry that she had published prior to becoming a teacher. In this modeling activity, Rose shared a personal story, explaining that she believed that writing had "saved" her.

After listening to Rose's story, students brought in their own reading artifacts, then sat in a circle and shared their artifacts and stories, following the norms of respect and solemnity that Rose articulated. An African American male, Jeffrey, showed a photo of a close cousin he had lost to gun violence and talked about their friendship when they were younger and how the death motivated Jeffrey to avoid some of the pressures to be involved in criminal activity in his neighborhood. A Samoan student named Sosa shared a photo that he had borrowed from the principal's office that showed him with a group of other students at the state capitol protesting budget cuts to education. Sosa discussed how this first experience with activism sparked an interest in continued social justice work.

Because of the modeling from Rose and the safe space that was created, students took risks in sharing their reading artifacts. During the activity, students both learned new information about their peers—some of whom they had known since early elementary school—and gained insights into the complexities of their peers' identities. In this activity, students' own narratives were legitimized in an academic setting, community was created through sharing stories and risk taking, and students were seen as competent through their participation in other social contexts.

Planning Activities Based on Students' Experiences and Interests

In this chapter, we describe how to plan activities based on an identity-focused ELA framework, emphasizing the need to draw on experiences students bring from their communities and homes to the classroom. For example, knowing that most of her students came from Latino families in which parents and grandparents moved between different cultures as immigrants led Rose to plan activities that built upon her students' familiarity with the identity practices of negotiating identities across different social worlds.

Planning activities based on students' unique background experiences in different social and cultural worlds represents a challenge to generic "teacher-proof" curriculum or textbook series that ignore how differences in these contexts shape students' identity construction.

Adopting an identity-focused approach also goes beyond knowing students based simply on their academic records or performances to also getting to know them as people with unique abilities, knowledge, interests, needs, and talents. While we recognize that acquiring this kind of information about every single student may be asking the impossible of teachers, what we're suggesting is a shift in the kinds of information teachers seek about their students, information that helps teachers plan activities that honor and build on students' experiences and connect with them on a personal level. Knowing, for example, that a teacher and a student both share a common interest in graphic novels can serve as a basis for building a relationship around that shared interest.

This involves finding out about students' particular popular cultural interests and experiences, so you can then make connections between your instructional topics and their interests and experiences. Jefferson High School student, Jacob, noted how his teacher, Elizabeth, drew on his familiarity with rap songs to connect the play to their own lives:

> The way that she teaches where she asks questions or throws in jokes or she relates things back to our lives. We were talking about *Hamlet*, and it's hard to process *Hamlet* because the setting happened a long time ago, and she uses today's examples. She actually played a rap song that was in *Hamlet* and that helped us understand it.

Knowing about your students' interests and experiences means that you can interact with them in ways that convey a genuine concern about them as people, leading them to reciprocate by sharing their interests and experiences with you. Hannah describes her perceptions of Elizabeth as

> someone you can talk to—most of the time, there's a wall between students and teachers and with her she's really engaged so sometimes you're sitting in class and you're taking notes and the teacher doesn't appreciate that because he or she is focusing on the kid on the phone but they don't care about the kids, but she cares.

At the same time, we also recognize the need to plan activities that invite students into new and different social worlds portrayed in literature, nonfiction, or films as actions and spaces that position them in new and different ways. Exposing students to these alternative social worlds provides them with opportunities to think about alternative ways of being and becoming as they move into different potential worlds.

You can also devise activities that give students choices based on their particular interests in certain topics or issues, as did Deidra Gammill (2014) in scheduling "Google Thursdays" as days for students to study and present topics to their peers for their high school English class in Petal, Mississippi.

Students are more likely to be engaged in activities when they are given a choice of topics, texts, and/or practices for completing a project, choices based on individual differences. As Joshua noted about Elizabeth's assignments, "I really like that the essays and writing and even speeches are open, as long as it's in the area of the topic, there aren't any boundaries; you can just say whatever you want to." Students learn how to select topics, texts, tools, and/or practices to achieve certain goals or purposes.

Constructing Curriculum Based on and With Your Students' Identities

In this book, we advocate for the need to construct an English language arts curriculum consistent with your students' identities. While creating your own curriculum certainly entails more work and effort than relying on a standardized, prepackaged curriculum or textbooks, building on students' unique experiences and ideas can enhance students' engagement.

You can also include students in co-constructing an identity-focused curriculum by drawing on their experiences and ideas and positioning them as "co-constructors of knowledge" (Fraser & Bosanquet, 2006, p. 275). For example, students researched the experiences of Latinos in Toronto schools and then developed curriculum and taught a class on conducting research about students' identity construction in schools (Guerrero et al., 2013). In another Toronto-based project, preservice teachers and students co-constructed curriculum about themes of racism, bullying, and homophobia related to responses to *Night* (Wiesel, 2006) that included an exhibition of paintings on book pages as well as curriculum for teaching about issues of social justice in *The Absolutely True Diary of a Part-Time Indian* (Alexie, 2007), curriculum that was then employed in schools (Simon et al., 2014). Students also shared their perceptions of the value of engaging in co-constructed curriculum, noting that they experienced displays of competence and agency in being positioned as "teachers" whose experiences and ideas were valued by both the preservice teachers and their peers.

Identity Practices and Psychological/Emotional Aspects of Identity Construction

We want to distinguish between our focus on social, cultural, and academic aspects of identity construction and other psychological/emotional aspects of identity. Your students are likely grappling with an array of psychological and emotional issues that influence their identities—their ability to interact with and relate to you and their peers, express themselves in a confident manner, focus on completing their work, and so forth. We don't want to suggest that you ought to attempt to address all of these psychological and emotional issues. These are typically better addressed by referrals to trained school counselors, therapists, and psychologists. Instead, as an English teacher, you can help students learn to use the resources of the ELA classroom to negotiate their identities across various academic and social worlds.

We realize that there is often a fine line between psychological assistance and pedagogical assistance, but we believe that focusing on the academic aspects of identity practices specific to interpreting and constructing texts in an ELA classroom will help to clarify that line. Although most ELA teachers find themselves faced with moments when personal, psychological issues are brought to bear in the classroom, and we recognize that focus on identity may in some cases open up space for these challenging moments, we argue that addressing identity construction in the ELA classroom is important enough that teachers should be willing to take these risks.

In fact, we believe that avoiding issues related to identity construction in the ELA classroom allows students to focus too narrowly on their own status-quo identities, which they tend to view as static and monolithic. Addressing identity can help students entertain alternative identities and begin to see the socially and culturally constructed nature of our shifting identities.

We also wish to distinguish between an identity-focused approach and a focus on promoting students' self-esteem. We certainly believe that engaging in an identity-focused curriculum will hopefully lead to enhancing students' self-esteem or self-confidence. However, attempting to enhance students' self-esteem as the focus of instruction based on praise for their own unique, individual abilities may foster an egocentric narcissism in students that, as some research indicates, can limit their ability to empathize with others (Sparks, 2014).

At the same time, an identity-focused approach does emphasize the importance of the social and emotional aspects of learning (SEL) as contributing to academic achievement (Finley, 2014). Programs employing a SEL focus as described by the Collaborative for Academic, Social, and Emotional Learning (CASEL, http://tinyurl.com/p2j5z7u) emphasize the importance of students' social interactions and relationships as well as their emotional development—for example, their gaining empathy through responding to complex literary texts, which, as recent research indicates, serves to enhance empathy (Djikic, Oatley, & Moldoveanu, 2013). A meta-analysis of 213 programs employing K–12 SEL programs found that student participation in these programs resulted in higher achievement scores as well as improved attitudes, behaviors, and motivation to learn and reduced emotional distress and social withdrawal compared to students who did not participate in the programs (Durlak et al., 2011).

Community Contexts

Knowledge about your students' lives in their community and school contexts underlies successful planning. Awareness of how such contexts shape students' identities promotes connections between their experiences in their community and school and their classroom learning.

In planning activities for responding to *The Absolutely True Diary of a Part-Time Indian*, Rose and Anthony drew on what they knew about the students' own tensions emanating from how they were positioned by their urban community and family worlds versus how they were positioned in their school worlds—tensions similar to those of the protagonist Arnold's own negotiations. When Rose's students read about Arnold's experiences in his White high school, they could then share how students can be positioned by certain racial attitudes in their own school experiences.

Understanding students' communities involves acquiring specific demographic information about their city, suburb, town, or neighborhood, as well as the "funds of knowledge" (Gonzalez, Moll, & Amanti, 2005) students bring from their families to school. In describing how identities are shaped by differences in race and class across the various urban, suburban, and rural communities in this book, we attempt to avoid stereotypical assumptions about the relationships between race and class—that low-income communities are largely diverse whereas middle-class communities are homogeneous. And we avoid generalizing that a given activity employed in a particular type of school would work as well if grafted on to another school setting.

One key community factor shaping schools is racial diversity. For the 2014–2015 school year, the majority of students in American schools will be students of color (Ross & Bell, 2014). While White student populations have been declining, Latino/Hispanic student populations have been increasing. Unfortunately the ELA literature curriculum has not kept pace with this increase in Latino/

Hispanic student populations, and few texts by Latino/Hispanic authors are included in the curriculum.

Within schools, and even among schools in the same district, students in the same grade level are sorted according to race, class, and achievement through ability grouping or tracking, so low-income students, students of color, and/or low-achieving students often are grouped in schools or classes taught by novice teachers; this sorting results in inequality of academic opportunity (Kalogrides & Loeb, 2013).

Demographic differences in students' family incomes and economic opportunities can influence students' engagement in school (Wang & Holcombe, 2010), engagement that declines from 7th to 11th grades as evident in less compliance to school rules, as well as reduced participation in extracurricular activities, lack of identification with the school, and subjective valuing of learning (Wang & Eccles, 2012). And, because students from low-income families often lack the cultural capital associated with success in schools constituted by middle-class norms and expectations, these students are more likely to report feelings of not fitting into school, particularly if the school emphasizes the need to conform to middle-class values that may be inconsistent with the values students bring to school (Crosnoe, 2011).

Addressing the Needs of Non-Dominant Students

Low-income students who do attend college are more likely to attend less-well-funded colleges, resulting in less support and lower college completion rates (Carnevale & Strohl, 2013). The 2013 Kids Count report noted that 82% of low-income 4th graders were not proficient in reading in 2011 versus 52% of their higher-income peers—reading difficulties that shape their success at the secondary level. As a result, a high percentage—34% of African Americans in 2009/2010—do not complete high school, which makes it difficult for them to acquire employment and transition into adulthood in an economy that now often requires college degrees for many jobs.

Unfortunately, given these low test scores, schools with high percentages of low-income students are more likely to receive "skill-drill" instruction geared toward preparing students for multiple-choice testing, while students in schools with higher-income students receive more academically challenging instruction (Ravitch, 2011). After teaching at SBH, one of our focal teachers, Rose, moved to Seattle, where she now teaches in a school with students similar to those in her SBH class. However, her new school has adopted a test-driven, standardized curriculum that contrasts with the identity-focused curriculum she was able to implement at SBH. Reflecting on this contrast, Rose explained:

> In my current context (teaching marginalized youth in the Seattle area) I am seeing the fall-out of this over-emphasis on standardization. I'm seeing the kids that this approach is not working for. These kids are great kids,

they are smart kids, and many are EL kids. Yes, they need specific skills, but the way it's being taught is so "work-booky" and so test driven and high stakes. And then, kids don't feel seen, are not feeling reflected in the curriculum, and then not buying in.

At the same time, in her Seattle school, she still applies aspects of an identity-focused approach in ways that have had positive effects on her students' learning:

I think the identity approach has influenced the way I make lesson plans, trying to find places for student choice, and then using some of the skill-building stuff more by group. Vocab and quizzes are done as groups, so treated as a social learning activity. My reading scores have gone up two and a half grades on average this year. The balance of self-selection of topics to study, paired with group learning and group projects, whenever there is an element of connect to self, bring yourself in, it works. The essays and the work are much better.

Public Acceptance of Critical Thinking

One key identity practice in an identity-focused approach is an emphasis on teaching critical thinking, as described in Chapter 6, an emphasis with strong public support. A May 2013 Phi Delta Kappan/Gallup Poll (Bushaw & Lopez, 2013) found that members of the American public completing the poll "strongly agreed" that schools should give priority to teaching critical thinking skills (80%) and communication skills (78%). Poll participants also strongly agreed the teaching should focus on setting meaningful goals (64%), motivating students (61%), fostering students' creativity (58%), teaching students how to collabo-rate on projects (57%), and promoting students' well-being (54%). We perceive the public's support for these goals as consistent with our identity-focused ELA curriculum, given an emphasis on engaging students in creative activities that involve in critical thinking, communication, goal-setting, and collaboration.

However, one challenge in fostering critical thinking is that it is related to another of our identity practices—adopting alternative cultural perspectives. In certain regions of the country, people are choosing to live in neighborhoods or communities that only include other people who share their perspectives, a pop-ulation trend defined as "way-of-life segregation" (Bishop, 2009). This means that in schools in certain communities whose members share the same homoge-neous outlooks, students may have difficulty voicing perspectives that challenge certain prevailing perspectives valued by that community's population.

Relating Community to Classroom Contexts

All of this points to the importance of planning instruction based on an aware-ness of how students' communities shapes their identities. Students are more engaged in classrooms if they sense that their teacher has some knowledge about their community and cultural contexts shaping their particular interests, outside-school activities, or knowledge (Wang & Eccles, 2012).

For example, now-retired Minneapolis teacher Jay Ritterson drew on his knowledge of his students' cultural backgrounds for teaching spoken-word poetry at Edison High School in Minneapolis, an urban school with a highly diverse population and a 95% free/reduced lunch rate. To devise a spoken-word unit for his students, he recognized the need to know more about his students as a group of diverse, urban students:

> My goal in doing a Spoken-Word Week has roots in my longstanding desire to do a better job of connecting with my students. I have always felt effective teaching, like effective parenting, is an act of mutual love. It is after all a very personal activity, nurturing personalities, shoring up vulnerabilities, meddling with a person's thinking. It has to do with feelings as well as cognition.
>
> Not only did I learn about them, I also learned a little about how to learn about others. As a survivor of the hippie years, "white, middle class, suburban, adult male" was something I had already done and had been moving beyond. Here was an opportunity to enrich my life enormously, because an asset almost all students have is that they are not locked into the "who" about themselves or others the way adults are.

To acquire knowledge about his students' cultural backgrounds, Ritterson took a workshop on East African history and culture in which he learned about the importance of oral poetry, as well as a workshop on uses of oral poetry grounded in local places for teaching Latino students. And he attended performances at a spoken-word open mic club as well as viewed YouTube spoken-word videos with

> messages confronting the denial, damage, and destruction of group and personal identity. Victims spoke out against their abusers. Oppressed spoke out against their oppressors. A few spoke out about the liberation of being able to speak out. The message was clear; who they were was not going to change and their identities were not going to be denied. That meant that how they were viewed was going to have to change. . . . Who they were and were going to become was up to them. These young poets stood up and declared who they were. They expounded a view of their world past and future that was theirs. They spoke with strength and pride, and that was just what my students needed to be able to do to break through the ceilings of race, language, culture, and poverty that limited their futures.
>
> I immersed myself in examples of spoken-word, listened, watched, and reflected. I read about spoken-word and its background and activity— Harlem Renaissance, beat poets, hip-hop, Nuyoricans, Gil Scott-Heron,

Bob Dylan. I read about the background of Somali poets and poetry, and contemplated the parallels to Western styles.

Based on what he learned about how spoken-word performances serve to foster students' agency, he perceived his goal for use of spoken word in his classroom as

[e]mpowering students to be themselves and assert themselves into the best life possible for them. Spoken-word poetry was the vehicle, their identity the engine, their personal and cultural experience the fuel that would carry them forward. Would this improve their language skills? Students learn to read and write according to their perceived need for these things. Would the power of words to set one free, and the opportunity to be accepted and respected as "who one is" help shape that perception? If this activity could open a door through which the possibility of a better life would appear, then walking through that door would indeed require one to develop one's language skills. Pedagogically then, this was a good thing to do.

Ritterson then developed his spoken-word activities by creating these written instructions:

- The lesson was simple: introduce with examples, discuss with open-ended questions, explore on the Internet for inspiration, write as groups—comparing and sharing as you go—refine and rehearse, present and listen to presentations.
- Start putting your ideas into words. Get the ideas first. Then the words. Then the way you want it to sound. Containing references to problems, conditions, or issues that impact your life or references to your cultural, national, or historical background.
- Your poem must be your own. (Do not use inappropriate language for the classroom. Ask if you are in doubt.) Do not use abusive, threatening, or demeaning language. (Anger is quite acceptable, but you must be respectful.)

To help familiarize students with the use of poetry to engage audiences and construct the persona of the speaker, Ritterson had students study Somali poetry, which is based on a rich oral tradition. He then had students work in groups to respond to Latino poetry. Then, students created their own work, with the options of just writing a poem, writing a poem that a peer performs, writing a poem that is read aloud, or writing a poem to recite and perform. Students rehearsed and performed poems within their groups before performing them for the class.

In reflecting on this activity, Ritterson noted that the activity was popular with his students:

The most requested activity from the same students in the following year in my junior classes and those of others was classroom or school-wide open mics for spoken-word. Their genre had been honored, their language had been honored, their words had been honored, and they had been honored, and they liked it. Several of the students participated in an emerging spoken-word club and a school-hosted, public open mic. A few participated in the citywide slam later in the spring.

One poet, using the piece she wrote for my class, won an award at the citywide slam. Hers was an intensely personal piece exposing the pain and rage from her sexual abuse and the eventual forgiveness of her perpetrator. Another of my students was able to leverage her college admissions the following year with the poetic skill demonstrated in my classroom, where she stunned her American classmates with an incredible, memorized poem expounding the endurance of national pride she held for her homeland and its people. Before her performance, she was simply another demurring Somali girl. From almost all, it was noted as the best, most remembered lesson of the year in my year-end survey.

I would have to say it worked because it changed their thinking about themselves and their capacities and about learning. And it worked for me because I modeled the joy of meaningful learning, supported students in directing their own learning, and honored all of the demonstrations of learning.

Students' Sharing Experiences and Knowledge

Central to an identity-focused approach is building curriculum based on students' experiences and knowledge that shape their identities. Another way to find out more about your students is by asking them to write about their experiences and knowledge. In a Funds of Knowledge Writing Project in his middle school language arts class, Chris Street (2005) had his students write about topics based on their own home experiences. For example, one of his students, Norma, wrote about her experiences with dangerous elevators in her family's apartment complex, an issue that had not been addressed by the apartment management for two years.

You can also ask your students to complete questionnaires and/or interview their students about their interests, hobbies, previous school experiences, and perceptions of themselves and others. For their interviews with SBH and JHS students, Anthony and Richard employed questions related to students' reading/ viewing interests, favorite subjects, self-descriptions, others' descriptions of them, experiences or factors constituting their identities, and how they vary their identities across different worlds. For example, prompts included "What do you think makes you who you are?," "One of my favorite memories from school is . . .," and "In what ways are you different or similar from your friends? Your family?"

Students can also share information about themselves with others within their classes by bringing in an artifact, image, photo, text, and so forth that represents some aspect of their identity. Working in pairs or small groups, other students can pose questions about how an item reflects an student's identity. Students can also create video blogs (vlogs) in which they share descriptions about themselves, using images, artifacts, or props. Vlogs allow students to use both audio and visual modes for sharing information about themselves (Taylor, 2013). To create vlogs, students simply use their computer webcam to record themselves talking about themselves, and then upload the video to YouTube. For example, students can hold up copies of their favorite books to share their reading interests. Or they can share certain autobiographical experiences or perceptions of school or community events. Or, if students are addressing certain issues or topics in group or class projects, they can share their ideas with each other using vlogs (Taylor, 2013).

After Richard interviewed individually a large number of Elizabeth's students, Elizabeth noted that the students indicated they rarely engaged in one-on-one conversations with their teachers about their own interests, needs, or goals. This suggests the value of meeting with students individually to talk about their interests, needs, or goals; these meetings can help build relationships with students.

Creating Safe, Supportive Classrooms

In planning activities, is it also important to consider whether students perceive the classroom as a safe space for voicing opinions or ideas perceived as unpopular or deviant by their peers. Students are more likely to engage and voice opinions and alternative perspectives when they perceive their classrooms as safe, supportive spaces in which they gain pleasure from sharing their responses to texts with peers as well as a means of defining their difference from peers. As Michael Smith (2013) notes:

> People read to affiliate with others. Or people read to mark their place in the world. They do a kind of identity work by using their reading to assert their difference from others. One of the informants in our study avoided reading the books that were most popular among her friends and instead read what she called dark fiction. That reading was an important part of how she understood herself. As she said "I'm weird in the way that [I don't have] inhibitions like most people. I can read dark fiction and not be disturbed by it."

This suggests the need to support both students' sharing their responses to socially bond with each other as well as their willingness to adopt alternative practices and stances unique to their identity construction. When students are comfortable challenging each others' responses reflecting status quo perspectives, they may then begin to explore alternative perspectives, something we discuss in more detail in the next chapter (Beach, Thein, & Parks, 2008).

You create a safe, supportive classroom community by setting certain guidelines for appropriate behavior in your classroom. And, by sharing your own experiences and alternative perspectives constituting your identities, you are modeling how students can share their experiences and alternative perspectives. Elizabeth notes, "What makes my class a safe classroom is that I try really hard to understand them. I think that I understand them because I've been them." For example, she recognizes that some of their behavior is the result of mimicking their peers:

> They are like parrots. As a teacher, I have to realize that the behavior that's happening is not always the person that's doing it. Sometimes they have one really powerful, charismatic friend and sometimes they are in a class with a person that they can't help but clown around with so it can be one other little person's personality that can make them go haywire.

She also knows that students are more likely to voice alternative, unpopular perspectives or opinions if they know that they will not be perceived negatively or ostracized by their peers for posing those perspectives or opinions. As a result, she directly addresses instances of unacceptable actions:

> If we're doing an online discussion and a kid writes like, "that's because you're gay," I will put it up on the screen in class and point it out that it happened in a public space and we need to deal with it publicly so when kids see that they will get called out about it. They don't want to get called out, but they know that I will do it when it has to happen, and I can switch easily between being fun-time lady and "no." I want my classroom to be a good learning environment, and it's not a good learning environment if only some voices get heard and if some people's radical ideas are discouraged. They know that I'm sincere, and I think that helps a lot.

In contrast to creating safe classrooms through constantly monitoring students' behavior, she establishes a tone in the class where students learn to respect each other.

Community Contexts: South Bay High School

To illustrate these planning processes, we now turn to describing how the teachers featured in this book planned activities based on their students' identities as positioned by particular community and school contexts. In addition, we note how students draw on identity practices to position themselves in these contexts and how the teachers' own identity construction has an influence on their students' identity construction.

Based on his earlier teaching experience and his dissertation research in Rose's class, Anthony had extensive knowledge about the urban community contexts of South Bay High School (SBH) (pseudonym), knowledge that was invaluable for his understanding of the students he was studying in Rose's (pseudonym) class. (Note: We have not disclosed specific information about the identity of the teachers, school, or community, given Anthony's dissertation research protocol agreement with the University of California, Berkeley; all SBH students are identified by pseudonyms.)

South Bay High is a bit like the "Little Engine That Could." At the time that Anthony conducted research at the site, the school had been in existence for fifteen years and had suffered through numerous changes at the administration level, struggled with teacher turnover yearly, saw the demographics of students change dramatically, had to make severe cutbacks due to decreasing enrollments, and even changed physical locations of the school building multiple times. However, SBH has, throughout all of this, had very high rates of graduates attend college, maintained a strong commitment to professional development of staff, worked toward equitable outcomes, and used traditional and alternative assessments in evaluating the students and their own work as a school.

South Bay High School occupies an area of a major city with a large working-class and immigrant community, primarily from Latin American countries. There is a strong Catholic tradition among the families that send their students to SBH; however, the students are quite diverse with regard to their own beliefs. Like many large cities, schools here have become increasingly segregated, "neighborhood" schools; however, SBH is one of the most diverse in the city with regard to ethnicity and race. Additionally, while much of the city is changing as a result of gentrification, the school's surrounding neighborhood remains ethnically diverse, working class and poor, and is saddled with problems including crime, gangs, police harassment, and drug-related violence. While students report feeling safe at the school itself, it is often the commutes to and from home that can potentially lead to dangerous situations.

SBH is in the shadow of a larger, comprehensive public high school with a checkered history of success. Some of the students at SBH were students who had been removed from the larger school for various reasons. Other students came to SBH because they wanted a small school where students would be known well by the adults and they were less likely to fall through the cracks. Given its smaller size, however, they lacked the funding and resources for many of the perks of larger schools—a football team, a library, and so forth.

Rose's Identity

In constructing her identity, Rose does not match the "White woman teacher" archetype. She often wore typically men's clothes, sported a very short haircut, and had many tattoos. Rose is open about her sexuality and is open to discussing this with the students and referencing her partner in casual conversations during and between classes, much the way that heterosexual, married teachers have the privilege to do without a second thought.

Rose's appearance and identity served a pedagogical purpose. Many students in her class had a distrust of White people, teachers, and schools in general, and yet the majority of the class stated a sense of affinity with Rose. Rose believes that her appearance signals to students that she is an outsider and is marginalized in some of the same ways they often are. As a result, her students confide in her and feel at ease with her in ways they might not with other White teachers. In fact, students who themselves come across as tough and have faced real hardships, for example, Tre and Andrea, have clearly formed very special relationships with Rose. Tre expressed in an early interview that Rose was "real," a good teacher, honest, and the only teacher in the school he believed really cared about him. Most of the students interviewed in the class reported feeling similarly about Rose.

Rose's relationships with students meant that her class was a gathering spot during lunch; when students were kicked out of other classes, they often found themselves at her door. She would also often take students to and from places—their homes, the courthouse, sports events, and so on. While Rose expressed the need for boundaries between her and the students, she was often the one who crossed these boundaries when she saw a student in need.

Rose's Class

Rose's fourth-period English 11 class is, like many at the school, lively, active, social, and not particularly academic or rigorous. Each class session, like classes in many places, seems to follow a familiar script. The top of the class involves the teacher posting an agenda, welcoming students in from the hall, and trying to organize materials. The classroom space is relatively sparse—the teacher has to supply her own materials, but she has also set up a cozy tea and cocoa corner. Students wander in at different rates, often with headphones on and phones out, and engage in conversations that began during passing period and end five to ten minutes later and after an equal number of reminders. They then settle in to begin the warm-up posted on the board.

At this point, the students who choose to engage, or not, or who find ways to do both, are usually the same students with a few exceptions. Of the students repeatedly discussed in this book, Alejandra is usually fully engaged, Tre and Andrea are rarely engaged in academic work and choose to be social, while Cat, Carlos, and Jeffrey tend to straddle a space in between. The class of twenty-two students is half female, all of whom are Latina students—primarily first- or second-generation Mexican; and half male, consisting of four African American males, one Samoan male, one mixed student, and five Latino males. While the class is generally close, they also have some clear groupings that tend to dictate daily interactions. The most dominant voices belong to one grouping of the Latinas, often led by Andrea, and three of the African American males (including Tre)—and the banter, flirting, and discussions between these groups are often the source of each day's off-task behavior. Rose, who is very much at ease with the students and who clearly enjoys her work, uses humor, lecturing, warnings, guilt trips, and the other resources available given the obvious care and community in the room to cajole as much production as she can each day.

Curriculum for *The Absolutely True Diary of a Part-Time Indian*

The curriculum for the Sherman Alexie (2007) novel *The Absolutely True Diary of a Part-Time Indian* was designed to be an intentionally different experience for the class. The product of a joint collaboration between Anthony and Rose, it was fashioned from various pedagogical approaches, the skills and needs of the particular students, and with a consideration of the class culture. The goals for the unit involved students in the following activities related to certain identity practices:

- choosing concepts or themes they deem to be authentic to guide their work and inform their final project in the unit related to *adopting alternative perspectives* and *engaging in critical analysis of texts and worlds* and *identifying long-term identity trajectories.*
- interpreting the characters' and their own identity construction in terms of how they were positioned by participation in different social worlds related to *negotiating identities across different social worlds.*
- engaging in deep reading of the novel and other self-selected texts related to *defining connections between texts.*
- writing in various genres, working collaboratively in groups, and "trying on" various discourses and narratives related to *building relationships with others.*

The pedagogical influences on the goals for this curriculum, when synthesized, might be characterized as a *culturally competent interpretive pedagogy* (Moule, 2012) designed to foster use of the different identity practices. The students in Rose's class, for the most part, struggled to see school as being particularly relevant, were below grade level as readers and writers, and, while they cared about each other and Rose, did not have a history of showing interest in the academic content. In addition, many students held strong social identities that provided them with a sense of power and success by adopting the identities of the class clown, a basketball star, and so on, but that was often at odds with being positioned as particularly academically oriented.

During the planning stage, *The Absolutely True Diary of a Part-Time Indian* was selected because it met the criteria reflected in the goals for this curriculum. The novel's appealing blend of cartoons, vivid and witty dialogue, emotional honesty and rawness, and taboo elements sufficed in keeping students of all reading levels engaged. It was also instrumental in creating optimal conditions to provide students with the opportunity to be exposed to new narratives, to be engaged readers, and to be willing participants in class. The selected text was determined after considerations about accessibility for students of varying reading skill levels, the potential the text would offer for being both familiar and unusual, and for its explicit focus on identity-related themes.

A very funny, at times moving book, the novel tells Arnold's story, a Spokane living on an Indian reservation struggling with the early years of being a teenager, some severe disabilities, and living in poverty. Motivated by a teacher who saw his potential, Arnold decides to attend an all-White school off the reservation, which initially only adds to his problems. By enrolling in the all-White school, Arnold feels alienated by both communities, seen as a traitor to the reservation and as a token minority in the White school. However, after some initial hardships he learns to exist and even thrive in both spaces. The fact that Arnold moves between these two incompatible worlds lent itself well to students exploring their own related identity practice of *negotiating identities across different worlds*. The novel is referenced throughout this book, often referred to as "the Alexie novel."

In addition, selecting a text such as *The Absolutely True Diary of a Part-Time Indian*, which was accessible and engaging to most students, and then allowing students to choose the themes or topics in the book as well as related "partner texts" that they saw as being in conversation with Alexie's novel helped to build student interest and engagement associated with the identity practices of *adopting alternative perspectives* and *making connections between texts*. Creating a curriculum that students would ideally perceive as relevant and engaging invites them to employ "literary interpretation practices [that] can transform imaginative occasions into productive insights" (Sumara, 2002, p. 5).

Rose's Eight-Week Curriculum

The following narrative captures the experiences, activities, and outcomes for the eight-week curriculum. First, consistent with the identity practice of *reflecting on change over time*, students wrote a literacy biography in which they discussed the various ways they are and have been literate, an activity that signaled early on that literacy in this unit would go beyond school texts and writing papers. The biographies included memories from reading in elementary school, engagement with digital literacies, embodied literacies like dance and fashion, favorite books read, worst and favorite memories of writing, and so forth. Sharing the biographies provided an opportunity for students' complex identities and histories to be recognized in ways that were in contrast to the ways they had been positioned in the class previously.

Next, a Native American guest speaker and local activist, Mark Anquoe, came to the class to share his views on the novel, American Indian history, and current issues regarding culture and society to help provide some context for the novel. Eager students peppered the guest speaker with thoughtful questions about the book, life on a reservation, and issues such as sports mascots and other topics.

Students were then provided their own copy of the book to keep, which served to build a sense of ownership and accountability and to encourage writing in the book itself. In a school where students often read books that were missing pages, covers, and were generally in poor condition, this act was meaningful for students. Next, we discussed and practiced (through role-playing) some of the norms and expectations we had for developing a "community of interpreters" that would ideally feel a bit different than the typical classroom community dynamics. This included being vocal, respecting other people's narratives, taking academic and social risks, and assuming ownership of one's own learning.

A final pre-reading activity was the human barometer game. This activity involved posting two signs at either end of the room, one stating, "strongly disagree," and the other, "strongly agree." Rose read statements that ranged from the innocuous (e.g., chocolate ice cream is better than vanilla) to the more controversial (e.g., everyone is a little bit racist). Many of the statements were related to the key ideas and issues tackled in the novel. Students then had to physically stand in different spaces in the room to indicate the extent to which they agreed or disagreed with the statement. Finally, students were called on at random to defend their position, and if others were convinced, they were given a chance to move. Beyond introducing concepts and themes in the novel, this activity offered an assessment of the students' attitudes on particular topics, allowing them to learn where some people stood alone, see what swayed students to change positions, and generally get to know the class and the individuals better.

Students did most of the reading of *Diary* at home, but early on, the class did a lot of collective in-class reading. During this time the teacher taught and modeled through think-alouds, doing annotations, re-reading strategies, and reading for deep engagement. The text is not a difficult read and is generally noted as being written for a 9th-grade reading level. However, like many quality young adult novels, it is the sort of text that presents few problems regarding comprehension, and it carries layers of wisdom that stronger readers can also grapple with to maintain engagement.

As they read the novel, students were also participating in numerous activities that aided comprehension, built engagement, encouraged interpretation, and prepared them for later assignments. Students worked in small "detective teams" in which they tracked some of the literary devices. Teams included the symbolism sleuths, the theme musketeers, characterization crew, and so forth. Close to the end of the book, each team presented their work for the class, supporting a jigsaw method of building a collective understanding of the novel. The literary device detective teams project is an example of how Rose was able to meet certain CCSS objectives while still leaving time to enjoy a more aesthetic response to the novel.

As they read the novel, students developed connections between the text and their own lives consistent with the identity practice of *making connections between texts and people*. For example, the group studying the novel's use of symbolism used culturally relevant parallels and examples in their presentation to the class. In addition, while still reading the book, students participated in Socratic discussions, written responses to prompts about the text, and other activities designed to encourage thoughtful engagement with the literature.

Students both created and brought into the class additional texts that Rose accepted as legitimate and instrumental resources for learning and applying to interpretations of the Alexie novel. Partner texts were works (poems, films, historical documents, songs, other books) that students brought to the class and shared with others; these were works that they viewed as being connected in some way to their understandings of the Alexie novel. Students also brought to the class reading artifacts, texts they perceived to be important in their lives— letters from parents, awards they had received, children's books that their parents had read to them, and so forth. The reading artifacts became shared, legitimate, additional texts that students used to make meaning of themselves, the class as a community, and their peers. A final text source, because of the salient role they play in Alexie's novel, were cartoons that students created either to depict scenes from the book or inspired by Alexie's cartoons but dealing with the students' own lives.

As the class reached the end of the novel, students were introduced to the final project for the unit, the Touchstone Text. The term "touchstone text" refers to those works that are shared and valued by a collective group (Davis, Sumara, & Luce-Kapler, 2000); as a text "inhabiting the reader and the reader, in turn, inhabits the text into his or her life" (Neilsen, 2006, p. 5). Touchstone texts can position identity through signaling a shift of self and/or the collective that occurred through engaging with the text, serving to create a "class chronotope" as a shared experience defining students' collective sense of increased agency over time (Bloome et al., 2009).

In this context, the Touchstone Text assignment was the final project. Students did a series of activities to determine an authentic, meaningful concept they hoped to explore and that the book could help them consider. The goal of the final project was to display a thoughtful, nuanced, original, and well-articulated line of thinking around the concept in a format selected by the student. While not the final word on the concept, it presents the audience with an advanced interpretive stance around a particular idea that struck the student as he or she read the novel or that he or she brought to the reading in advance.

Students' Final Projects

While the projects are discussed at other points in this book, here is a brief introduction to some of the featured students from Rose's class at SBH did for their Touchstone Text. Because the project invited students to select both the content and the format of their touchstone text, students' identities really came to the surface in surprising ways. Also of note is that because the students selected the format (and chose formats they were already comfortable with), the emphasis with regard to rigor and assessment was on the complexity and depth of critical thinking about the concept, as well as how they expressed their thoughts.

Jeffrey's PowerPoint reflected his thoughtful journey on issues of race, included sharing some painful stories about his own life, but also ended with an image of Spider-Man sitting in a tree as a reflection of his playful and youthful spirit. Asked about his interest in the topic, Jeffrey said, "Honestly, I think racism is really real—like, people just expect me to fail because I'm black, like they expect me to be in the street. If people think you're supposed to fail then nobody really cares if you do."

Andrea, not known to be at all sentimental, shared a letter she wrote about love that she transformed into an essay. It was written initially as a response to people in her family who disapproved of her romantic relationship with a young man, and it was then revised to be a treatise on young love. Later, she shared in an interview that she had not intended to do her project on the topic of young love, but then because she was dealing with "drama from other people" about her boyfriend at the time, she channeled her anger toward this project and it helped her to cope.

Cat, the young shy Latina with the artist's soul who felt like an outcast in the school, wrote a series of poems about feeling alienated, losing loved ones, depression, and, ultimately, her hopes for peace and joy in her life. Later, she would share in an interview that reading the poems in front of the class was extremely scary for her but it was something she was proud of and that it helped her heal and feel less intimidated. Bolstered by the experience, she recently shared with Anthony that she took another step as a poet, performing in front of a crowd at a spoken-word event for the first time.

Carlos, in a highly personal piece, created a story line about two families facing similar hardships and explored how the healthier family of the two used humor and communication whereas the other family turned to substance abuse and silence to cope. He then turned this into a comic book for his final project and later confided in Anthony that the project helped him get over the anger he had toward his mother for divorcing his father.

However, the most polished, well-researched and impressive project came from Alejandra. She had been struggling with finding balance between her social life, where she enjoyed having diverse friends, exploring her sexuality, and generally looking for new experiences, with her family life, where she was growing up in a highly religious family that had placed her on a pedestal she found restricting. Her project was a scrapbook that she created exploring interracial marriages, including landmark cases and local and national statistics, where she referenced the various sides of the debate on the merits or pitfalls of interracial marriage. Finally, she made some very astute connections between the history of that issue and the current debates around gay marriage. She shared that she loved the freedom to be creative with producing the scrapbook and that working on the scrapbook helped her feel less burdened by her family's narrow views.

In all of these projects, the Alexie novel, outside research, interviews of peers and adults in their communities, and additional resources all informed the final product. Rose's recognition that the students had latent talents not being accessed in school, and her ability to create a safe classroom where students could share personal and meaningful feelings and ideas with other students, created an assignment and an academic space for transformative work to occur.

Community Contexts: Bloomington, Minnesota

Jefferson High School (JHS) is located in Bloomington, Minnesota, an older, inner-ring suburb of Minneapolis with a population in 2010 of 82,893, making it the fifth largest city in Minnesota. Seventy-seven percent of JHS students are White, 6% Asian American, 4% Hispanic/Latino, 9% African American, and 4% other (U.S. News and World Report, 2015). On the 2013 statewide reading tests in which 67% of students were rated as proficient, 82% of JHS students were rated as proficient, with 87% of students still enrolled in college after their second year, data indicating a relatively high level of academic success.

To acquire information about her students' perceptions of Bloomington, Elizabeth Erdmann, our focal JHS teacher, had her 12th- and 10th-grade students complete an anonymous questionnaire regarding their perceptions of their community, school/school groups, and classroom. Her students described Bloomington as a relatively supportive, friendly suburban community. At the same time, they noted differences between the more upper middle class, largely White western section of Bloomington in which Jefferson High School is located versus the lower middle/working class, more diverse eastern section in which the other district's high school, Kennedy High School, is located—income differences that provided certain advantages for JHS students.

The JHS teachers noted that while most of their students had acquired certain resources from their family experiences, some of their students experienced strong family pressure to succeed academically so that they could be accepted at elite colleges, pressure that served to narrow their school experience to "getting good grades" at the expense of exploring the emotional and social aspects of their identities.

Jefferson High School

Jefferson High School has an enrollment of about 1,700 students in grades 9 through 12. It has won a number of awards including the 2009–2010 National Blue Ribbon School of Excellence and the U.S. News & World Report National Bronze Winner award (Jefferson High School, 2015). Its average English ACT score of 24.1 was higher than the state average of 22.1 and the national average of 20.5. Sixty-seven percent of the teachers have their master's degrees. It also has an active athletic program, with 1,243 students participating in thirty-four programs in 2011.

One aspect of high school culture is adherence to rules. In their questionnaire responses regarding perceptions of the school, Jefferson High School students noted that, while adherence to rules resulted in a sense of order, because some of the rules were arbitrary and inconsistent, students didn't follow certain rules.

In designing classroom activities, the JHS teachers drew on how the school context positioned their students' identities. For example, given her students' conflicting attitudes toward school rules, in studying the novel *Speak* (Anderson, 2011), which portrays students' resistance to school rules, Kristen Varpness had her students examine how rules operate in high school cultures. She first had students write about their responses to the opening chapter of the novel:

> Describe your first day of high school. Do you remember what you wore? How did you get to school that day? Was there an opening day pep fest? What were your impressions and feelings? Please reference the first chapter: WELCOME TO MERRYWEATHER HIGH. After reviewing the list below from pages five and six, write your own list of things you've been told that you feel like are lies:
>   "The first ten lies they tell you in high school:
>
> 1. We are here to help you.
> 2. You will have enough time to get to your classes before the bell rings.
> 3. The dress code will be enforced.
> 4. No smoking is allowed on school grounds.
> 5. Our football team will win the championship this year.
> 6. We expect more of you here.
> 7. Guidance counselors are always available to listen.
> 8. Your schedule was created with your needs in mind.
> 9. Your locker combination is private.
> 10. These will be the years you look back on fondly."

Students then used these rules to examine how students are labeled according to different categories related to their alignment with certain groups, alignment associated with adherence to school rules. Kristen then gave students a slip of paper with a label. To reveal their label to their peers, they made a list of adjectives, nouns, verbs, and so forth to describe their label. They then stood around the room and read one of the words they used to describe their label. They then grouped up according to similarity of these words, leading to students sharing their labels with the class. Through this activity, students were reflecting on how the norms operating in their school culture can position them to adopt certain identities related to group labels.

Elizabeth Erdmann's Identity

Elizabeth Erdmann, our focal JHS teacher and one of five JHS English teachers who were employing an identity-focused curriculum development project during the 2012–2014 school years, had been teaching for eleven years at the school. She completed her licensure and master's program at the University of Minnesota, working with Richard as her advisor. She taught TV Production, College

Writing, Introduction to Creative Writing, Advanced Creative Writing, Public Speaking, English 10, and Teen Literature, as well as English 9, 10, and 12 during summer school.

Elizabeth was a semifinalist for 2009 Minnesota Teacher of the Year, received an NCTE Teacher of Excellence Award from the Minnesota Council for Teachers of English (MCTE) in 2009, and served as MCTE's executive secretary. In 2010, she received the National Council of Teachers of English Media Literacy Award for her integration of media literacy in her curriculum.

Students in her classes value how she established individual relationships with them in ways that served to enhance their learning; they noted that:

- She understands our feelings, attitudes, and thought processes.
- She relates to us a lot and she actually helps us when we need help and we learn from that help given.
- She interacts with us and cares if we are getting the subject, and if we aren't she explains it in a way so that we do get it.

In Elizabeth's class, students are encouraged to engage in discussions and sharing of their work in ways that value their contributions as members of the classroom community, active listening consistent with the Common Core Speaking and Listening Standards (Council of Chief State School Officers and the National Governors Association, 2010). To do so, she has students restate others' discussion contributions to foster active listening. Similarly, in working with middle school students, Alicia Sullivan (2013) provided her 6th-grade students with stems such as "My partner _____ said . . ." and "Talking with _____ changed my thinking because _____ . . ." and "_____ suggested," so that her students would be restating their peers' statements versus their own in discussions.

Elizabeth also frequently shares anecdotes about her own daily past and present experiences to encourage students to share their experiences. And she challenges students to voice their opinions about events in the school or community, as well as eliciting alternative perspectives about those events, activities that serve to foster use of the different identity practices. As the students in an anonymous survey noted:

- This class has done a lot to show the differences in people's identities and this has shown me to accept diversity and embrace differences in people because that's how they identify themselves, and I have seen people embrace the differences I have and it's like everybody brings something to the class that makes the class exciting and interesting.
- In this class, they encourage us to show what we believe and feel like we won't be judged. We all have our own unique identities, and we can show that without being made fun of.

- People are comfortable talking in the class and to the teacher. Everyone will listen to what each other has to say and Erdmann always has a good understanding of what we are saying and good commentary. This shapes my identity because I can say what I want to in this specific class and know others are listening for once.

Elizabeth also recognized the need to model how students' identity practices position their responses to texts and how texts position their adoption of certain identity practices, as well as the need to connect their instruction to the Minnesota Common Core State Standards. For example, to address the CCSS reading standard, "Analyze how two or more texts address similar themes or topics in order to build knowledge or to compare the approaches the authors take" (Minnesota State Department of Education, 2010, p. 56), Elizabeth asked students to write about a common theme or topic related to characters' identities in three texts students read during the school year, an assignment that involved their use of the identity practice of *making connections between texts* to interpret texts.

Elizabeth knew that some of her students would have difficulty in completing the assignment, so she modeled this process for them with an illustrative example:

> If you think back to the literature you read in 11th grade, *Death of a Salesman*, *The Great Gatsby*, and *The Crucible* deal with characters whose desires lead to their eventual destruction (this is an example of a thesis statement). After you settle on a solid thesis statement, you need to explain in the body of your paper (using specific examples from the texts) how this concept is reflected in each work.
>
> Here is a very condensed example of the kind of reasoning I will look for in your paper, based on the above example thesis statement. I explain HOW each character's desires lead to his/her destruction:
>
> Willy in *Death of a Salesman* wishes that his son Biff would follow in his footsteps, so much so that he purposely kills himself in a car crash so Biff can use the life insurance money to start his own business. The irony is that Biff does not want a career in business, and even after his father's death, does not pursue that path. Jay Gatsby in *The Great Gatsby* goes to extreme lengths to gain wealth so he can achieve his dream and reclaim Daisy, his lost love. Ultimately though, this leads to his untimely death. Finally, in *The Crucible*, John Proctor's death is indirectly caused by his illicit affair (desire) with Abigail Williams during the paranoia of the Salem witch trials.

In planning her instruction, Elizabeth also recognized that her students would have difficulty employing the identity practices of *negotiating identities across different social worlds* or *engaging in critical analysis of texts and the world*, because, as fish in water, they do not recognize how their identities are positioned by larger social worlds. She noted that one student

> wrote [on the questionnaire], "Nothing shapes me." That's like saying, "Nothing gives me my identity." But the institutions, the country we live in shapes me. This is normal; they just think that it doesn't affect them in any way. My neighborhood is normal or regular, like, what does that mean? They don't see beyond right here.

To help students examine how social worlds position their identities, Elizabeth had her 12th-grade students conduct mini-ethnographies describing people's practices within a certain place or site. This involved them in the identity practice of *adopting alternative perspectives*, in this case the cultural perspectives constituting people's practices in a place or site, a project we describe in more detail in Chapter 4 with examples of some of the students' ethnography reports. In planning literature instruction for her 10th-grade English class, to have students engage in the identity practice of *adopting alternative perspectives* in response to a text, for responding to character identity construction in *The Kite Runner* (Hosseini, 2004), Elizabeth had her students work together in groups to conduct research on the historical, cultural, and institutional forces positioning characters in the novel.

To have students engage in the identity practice of *making connections between texts and people*, in the 12th-grade assignment noted above, Elizabeth asked students to draw connections between three of the books they had read during the year—*1984, Lord of the Flies, The Alchemist, The Tao of Pooh, Candide, Macbeth, Beloved, Ordinary People, Hamlet*, and *Catcher in the Rye*—in terms of a certain common "motif, theme, situation, relationship, topic of concern, view of humanity, or some other connection you see."

Our Framework and the Common Core State Standards

Given the widespread adoption of the English Language Arts Common Core State Standards (Council of Chief State School Officers and the National Governors Association (2010), it is important to consider how our framework seeks to address these standards. You can align use of our five identity practices by designing activities involving them in ways that address particular Common Core State Standards (CCSS) related to reading, writing, speaking/listening, and language. To do so, you need to recognize that the CCSS do not dictate what and how to teach; they identify certain goals to be addressed through classroom activities associated with use of the five identity practices (Beach, Haertling-Thein, & Webb, 2012). The CCSS are particularly useful for clarifying specific criteria students can use for understanding expectations for their participation, as well as for self-assessing their participation in activities and changes in their learning over time.

At the same time, it is important to avoid the propensity for standardization associated with any adoption of academic standards, standardization that undermines an identity-focused approach by ignoring individual differences in students' knowledge, abilities, and dispositions.

You can avoid standardizing instruction by involving students in collaboratively planning activities or sharing resources so that students assume that they have some ownership in developing these activities. For example, in teaching *The Absolutely True Diary of a Part-Time Indian*, SBH students brought in "partner texts"—rap lyrics, poems, photographs, other books—a process referred to as *juxtaposing* (Sumara, 1996) of texts with the Alexie novel. Consistent with the identity practice of *defining connections between texts and people*, these outside texts and students' writing led to students explaining the connections between their texts and *Diary*, reflecting their ability to use connections to interpret the novel based on their own resources. By inferring connections between three texts, students were comparing how the different worlds of these texts shaped the main characters' identities, a focus involving use of intertextual connections that address the Common Core literature standard:

> Analyze how two or more texts address similar themes or topics in order to build knowledge or to compare the approaches the authors take.
> *(Council of Chief State School Officers and the*
> *National Governors Association, 2010, p. 35)*

And, for her 10th-grade students, based on their reading of *Night* (Wiesel, 2006) and *Persepolis* (Satrapi, 2004) as guides for storytelling and memoir, she had students create a visual, comic-book memoir with images and speech bubbles portraying a key event in their life, an example of recontextualizing their prior experience with literary texts to connect to writing a multimodal memoir that addressed the Minnesota Common Core standard for descriptive, narrative writing:

> Write narratives and other creative texts to develop real or imagined experiences or events using effective technique, well-chosen details, and well-structured event sequences.
> *(Minnesota State Department of Education, 2010, p. 75)*

Consistent with the identity practice of *adopting an alternative perspective*, she asked students to go beyond simply writing an autobiographical description of the event to reflect on how the event itself "transcends the author's personal experience and comments upon ideas and issues from important events in our modern society," so that students were applying the perspective of the social significance of the event. For example, one student described talking with a friend about a range of larger issues facing the world—hunger, terrorism, gay marriage—only to end up focusing on "Facebook overuse," a commentary on students' perspective on the world.

Adopting the Common Core Standards
for Teaching *Ordinary People*

To illustrate the application of the Common Core standards to teaching literature based on an identity-focused approach, we describe Jackie Van Geest's unit for teaching the novel *Ordinary People* (Guest, 1982) to 12th-grade students at Jefferson High School, Bloomington, Minnesota. This novel, set in a similar middle-class suburb in the 1970s, portrays Conrad, a high school student, coping with conflicts between his father, Cal, and mother, Beth— conflicts precipitated by his brother's accidental drowning. Conrad is also dealing with conflicts in his relationships with his high school peers, including his girlfriend.

As tensions increase between his parents as well as between him and his mother, Conrad experiences depression and attempts suicide, leading him to seek help from a psychiatrist. Beth eventually leaves Cal, but Conrad emerges a stronger person at the end of the novel. Because of its portrayal of the characters' issues of identity construction around the difficulties of adopting the roles of father, mother, and son/brother within a dysfunctional family, the novel created a space for students to discuss the characters and their own identity construction. As we note throughout this book, students responded to the characters' identities by drawing connections to their own experiences and attitudes related to their identities within their own family relationships, for example, by contrasting the tensions between Conrad and Beth with their own positive relationships with their own parent(s).

It is important to recognize that students are continually developing in their use of these identity practices. In our descriptions of each of the five identity practices discussed in Chapters 3–7, as summarized below, we will also discuss ways in which teachers can conceive of student development for each of these practices and design activities consistent with certain relevant ELA Common Core State Standards (Council of Chief State School Officers and the National Governors Association, 2010) to foster such development.

For her *Ordinary People* unit, Jackie drew on the Minnesota English Language Arts Common Core State Standards (Minnesota State Department of Education, 2010) reading, writing, and speaking/listening/media literacy standards for planning her unit and providing feedback during the unit on students' development in addressing these standards:

- Cite strong and thorough textual evidence to support analysis of what the text says explicitly as well as inferences drawn from the text, including determining where the text leaves matters uncertain.
- Analyze a complex set of ideas or sequence of events and explain how specific individuals, ideas, or events interact and develop over the course of the text.
- Draw evidence from literary or informational texts to support analysis, reflection, and research.

- Make strategic use of digital media (e.g., textual, graphical, audio, visual, and interactive elements) in presentations to enhance understanding of findings, reasoning, and evidence to add interest.

(pp. 61, 65, 67, 84)

For example, for the students' final essay assignment, Jackie had students use evidence from the novel to interpret characters' perceptions of and interactions with each other to interpret those characters' identity construction over time. In her feedback, she then noted how students demonstrated change in their ability to interpret characters' perceptions and interactions.

And, given our framework's focus on how identities are constructed within particular sociocultural contexts, for planning these activities we emphasize the importance of creating authentic, purposeful contexts for interpreting and producing texts. In writing to her school administrator regarding the need for an anti-bullying policy, a student has some purposeful reason for engaging in writing: to attempt to achieve change in her school.

Further, the specific grade-level Common Core standards presuppose certain developmental differences in students' cognitive ability to employ certain practices—that 9th graders are able to engage in more cognitively advanced writing than 6th graders. Our framework invites teachers to avoid such developmental presuppositions regarding students' abilities by determining and building on students' unique strengths and talents in planning activities.

Summary

In this chapter, we described how teachers in both an urban and a suburban school planned their activities based on their knowledge of how these different communities and schools position students' identities. By doing so, they were fostering their students' awareness of how larger social worlds position characters' and their own identity practices; for example, how Arnold's school and reservation worlds portrayed in *Diary* influenced his identities in ways that connected to students' own negotiation of identities between community/home and school world. Through effective planning of these activities, students were learning to employ certain identity practices to position themselves in the classroom in ways that served to enhance their sense of agency as academically and socially successful students. (For additional resources, activities, and further reading, see http://tinyurl.com/lw789fe.)

In the next five chapters—each addressing one of the five identity practices—we describe in more detail how these and other teachers fostered students' identity construction through use of these practices.

References

Alexie, S. (2007). *The absolutely true diary of a part-time Indian.* Boston: Little Brown.
Anderson, L. H. (2011). *Speak.* New York: Square Fish.

Beach, R., Haertling-Thein, A., & Webb, A. (2012). *Teaching to exceed the English language arts Common Core State Standards: A literacy practices approach for 6–12 classrooms.* New York: Routledge Press.

Beach, R., Thein, A., & Parks, D. (2008). *High school students' competing social worlds: Negotiating identities and allegiances in response to multicultural literature.* New York: Routledge Press.

Bishop, B. (2009). *The big sort: Why the clustering of like-minded America is tearing us apart.* New York: Houghton Mifflin Harcourt.

Bloome, D., Beierle, M., Grigorenko, M., & Goldman, S. (2009). Learning over time: Uses of intercontextuality, collective memories, and classroom chronotopes in the construction of learning opportunities in a ninth-grade language arts classroom. *Language and Education, 23*(4), 313–334.

Bushaw, W. J., & Lopez, S. J. (2013). Which way do we go: The 45th annual PDK/Gallup Poll on the public's attitudes towards public schools. *Phi Delta Kappan Magazine, 95*(1). Retrieved from http://kappanmagazine.org

Carnevale, A., & Strohl, J. (2013). *Separate and unequal: How higher education reinforces the intergenerational reproduction of White racial privilege.* Washington, DC: Georgetown University Center on Education and the Workforce.

Council of Chief State School Officers and the National Governors Association. (2010). Common Core State Standards from English Language Arts. Authors. Retrieved from http://www.corestandards.org/ELA-Literacy

Crosnoe, R. (2011). *Fitting in, standing out: Navigating the social challenges of high school to get an education.* New York: Cambridge University Press.

Csikszentmihalyi, M., & Larson, R. (1986). *Being adolescent: Conflict and growth in the teenage years.* New York: Basic Books.

Davis, B., Sumara, D., & Luce-Kapler, R. (2000). *Engaging minds: Changing teaching in complex times.* New York: Routledge.

Djikic, M., Oatley, K., & Moldoveanu, M. (2013). Reading other minds: Effects of literature on empathy. *Scientific Study of Literature, 3,* 28–47.

Durlak, J. A., Weissberg, R. P., Dymnicki, A. B., Taylor, R. D., & Schellinger, K. B. (2011). The impact of enhancing students' social and emotional learning: A meta-analysis of school-based universal interventions. *Child Development, 82*(1), 405–432.

Finley, T. (2014, August 13). The research behind social and emotional learning [web log post]. Retrieved from http://tinyurl.com/la8ujlt

Fraser, S., & Bosanquet, A. (2006). The curriculum? That's just a unit outline, isn't it? *Studies in Higher Education, 31*(3), 269–284.

Gammill, D. (2014, July 11). Google Thursdays and the power of self-directed learning [web log post]. Retrieved from http://tinyurl.com/lqdevva

Gonzalez, N., Moll, L. C., & Amanti, C. (Eds.). (2005). *Funds of knowledge: Theorizing practices in households, communities, and classrooms.* New York: Routledge.

Guerrero, C., Gaztambibe-Fernández, R., Rosas, M., & Guerrero, E. (2013). *Proyecto Latin@* on stage and under the magnifying glass: The possibilities and limitations of a high-profile institutionally sponsored youth participatory action research project. *International Journal of Critical Pedagogy, 4*(2), 105–126.

Guest, J. (1982). *Ordinary people.* New York: Penguin.

Halpern, R. (2013). *Youth, education, and the role of society.* Cambridge, MA: Harvard University Press.

Hosseini, K. (2004). *The kite runner.* New York: Penguin.

Jefferson High School. (2015). About our school. Author. Retrieved from http://tinyurl.com/kyuhsrb

Kalogrides, D., & Loeb, S. (2013). Different teachers, different peers: The magnitude of student sorting within schools. *Educational Researcher, 42*(6), 304–316.

Kids Count report. The Annie E. Casey Foundation. (2013). *Early reading proficiency in the United States.* Baltimore, MD: Author. Retrieved from http://www.aecf.org

Minnesota State Department of Education. (2010). Minnesota K-12 Academic Standards in English Language Arts. St. Paul, MN: Author. Retrieved from http://tinyurl.com/72fzzr9

Moule, J. (2012). *Cultural competence: A primer for educators* (2nd ed.). Belmont, CA: Wadsworth.

Neilsen, L. (2006). Playing for real: Performative texts and adolescent identities. In D. Alvermann, K. Hinchman, D. Moore, S. Phelps, & D. Waff (Eds.), *Reconceptualizing the literacies in adolescents' lives* (2nd ed., pp. 5–28). New York: Routledge.

Ravitch, D. (2011). *The death and life of the great American school system: How testing and choice are undermining education.* New York: Basic Books.

Ross, J., & Bell, P. (2014, July 1). School is over for the summer: So is the era of majority White U.S. public schools. *National Journal.* Retrieved from http://tinyurl.com/ofbot74

Satrapi, M. (2004). *Persepolis: The story of a childhood.* New York: Pantheon.

Simon, R., Brennan, J., Bresba, S., DeAngelis, S., Edwards, W., Jung, H., et al. (2014). The Teaching to Learn Project: Investigating literacy through intergenerational inquiry. In H. Pleasants & D. Salter (Eds.), *Community-based multiliteracies and digital media projects: Questioning assumptions and exploring realities* (pp. 159–180). New York: Peter Lang.

Smith, M. (2013, August 28). A question about reading and motivation. eXtended Mind, Culture, Activity listserv.

Sparks, S.D. (2014, August 10). Can schools respect individuality without cultivating narcissism in students? [web log post]. Retrieved from http://tinyurl.com/krw85dy

Street, C. (2005). Funds of knowledge at work in the writing classroom. *Multicultural Education, 13*(2). Retrieved from http://tinyurl.com/nxgu88h

Sullivan, A. (2013, September 3). Phew! They're chatty! [web log post]. Retrieved from http://writesolutions.org/chatty

Sumara, D. (1996). *Private readings in public: Schooling the literary imagination.* New York: Peter Lang.

Sumara, D. (2002). *Why reading literature in school still matters.* Mahwah, NJ: Lawrence Erlbaum Associates.

Taylor, S. (2013). Vlogging composition: Making content dynamic [web log post]. Retrieved from http://tinyurl.com/qz6atlo

U.S. News and World Report. (2015). Education rankings and advice: Jefferson High School. Author. Retrieved from http://tinyurl.com/nouz43w

Wang, M-T., & Eccles, J.S. (2012). Social support matters: Longitudinal effects of social support on three dimensions of school engagement from middle to high school. *Child Development, 83*(3), 877–895.

Wang, M-T., & Holcombe, R. (2010). Adolescents' perceptions of school environment, engagement, and academic achievement in middle school. *American Educational Research Journal, 47*(3), 633–662.

Wiesel, E. (2006). *Night.* New York: Hill & Wang.

3

ADOPTING ALTERNATIVE PERSPECTIVES

> Identities provide us with particular perspectives on shared social worlds . . . what we "know" is intimately tied up with how we conceptualize that world and who we understand ourselves to be in it. Our conceptual frameworks are thus inseparable from how we comprehend ourselves in terms of gender, culture, race, sexuality, ability, religion, age, and profession—even when we are not consciously aware of how these aspects of ourselves affect our points of view.
>
> *Paula Moya (2006)*

Introduction

In this chapter, we describe activities designed to foster students' use of the identity practice of adopting different, alternative perspectives to expand ways of believing and knowing. We believe that this is an important identity practice for constructing identities. To begin to entertain alternative identities, students need to experiment with adopting new ways of perceiving themselves and the world in ways that challenge fixed, status quo self-perceptions. Experimenting with alternative ways of believing and knowing leads to imagining alternative ways of being and becoming as students construct identities.

The ELA class is potentially fertile ground for such activity to occur because the languages for unfamiliar beliefs and knowledge are available in the forms of literature, as well as in students' talk and writing, that encourage the adoption of alternative ways of believing and knowing. In Anthony's analysis of students at SBH, one finding was that while students appreciated being seen by others in complex and nuanced ways, they often lacked the capacity or language to apply a sophisticated lens of identity to themselves or peers. In a survey given to students at SBH, they were asked to respond to the following prompt: "If asked what your identity is, what would you say?" The greatest number of descriptors used was eight (by Andrea) and the fewest was one, with the average number of descriptors being three. For example, when asked to share his identity, Carlos described himself as "a gamer," who is "chill and likes to make people laugh." When encouraged in a later interview to expand on these descriptions of self, students struggled to provide more detail about themselves. In many ways, Carlos's description is emblematic of the affordances—stability, presentation of self, status and position among peers—as well as the constraints, that is, seeing the self as limited, identity as fixed, selecting self-definers that may limit academic or social success, which are inherent in limited perceptions of the self.

While the identities that students adopt may or may not be conducive to academic success, finding a stable description of self is reassuring as students consider who they have been and imagine who they might become. While offering a modicum of security, such self-descriptors can also limit youth, inhibiting the sort of identity experimentation that adolescence ought to provide.

We believe ELA can be a place for students to try on alternative perspectives about the various realms that inform the descriptors we use to understand the self. At the same time, we offer activities and language for teachers and students to use so they will be equipped with the skills and resources necessary to reimagine the self.

Different Perspectives on Identity Construction

Despite a wealth of new imaginings about identity in various spheres of society, schools (in large part due to their institutional structures and traditions) hold a relatively simplistic and narrow view of identity for students. However, we discuss the benefits of instructional activities that support the adoption of alternative perspectives, providing examples from our research that illuminate instruction. First, we apply James Gee's (2000) discussion of the four realms of identity—affinity, discourse, institutional, and nature identities—and consider how students might benefit from applying Gee's heuristic both to characters in literature as well as to themselves.

Gee's notion of identity involves asking, "*Who am I?*" To consider how to explore this question with students, we examine perspectives about race, class, and gender and affinity identities to consider how the relevance of said perspectives are informed and shaped by cultural, social, and historical contexts.

Next, we consider how we can encourage students to ask, "*Who are others?*" during which we look at the benefits of encouraging empathetic and critical adoption of alternative beliefs and values. In this section we consider adopting varied ethical and moral perspectives, adopting outsider perspectives, and the perspectives of characters found in literature.

Finally we ask, "*Where and when am I?*" during which we examine historical, economic, space, and place discourses, institutional contexts, and the roles they play as individuals construct the self. As we explore each of these thematic questions, we offer activities and examples of lessons to support instruction and encourage engagement.

James Gee's Four Identity Sources

In his definition of identity, James Gee (2000) emphasizes the importance of social and cultural perspectives associated with how students are "recognized as a certain 'kind of person,' in a given context . . ." (p. 99). Gee offers a model of identity consisting of a cross-section of four specific identity sources most individuals carry: affinity, discourse, institution, and nature (Gee, 2000)—sources that inform one another and are subject to changes due to varied social contexts and cultural practices.

The *affinity* aspect of one's identity is described as the groups, causes, or communities a person feels a sense of community with. This aspect is informed by the activities and experiences an individual has participated in with other social actors. For example, one might describe himself as an American because he lives in the United States, or one might identify herself as being a Deadhead because she went to many Grateful Dead concerts. One's *discourse* identity includes the personality traits that are recognized by others and are associated with an individual, such as having a good sense of humor. The *institution* identity is how one is positioned by authorities within institutions. This could be one's professional status (teacher, lawyer, dancer) and also includes positions that are situated in additional institutions—for example, being working class (economic institutions) or being Hispanic (social construction of race). Finally, Gee discusses one's *nature* identity—that is, the biological state developed from forces in nature, such as being left-handed, having green eyes, having a predisposition to heart disease, or being an identical twin. Taken together, it is difficult to imagine a descriptor of self that would not fall into one of the above identities, and thus it is a useful formula for engaging students in a thoughtful discussion on identity.

Depending on the cultural and historical context, one identity characteristic might fall into all four identities. Gee (2000) gives the example of attention deficit/hyperactivity disorder (ADHD). Saying one "has ADHD" is an act of labeling that identifies the person as possessing a particular condition associated with a medical condition. With this label comes an institutional identity—being afforded particular protections under the law; authorizing various forms of treatment and support; and, for a student in a school, being classified in a particular way by people in authority.

Additionally, regardless of the debates around the causes of ADHD—be they genetic, environmental, lifestyle, prenatal care—the label suggests abnormal functioning of the brain's neurotransmitters and therefore is related to one's nature identity. Having ADHD affects behavior, moods, attention, and learning, all of which others observe and attach meaning to, so these behaviors can be considered relatable to one's discourse identity. Finally, people who have ADHD may feel a bond with others who have the same condition, perhaps belonging to support groups or regularly visiting particular websites where ADHD is discussed—all actions that fashion one's affinity identity.

In each of these identity realms, what matters for the construction of identity are those indicators or characteristics that are recognized by others as having meaning, a recognition that positions one's identities. Consider the differences between the current social and cultural meanings we attribute today to being identified as a hipster (affinity identity), or being gay (nature identity), or being a teacher (institutional identity), or being macho (discourse identity) versus fifty years ago for each. Clearly, the four identities Gee notes vary in salience depending on the social and historical context. These identities not only inform one another, they are also socially and historically defined, and due to connotative reasoning, they are often understood in terms of one another (Gee, 2000). People are, of course, combinations of these identities, and apply different emphasis of importance given the context or activity in which they consider the self. While all of these identity sources relate to our work in the book, the notion of affinity identity seems particularly salient. Of the four, it is perhaps the most susceptible to re-creation based on an individual's agency.

Bringing Gee into the Classroom

In Anthony's research, he found that students appreciate being seen in complex ways and yet struggle to see themselves or their peers beyond limiting or narrow labels that are available in high school contexts ("stoner," "nerd," etc.). In order to encourage a more complex understanding of identity, the students at SBH were introduced to the four identity categories identified by Gee (2000) discussed above and applied them to characters from literature.

In response to *The Absolutely True Diary of a Part-Time Indian* (Alexie, 2007), students constructed an identity chart to analyze the protagonist, Arnold, and his different identities. According to the students, Arnold's *biological* identity included his birth defects, his hair and skin color being particular shades of brown, being a younger brother, and being skinny and tall with big feet. They viewed his *institutional* identity as being labeled as an Indian, living in poverty, being a student, being seen as a mascot or savage at his White school and as an "apple" on the reservation. In addition, Arnold's personality—being seen as smart, awkward, funny, and very earnest—reflected his *discourse* identity. Finally, the students noted that the following details—Arnold being on the basketball team, his passion for books and comics, his friendship with Rowdy, and his bond to the reservation—all revealed parts of his *affinity* identity.

Next, the SBH students created similar charts for themselves as illustrated in Cat's identity chart in Figure 3.1, and then followed that up with the identities (those they could change) they hope to have in ten to twenty years.

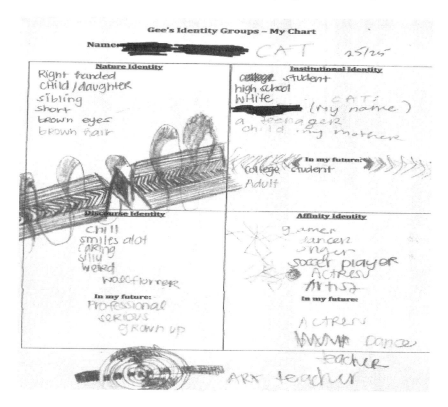

FIGURE 3.1 Cat's Identity Chart

In the above image, Cat's choices for how she identified herself within Gee's framework are illustrative of her identity in multiple ways. Cat is Latina, her mother and father are both of Mexican descent, and yet Cat elects to refer to herself as "White" because she is often referred to as White by her peers and she makes efforts (in her appearance, interests, manner of speaking) to distance herself from Latina cultural markers. Her name is also meaningful to her. While her pseudonym for this book is Cat, her actual name is French in origin, is very unusual, and is something she sees as appropriate given the self-described "weird, wallflower, artist" status that she claims.

Her choice to use the term "wallflower" is an example of how literature has the potential to provide students with additional narratives to author the self. Cat's favorite book is *The Perks of Being a Wallflower* (Chbosky, 1999), a story about a young man who, like Cat, is an outsider, shy, and introspective. Also like Cat, he is a junior in high school struggling with many of the usual themes that accompany this period and, particularly salient for Cat, feeling completely disconnected from the teens that surround him. Cat's notes about her imagined future reflect her sense of agency associated with being a teacher, an artist, an actress, or so forth, which Cat believes will require her to be "serious" rather than "silly" and "professional" rather than "weird." Even her drawings all over the chart can be seen as an identity display through her abstract, playful images that enhance her worksheet.

The activity of completing Gee's identity chart was a generative event in Rose's class. As we discussed about planning curriculum around students' identities, this activity provided the teacher with a better understanding of Cat's identity as classroom student, and provided students with a language with which to discuss and challenge fixed notions of identity. For example, Jeffrey was surprised to learn that race was a social construct and not simply one's nature identity.

The chart also provided a space for adolescents to think about the ways that they are positioned by others, and a space to resist such positioning. Anthony noted to students that if they were left-handed and had been born one hundred years earlier, this trait might have carried a negative connotation about being inferior that needed remedying. Finally, the important lesson in Gee's identity theory is that identities are unstable, historically and socially produced, and open to change and transformation. This last benefit is perhaps most salient, given that for so many students, like Cat, adolescence involves struggling with feelings of alienation, marginalization, and hopelessness.

Who Am I?

We explore how to discuss and teach the question of "Who am I?" in a necessarily incomplete and problematic way. While we recognize the problems associated with labeling students solely on the basis of gender, race, class, or affinity groups, we also recognize that students need to be given an entry point into a necessary conversation if they are to develop the critical thinking required to challenge the labels they use. In addition, these labels are not seen in a vacuum; the significance given to each label is very much determined by what other labels a person possesses. For example, culturally defined understandings of what it means to "be a man" are informed by other identity characteristics—such as class, nationality, and religion. Finally, while we would argue that nature identity-related terms (having red hair, being overweight, needing glasses, being very tall) are all important labels that shape identity, we also believe that they all deserve critical scrutiny.

Who am I? is about exploring the ways in which language positions identities in terms of race, class, gender, or sexuality as common descriptors that individuals tend to access, and that can serve to invite processes of becoming and developing, but that can also marginalize and oppress. Because the young people around youth are also students, the institutional identity of being a student is taken as a given, as opposed to the ways that adults reference their profession when answering, "Who am I?" In creating their charts, none of the students at SBH actually used the word "student." Not being locked into an institutional identity in the same way as adults, students can have the freedom to resist external labels and also attempt to adopt new identities to see what fits.

Who Am I as Defined by Race, Class, and Gender

With these considerations in mind, the use of terms such as gender, race, class, and the terms associated with affinity groups are discussed, followed by activities that invite students to challenge these constructs and arm them with the skills and tools to relabel themselves.

Race

Examining discourses of race in their own lives and literature requires students to go beyond perceiving race simply as a matter of their individual prejudices or "colorblind" notions that "we are inside all the same," to examine how institutional racism itself shapes beliefs and knowledge about racial identities (Bonilla-Silva, 2001). In addition, issues of race and racism are entrenched in media representations, often in ways that tend to reify stereotypes and reproduce simplistic or problematic analyses (Shohat & Stam, 2013).

What would it mean to adopt an alternative perspective about race? How can students be supported to imagine what it means to be a particular race? Critical race theory offers many strategies for students to develop a more complex and thoughtful understanding of race issues, almost always emphasizing the need to look beyond status quo representations of and discussions about race (Delgado & Stefancic, 2013). In considering institutional racism, students could study the roles that legal, governmental, economic, and political systems play in positioning people based on race. For example, students might examine how the real estate industry created segregated "desirable neighborhoods" through restricted housing laws. Or how the legal and political systems in the 1970s and 1980s created the "war on drugs" and mandatory drug sentencing laws to construct the stereotypical presupposition that African American males are more likely to engage in the practice of committing crimes or using drugs—a reflection of a discourse of institutional racism that shaped the legal and prison system.

As documented in Michelle Alexander's (2012) *The New Jim Crow: Mass Incarceration in the Age of Colorblindness*, this particular discourse of institutional racism became the "war on drugs." Developed during the 1970s by conservative politicians, this discourse defined African American males as potential or active drug addicts requiring criminalization. This "war on drugs" included passage of harsh drug laws, particularly for crack cocaine that was in use in African American, urban neighborhoods, resulting in racial profiling, higher arrest rates, and long-term incarceration of African American males, despite that fact that drug possession and use was no higher for African Americans than for other demographic groups.

It is therefore the case that the construction of African American males as "drug addicts/criminals" was an institutional, political, and cultural effort to challenge African Americans' growing sense of agency during the 1970s and 1980s, agency evident in the fact that, across measures of self-esteem from 1991 to 2008, 8th-, 10th-, and 12th-grade African Americans had the highest self-esteem scores, followed by Whites, then Hispanics, then Asian Americans, with males scoring slightly higher than females (Bachman et al., 2011).

Similarly, as portrayed in *The Absolutely True Diary of a Part-Time Indian* (Alexie, 2007), given the construction of the Native American identity in popular culture as the "savage enemy," Native Americans were relegated to live on reservations in ways that limited their economic, educational, and political opportunities. Or, as evident in debates about immigration reform, immigrant Latinos are portrayed by conservative politicians as competing for their White constituents' jobs, a discourse based on a divide-and-conquer political strategy.

As we noted previously and later in this chapter, it is possible for students who initially subscribe to problematic discourses of race to change their perspectives through discussions of race in multicultural literature in which these problematic discourses are challenged by their peers (Beach, Thein, & Parks, 2008).

Class

While class differences are typically described in terms of the categories "working class," "middle class," "upper middle class," and so forth, these categories often frame identity practices in essentialist ways based on economic structures. For instance, if someone is identified as "working class," there is an assumption that this person must have certain identity practices, which is often not the case (Vagle & Jones, 2012). This suggests the need to complicate these categories in terms of how people adopt a range of different identity practices associated with allegiances to different spaces defined by class difference (Gibson-Graham, Resnick, & Wolff, 2000). For example, while the notion of being self-reliant is often associated with being "middle class," in her study of working-class young adults, Jennifer Silva (2013) found that these young adults have had to adopt a self-reliant attitude toward life because they have limited support systems for helping them gain employment.

Related to Silva's findings, Anthony found that the majority of students at SBH state that they intend to go to college and become professionals in the working world. Most of them hope to be the first in their low-income families to attend college, some hoping to be the first to graduate high school. However, when asked to articulate what this process involves, they often seemed at a loss. Although students may have teachers who have articulated this process for them, it was evident that nothing can substitute for being able to witness other siblings, parents, and friends who have successfully attended college as role models to emulate.

Many families are also struggling given the decline of jobs—with only 58.7% of the adult population holding full-time jobs, leading to an increasing income inequality in America as hourly average wages have been stagnant or even declined since 1973, and with 10% of Americans owning 80% of the total financial assets (Young, 2013). While in 1970, families living in middle-class neighborhoods comprised 65% of the population, that percentage in 2013 decreased to 44%, and over the same period the number of families living in poor neighborhoods increased from 15% to 30% (Young, 2013).

Unfortunately, discussion of class difference rarely enters the classroom context (Vagle & Jones, 2012). A number of reasons contribute to reluctance on the part of teachers to discuss a sensitive issue: anti-union and anti-labor sentiment repeatedly expressed in corporate media, a lack of language on the topic, and, unlike race and gender, class is less visible. Additionally, within a single school in a particular neighborhood, the economic status of the students may be relatively heterogeneous. While Dorothy Allison's (2012) novel, *Bastard out of Carolina*, provides students with the perspective of Bone as a young female in her rural, working-class family's world who struggles with sexual abuse, neglect, and poverty associated with being poor "white trash," this important novel is infrequently taught due to censorship concerns.

Despite these challenges, an important issue to raise with students of all economic backgrounds is a consideration of the affordances and constraints of being identified with a particular class. How class shapes one's identity is not considered as frequently as other potential mechanisms, yet students are surrounded by uncritical depictions of class on a regular basis through the media and other institutions.

Consider the recent trend of reality television shows designed to exploit and poke fun at rural people who struggle with obesity and poverty. Or the daily talk shows where poor, undereducated people are often pitted against other poor people for the viewing pleasure of the audience. Or note the problematic adoption of "working class" culture by young people who enjoy upper- or middle-class privilege. For example, the hipster obsession with "authenticity" means they are often just affecting whatever trappings of working-class life they like. Current trends include wearing "trucker hats," drinking Pabst Blue Ribbon beer, and eating at fancy mac and cheese restaurants. It is important to note that low-income students, while keenly aware of this behavior on the part of people with privilege, do not have the access, resources, or opportunities to "adopt" upper-class culture in similar ways. How do these representations or opportunities, or lack of representations or opportunities, shape students' identities across economic classes?

While markers of class difference are less salient than for race or gender, Jefferson High School students often described how class differences intersected with race and gender differences. For example, Josh Cornes contrasted his previous life in England with his current life in Bloomington, Minnesota, by noting that Bloomington was less racist, at least from his perspective as a White person, than his British working-class town:

> Back in England, it was pretty racist. Bloomington is a kind of well-off place, so they would have been brought up so that everyone here is pretty accepting. There are not many fights here, where back in England, there was a fight every day. [My school] was similar, but some people were not as well-off as here.

Students were also aware of how identities constituted by discourses of class through certain "embodied dispositions" (Scollon & Scollon, 2003) reflected in students' dress, appearance, physical walk, or gestures. In their interviews, Jefferson High School students consistently noted that the cheerleaders in their school represented upper-middle-class backgrounds as manifested in their dress, appearance, and attitude of superiority. As Nicole noted, "They always feel like they are on top and can do what they want and wear what they want and say what they want." She was also aware of how these class differences positioned her own identity. In describing her afterschool work at a local country club, Nicole described how her perceptions of the upper-middle-class male golfer clients shaped her own identity within the country club space, an identity that differed from her home or school identities:

> I work down in the Pro Shop and that world is just different—everyone feels like they are very prestigious, like, I'm here and I belong to a country club. So, I'm working here and these guys are good and you have to really serve them and be there for them, so you put on a different face, so, alright, I'm here and have to be proper; I can't make these funny jokes. I have to display myself well.

Class differences may also shape students' values, whereby upper-middle-class students place a high value on achievement and documentation of success as "portfolio shape-shifting" people, while working-class students may value fairness and loyalty to friends (Gee, Allen, & Clinton, 2001). For example, a number of the JHS students perceived their primary goal in school was to build their resume based not only on getting good grades, but also through active participation in school organizations and athletics for the primary purpose of college admissions, while other students were critical of what they perceived to be an obsession with achievement-orientation at the expense of building strong friendships with peers.

Gender

Students construct themselves in terms of gender differences by adopting, enacting, or resisting discourses of femininity and masculinity through use of language, gestures, dress, reading/viewing preferences, and so forth. Students could examine how up until the mid 20th century, in American society, being male was associated with the workplace, while being female was associated with the home/family (Hall, 1997).

It is important to move beyond these essentialist notions of gender differences to perceive gender less in terms of category differences and more in terms of enacting or performing certain gendered identity practices associated with femininity or masculinity. In describing her planning for teaching a gender and women's studies college course, Kate Drabinski (2011) notes:

> In my experience, very few students are used to thinking about identity in terms of practices. Even if they recognize themselves as occupying an identity category, the practices that produce that identity are not automatically legible to them. For traditional college-aged students reared in educational settings that think about difference largely in terms of tolerance and diversity models, identity is a given, and having oneself recognized for who one is remains a primary goal of political identity formation . . . I then organize class discussions and activities to get students to see how they too are implicated in social practices of gender, no matter how "natural" gender might feel to them.
>
> *(p. 13)*

To construct gendered identities, students draw on popular culture and advertising representations of gendered performances, for example, advertisements by the beauty industry constructing images of idealized femininity or sports promotions or alcohol ads constructing images of masculinity. These discourses of masculinity and femininity shape students' perspectives of characters in literature, television, films, and online representations of gender difference (Guzzetti & Bean, 2012). For example, an analysis of a 10th-grade female student's perceptions of online advertising indicated that she adopted a consumer stance in responding positively to the gendered representations of advertised products (Alvermann, 2012), while at the same time, students in this study also adopted critical stances toward online gendered representations (Alvermann et al., 2012). Through constructing their own texts in the form of zines, manga/graphic novels, hip-hop videos, or websites, students create complex gender representations of females as means of challenging stereotypical representations (Joaquin, 2010).

All of this suggests that students can interrogate the ways in which gendered identities are positioned by larger commercial and cultural forces, leading them to appreciate how gender itself is a cultural enactment rather than simply a biological given.

Who Am I as Defined by Affinity Group Membership

> All passionate affinity spaces are organized first and foremost around a specific passion [involving] supportive interactions because people in the space accept a

theory of learning that says that expertise is not in a person but in the affinity space and that no matter how good you are there is always something more to learn and someone else from whom to get help and mentoring.

James Paul Gee (in an interview with Henry Jenkins, 2011)

As we discussed earlier, Gee defines *affinity* identity as being a reflection of the experiences a person has by engaging in a particular practice with others. Unlike institutional or nature identities, the authorizing agent of one's affinity identity is the affinity group of which one is a part. Participants of an affinity group may live far from one another, may not be connected in ways beyond the shared affinity, and yet because of a mutual interest in, and allegiance and access to, a practice, those participants feel connected to one another in ways that influence identity construction. Of the four identity categories, affinity seems most salient for the potentials of agency, ownership, and transformation.

On the one hand, the notion of affinity groups seems promising and perhaps even liberating in terms of providing spaces for students to engage with others in purposeful work, as reflected in participation in online affinity groups (Gee, 2013). On the other hand, a critical look at this identity construct suggests that some students, particularly those lacking in power or status, are often assigned to affinity groups as they are marginalized based on race, class, gender, sexuality, and appearance. For example, Tre, as a young black man growing up in poverty who made some poor choices and broke the law, was forced to wear an ankle bracelet, which affected his identity. This act, while having obvious legal purposes that constitute Tre's institutional identity as a criminal, also served as constant reminder of this status and informed his own affinity toward being a "survivor, doing what I gotta do."

Activity: Social Languages and Identity Construction in Affinity Groups

Students can reflect on their use or others' uses of social language related to their identity allegiances to certain affinity groups. To do so, they could describe their uses of language within a particular peer group, class, family, organization, or workplace affinity group in terms of use of a certain register, style, and dialect, and then note how those features serve to constitute their own or others' identities. For example, a Jefferson High School student, Brian Southwell, describes his use of language as a member of an "Obscuritan" peer group who share a strong interest in certain unusual indie music or viewing several movies in a theater on the same day:

> Obscuritan is a term coined by a group of Hipsters who don't like to be called "Hipsters." Obscuritans are very plain on the surface, speaking in a very boyish way, but the words spoken contribute to a life of cultural appreciation. Whether it be through listening to copious amounts of new

music, or seeing nearly every movie in theaters, Obscuritans express themselves by displaying interests that differ from the norm.

Activity: Self-Perceptions and Beliefs: "Chalk Talk" Descriptors

Students also adopt social language to define their beliefs and attitudes constituting their identities associated with membership in certain affinity groups. To encourage people to publicly share how their identities are constructed and recognized by others, photographer Wing Young Huie (http://www.wingyounghuie.com) organized a "Chalk Talk" project in which he took photos of people holding up a chalkboard on which they wrote responses to the following questions: "What are you? How do you think others see you? What don't they see about you? What advice would you give a stranger? What is your favorite word? Describe an incident that changed you. How has it changed you?" (Huie, 2012). One of Huie's agendas is to use photography of different, diverse people to demonstrate how their identities are constructed through how they are perceived or recognized by others.

People wrote the following on their chalkboards, "Race makes people doubt me," "I'm a rook in the chessboard of life," "I'm just a kid in a big world. I'm not capable of everything. But I am not capable of nothing," "Knowledge is the most powerful weapon that nobody can take away," "I'm Muslim as they think terrorist," "Don't hold onto things that hurt you."

Based on this project, students could take photos of each other or themselves with their beliefs about their identities on chalkboards. They could then discuss how they acquired these beliefs and how the beliefs shape their identities. This use of photography and images constituting identity construction serves to address two of the Minnesota Common Core Speaking and Listening Standards:

> Make strategic use of digital media (e.g., textual, graphical, audio, visual, and interactive elements) in presentations to enhance understanding of findings, reasoning, and evidence and to add interest.
>
> *(Minnesota State Department of Education, 2010, p. 84)*

To help students go beyond their perspectives on race and class as simply a function of their own individual prejudices to recognize the influence of discourses of institutional racism or class difference, students can first identify the systems constituting their own or characters' identities: schooling, housing, economic, military, entertainment, political, justice, communication, transportation, health care, retail, and so forth. For each of these systems, they could then discuss how certain practices, norms, or tools operating in these systems serve to support racial inequality or strive for an equitable society.

For example, students in a multicultural literature course in an urban, working-class high school debated the impact of affirmative action programs on fostering racial equality (Beach, Thein, & Parks, 2008). Some of the White students argued that affirmative action programs limited their own opportunity for financial support for college or for jobs—the fact that, in applying for college or a job, they may not receive the same preferential treatment as applicants of color. Other students argued that, given the lack of high-quality schooling preparation for students of color, and the need for advanced degrees leading to economic success, students of color need preferential treatment in terms of college admissions.

Underlying these students' stances was a discourse of individualism—that everyone has an equal chance to be successful if they just work hard without assistance from the government or programs such as affirmative action, that people need to "make it on their own." For example, one 12th-grade White male student in our research, Corey, adopted an individualist perspective (Beach, Thein, & Parks, 2008; Thein, Beach, & Parks, 2007). He therefore posited that Bone, the young female protagonist in *Bastard out of Carolina* who lives in poverty and is abused by her stepfather, could overcome her difficulties if she made a concerted effort to become successful by going to school and exerting herself. He was challenged by another student in the class, Kayla, who posited that people do not necessarily have the same opportunities within a class-based society, particularly those who have had a difficult childhood.

COREY: I just think that she has a chance like anybody else. *Anybody* [his emphasis] can, if you do the right stuff and work hard your whole life.

KAYLA: In class, Mr. Parks was talking about how everybody doesn't have the same chances.

COREY: Yeah, but . . . that's probably true, so I don't know. It's hard to say. I think that you can achieve goals in life if you work hard at it. . . .

KAYLA: Page 178 . . . I guess this one talks about growing up to be rich, like "what are the chances?" Do you think that Bone could grow up to be somebody or be rich?

COREY: I think she could if she stayed in school and went to college after, just like anybody else could. But, I don't know, the things that went on in her life might mess her up a little bit. She might need counseling or something, but I still think that she could probably get through it.

(Thein, Beach, & Parks, 2007, p. 56)

In this exchange, Corey maintains his stance regarding the value of self-initiative, but, when challenged by Kayla that people's opportunities can be limited, he does modulate his stance, conceding that "that's probably true, so I don't know," an indication that he was open to considering alternative perspectives.

Activity: Defining Gender as Practices or Embodied Performance

To help students perceive gender as enacted through the use of particular embodied performances, teachers can create activities in which students reflect on how people adopt and perceive certain practices as gendered. In her class, Kate Drabinski (2011) has students describe how they determine whether their peers are male or female, resulting in descriptions of physical features, names, interests, artifacts, and physical behaviors such as how they sit in classroom desks. (For an animation video in which a male adopts a female identity based on acquiring certain feminine attitudes or behaviors, see http://tinyurl.com/n4zp6zz.)

She then has students view other students in the class to discover contradictions to these notions of gender differences and actual practices—for example, that female students may be slumped down in their seats or male students may have purses—leading students to interrogate how discourses of female gender shape their perceptions of gendered identity practices.

She then has students write about how certain advertisers promote certain products based on stereotypical gendered practices, such as beer for males and martinis for females, which leads her students to further interrogate and critique not only how the advertising industry shapes representations, but also how students' perspectives are acquired through socialization by institutional and cultural forces.

Activity: Examining Gender and Power

Students can also examine how gendered practices are shaped by particular cultural contexts in terms of power hierarchies related to femininity and masculinity. In Rose's class the issue of gender was very relevant to the Latina students in particular. During a Socratic Seminar about *The Absolutely True Diary of a Part-Time Indian* (Alexie, 2007), the topic of cultural markers was raised. Andrea and a number of other Latina students discussed what they saw as a cultural marker in the Latino community of a common double standard in their families—that Latino boys have freedom and that Latina girls have responsibilities that limit freedom. The Latinas talked about having to care for younger siblings, having to cook and clean and, in some cases, join their mothers on the weekends to help clean the homes of other people.

At the same time, they argued that their male counterparts could go on dates, had few to no chores at home, and were generally spoiled. Carlos, who was in the Socratic, actually presented an interesting shift of political stance during this heated discussion. At first he joked, double-voicing a stereotypical gendered discourse: "Yeah, woman, make my burritos and tamales! Cook my food!" However, by the end, he adopted the beliefs of his Latina peers and was cheering on Andrea and the other young women by raising a fist to show solidarity, nodding, and giving utterances of support. The strongest voice in the discussion was Andrea, who in some ways displayed "male" associated embodied performances through dressing in sports clothes, using lots of swear words, staying out late to party, and getting into fights—displays that gave her a sense of power in a Latino community where young women had very little.

When asked if she thought this double standard would come to an end in future generations, she seemed skeptical. In response to the question as to whether her generation might change things, she points out: "But then again, there's the boy [you marry]. The way he was raised and saw his sisters raised is all he knows. So, women might want to change things, but we are taught you can't defy your husband."

Andrea's analysis suggests a growing feminist awareness that Rose supported by welcoming diverse viewpoints in the class, supporting and often leading spirited debates, and acknowledging the interests, passions, and intellects of her students.

This suggests the benefit of having students respond critically to gender representations in literature in terms of the level of complexity of the representations. Students in Rose's class found that women in *The Absolutely True Diary of a Part-Time Indian* (Alexie, 2007) lacked the complexity of the representations of male characters—a point of emphasis by a few Latina students who expressed displeasure about the book choice. Based on the identity practice of *making connections between texts and people*, Rose's decision to allow students to "step back" from the text to make text-to-self connections both validates the narratives students bring to the classroom and also creates a space for students to apply their schematic ideas about gender inequalities to gain a richer understanding of the novel. This led the students, particularly the Latina students, to recognize that sexism and gender representation problems exist in contexts other than their own.

Students can also connect gender perspectives to larger cultural values operating in a certain society. In studying *The Kite Runner* (Hosseini, 2004) in Elizabeth's class, students were asked to write about how "one aspect of a society: economy, foreign policies, gender roles, geography, history, politics/government, race/ethnicity, religion, family values, education, health, warfare, etc. most affected one (or more) characters and the choices they made in their lives." In her essay response to the novel, Jackie examined the influence of Islamic beliefs about the role of women in Afghanistan and perspectives on women:

> Women were treated as property, they were also judged harshly for their mistakes, and they were always supposed to have a husband. It has always been that way, until recently. There were always rules they had to follow according to society. . . . For years it seemed wrong for a women to not have a husband. It would look like there was something wrong with the girl. Then once they were married society believed that husband could tell his wife what to do. "Every women needed a husband. Even if he did silence the song in her" (p. 178). . . . Even today the stereotypical

housewife is a cook, maid, consumer, mother, and loyal wife. While the stereotypical husband is lazy and doesn't do a lot of work. People feel that they have to play these parts to fit in society.

Activity: Analyzing Media Representations of Identities

People acquire different discourses of race, class, gender, and sexuality from the media that not only represent but also perpetuate ways of believing and knowing about race, class, gender, and sexuality (Hall, 1997). Working in groups, students can select images from movies, television programs, advertising, magazines, popular fiction, and video games. They then identify certain consistent patterns in how those images and/or characters represent identities in terms of the use of social markers, physical appearance, dress, status symbols, setting, practices portrayed, and so forth related to race/ethnicity, class, gender, and age differences. They can then share their findings using a VoiceThread screencasting tool (http://voicethread.com) or create an iMovie production. For example, students may examine gender representations in terms of whether males or females are assuming major roles in Hollywood films, as well as how males and females are portrayed. One study found that of the hundred top-grossing movies of 2008, men had 67% of the speaking roles and women had 33% of those roles (Smith & Choueiti, 2010), with female characters being more likely to wear sexy, provocative clothing than men.

Students could also create parodies of how people are portrayed in the media based on race, class, and gender difference. JHS student Malaz Ebrahim created a parody video, "A Day in the Life of a Boy" (http://tinyurl.com/l6m6xb6), that portrays stereotyped assumptions as to

> what we girls think guys do all day. It is kind of a way to poke fun at guys and their daily routines. All the things we act out might not be all true, but it is the "stereotype" of what guys do. The theme of the story will be comedy and we will try to make viewers laugh while they are watching it.

In the video, two boys, portrayed by girls, are eating a large breakfast, weight lifting, high-fiving, male bonding, playing video games, making frequent potty stops, having a female serve them lunch, playing guitars in the basement, and viewing porn.

Malaz also noted how the use of music in the video served to enhance the parody: "The strength of our video is it had music that explained the situation that was going on and you knew what was going on at all times."

Who Are You?

Asking, "Who are you?" can be simply another way of asking, "Who am I?" A valued African moral principle is Ubuntu Botho. The term relates to notions of community, compassion, and humanity, and for Africans, it means "that my humanity is bound up in yours, for we can only be human together" (Tutu & Tutu, 1989, p. 69). Roughly translated, the expression means "I am, because you are." In other words, my value as a person is directly related to the value I have in the eyes of others.

As we noted in Chapter 1, identities are constructed through how others recognize that identity, emphasizing the importance of how students learn to perceive or empathize with others, something they experience in adopting the minds and perspectives of characters. Through adopting characters' uses of language portraying alternative perspectives, students are learning to move away from their own perspective to consider how others may perceive the world in ways distinct from their own perspectives, reflecting their ability to empathize with others (Zunshine, 2006). A report comparing adults' responses to literary fiction versus more popular fiction across five different studies found that readers responding to literary fiction scored higher on emotional intelligence perception for empathy than readers of popular fiction or nonfiction, even for readers who did not enjoy literary fiction (Kidd & Castano, 2013). One essential difference between literary and popular fiction texts is that in responding to literary texts, readers are experiencing multiple alternative perspectives, while readers of popular fiction are focusing more on the story development.

Given the need to have students experience characters' perspectives distinct from their own, this raises issues about what texts should be read by whom. Too often, teachers assume that students only want to read books by authors or with characters that "look like them." While it is notable that some students may be more likely to read if this occurs, it also inhibits the potential literature offers to engage in the identity practice of *adopting alternative perspectives*. Researchers suggest that adolescents are open to reading about characters quite different from themselves when the themes or issues in the text seem relevant to their lives (Athanases, 1999; Moje et al., 2008).

Recall that the students at SBH could only think of three descriptors to describe themselves on average. As one might expect, they also limited descriptions of their peers to just one or two words. Encouraging students to think about themselves as complex, developing, and possessing multiple identities helps them perceive others as also complex, developing, and possessing multiple identities. While the discussion of race, class, gender, sexuality, and affinity groups extends to this section, as well as the usefulness of the above activities, this section includes activities that invite students to adopt the perspectives of others.

Activity: Adopting Ethical/Moral Perspectives

Essential to engaging alternative perspectives is the ability to adopt ethical or moral perspectives that address societal issues. Adopting ethical or moral perspectives goes beyond a social science focus on cultural, historical, or institutional perspectives to address the question of what makes a person via one's ethical and moral stance on what is valued in life and how one can make changes in one's own and others' lives (Smith, 2011). In adopting Arnold's perspective in *The Absolutely True Diary of a Part-Time Indian*, students can begin to understand how systemic racism and oppression have real, significant effects on the ability of any given person to gain economic or social agency. Reading texts like this one often leads students to ethical wonderings, questioning how the status quo might be changed. Entertaining the need for change then allows students to try on the identity of a "change agent"—someone who is dissatisfied with the status quo and wants to work to make change.

At SBH, many of the students have friends, or are themselves, like the "Rowdy" character in *The Absolutely True Diary of a Part-Time Indian* (Alexie, 2007). Rowdy is the protagonist's best friend, who is often angry and getting into fights and suffers violent abuse in the home. When Arnold decides to attend the White school, their friendship is severely tested because Rowdy feels betrayed. Having a friend who is violent and who engages in destructive behavior can create moral and ethical issues for students. Anthony's study focal participants, Carlos and Andrea, enjoyed Rowdy's character because of his unapologetic "misbehavior" and admired Arnold for continuing to care about him even when he had problems of his own or when their friendship was suspended. They appreciated that a character like Rowdy was not presented as a "cautionary tale" in ways that one might expect from a young adult novel.

Carlos made some thoughtful connections between Arnold and Rowdy's friendship and the ones he saw young Latino men making with one another. Carlos describes the role of guy friends as having someone to "share opinions with . . . find out what is right and wrong . . . and someone to tell things to." While the dynamics of childish humor, anxiety about girls, competition around sports, and shared interests in comics are present in the book, so too are more subtle dynamics such as having a friend who will "have your back," someone who will keep secrets, and someone whose own struggles provide spaces for empathy, reflection, and kinship. Given the media (primarily video games) and the machismo culture that Carlos and his friends experience, the novel provided a rare space to examine these highly valued relationships in a thoughtful way.

Adopting this ethical perspective therefore supports a reflection of one's ethical or moral concerns about the world, for example, concerns about a lack of fairness or equality (Gee, Allen, & Clinton, 2001). In his autobiographical narrative, JHS student Brian wrote about his conflicted relationships with a gay coworker, Ben (pseudonym), when he was working in a restaurant in a small Idaho town. In this town, Ben was perceived in a negative manner by his other coworkers given his flamboyant behaviors and appearance. When Ben brought in some brownies to share with other coworkers, and Brian reached to take a brownie, Ben told him with sass: "Sorry, I don't give brownies to people who hate gay people." A few seconds of silence passed, and Brian finally managed to drum up a response to this largely new social experience. "Do you have any idea where I come from, Ben?" Brian said loudly but shakily. "Where I live, people go out of their way to accept people who are different, and I am proud of that." After this exchange, Brian and Ben went outside the restaurant, where Ben apologized, leading them to discuss reasons for his reactions: "Ben told me about growing up in Wallace and how he became extremely defensive of his sexuality as a result of childhood ridicule."

Brian also shared his own negative predispositions about Ben based on his flamboyant actions. Through discussing the ways in which they perceived each other and how the town perceived Ben, Brian recognized that he "had much more in common with Ben than I ever would have imagined. We shared stories of all sorts and came out of the evening as friends." This camaraderie carried over into work. Through recognizing how their perspectives of each other influenced their actions, both Brian and Ben realized the limitations of those perspectives influencing their relationship.

Activity: Adopting Outsider Cultural Perspectives

Many secondary students live in their own homogeneous cultural world given their lack of exposure to alternative cultural worlds, exposure that would lead to their recognizing the limitations of their own homogenous culture. By living in the Philippines, JHS student Ruby experienced a different cultural perspective that led her to critique her peers' cultural perspectives:

> I had a little stint in the Philippines and we lived there for two years. When you live in third-world country you get a taste of what it's like to be alive and then you move back here where everybody is super privileged; everyone has a problem, it's a first-world problem like there's no real problems for me. I had little kids coming up to me when I was 12 begging me for pennies and you're complaining to me that your iPhone died. I have a view that most people in JHS don't have. The kids [in the Philippines] care more about school and they do their homework.

She was therefore very open to entertaining alternative perspectives, something that was important for her success on the school's debate team. She notes "debaters have to defend something they can do it correctly with evidence to back it up but they can also thoroughly understand the opposing sides and that when you understand both sides then you can make an educated decision about which opinion you have which is why I don't have opinions."

Risk Taking, Self-Confidence, and Difference

When students identify challenging goals, they need to be willing to take risky actions to achieve those goals—risks that may vary according to gender. While male students are often more likely than female students to engage in deviant, risky actions that result in critique and ridicule, doing so helps them become more resilient and gain confidence in their ability to cope with failure (Dweck, 2012). In writing about his summer experiences in the late 1970s in Dubuque, Iowa, John Beckman (2014) recalls his engagement in activities involving risky behaviors with his male peers, such as jumping off a large dirt pile in their neighborhood. In contrast to contemporary summertime experiences scheduled and monitored by adults, these activities were initiated by Beckman and his peers, so they experienced the consequences of their own self-initiated behaviors. As Beckman notes:

> By making things, breaking things and taking real risks, by becoming citizens in our ad hoc community, we used the fallow days of summer to put our Catholic-school education, and our parents' parenting, to the test. Trial and error often proved that they were right. But in discovering what we enjoyed most—not what we were taught to enjoy—we also discovered new parts of ourselves: artists, engineers, combatants, daredevils, explorers, criminals, comedians and more. Our summer fun was a field study in life, which is the last thing we would have thought at the time.

In contrast, female students may be more concerned about complying to norms associated with being accepted by peers and teachers and succeeding in school (Dweck, 2012; Kay & Shipman, 2014). As JHS student Jackie notes:

> In school, I am quieter because I don't feel like I can be my real self. I hear a lot of people judging others and I don't want them to judge me the same way. The person I want to be isn't the person I am because I would love to play orchestra . . . I feel like if I would be given the same opportunities as someone else I would be more outgoing and wouldn't care that much about what other people thought.

One result of this gender disparity in the willingness to engage in risky actions is that although women are more likely to attend and succeed in academia, males are more likely to succeed and hold positions of power in the workplace, disparities that may be a function of differences in self-confidence, but not necessarily ability or competence (Kay & Shipman, 2014). However, if given *opportunities* to engage in risky actions, females do as well as males. As Kay and Shipman (2014) note:

> When women don't act, when we hesitate because we aren't sure, we hold ourselves back. But when we do act, even if it's because we're forced to, we perform just as well as men do . . . women need to stop thinking so much and just *act* . . . if we channel our talent for hard work, we can make our brains more confidence-prone.

(p. 66)

However, because this variation in the willingness to take risks may involve more than simply gender difference, students could discuss individual differences in their own willingness to engage in risky actions and how doing so may or may not enhance their self-confidence.

It is also useful to consider how you can support students' taking risks in their discussion participation or writing. In giving feedback to her students at Fortuna High School, Fortuna, California, Ann Conley (2014) focuses on fostering what Dweck describes as a "growth mindset" by noting instances of their taking risks by working through difficult material in a descriptive, nonjudgmental manner, for example, by using the word "yet," as in "Your sentence structure does not yet match the tone you are trying to achieve," or "Those drafts paid off in sentence variety and imagery."

Colleen described how her participation in the orchestra—what she described as the "orch dork community"—provided her the opportunity to display competence through working collaboratively with peers. "We get up on stage and play pieces together that we've been working very hard on for months and have perfected. . . . This is when we can really show all of our talents, and respect the different talents that we have." From this experience, she acquired "teamwork and self-motivation" as well as communication skills:

> I use communication in many classes and my job, which allows me to understand and do the best that I can. Being accepted into this group makes me feel happy . . . being a part of the orch dork community is what keeps me going during the day.

Students can display competence through making positive contributions to an event, group, organization, or community through problem-based learning or service learning activities.

In problem-based learning, students investigate problems and reasons for the problems, and then they propose alternative solutions to address these problems. For resources on problem-based learning, see the Buck Institute for Education website (http://bie.org) and the Expeditionary Learning site (http://elschools. org). To identify local or global problems, students can participate in Quest-2Matter (http://tinyurl.com/oeb9olb), a project in which they propose "quests" for addressing those problems.

Activity: Recognizing How Identities Are Constructed in Cultural and Historical Contexts

Central to the students' shift in their perspectives in Daryl Parks's multicultural literature course (Beach, Thein, & Parks, 2008; Thein, Beach, & Parks, 2007) was the students' increasing awareness, fostered by their responses to literature, that identities are constructed in cultural and historical contexts, including a meshing of English and social studies perspectives central to the Common Core

State Standards (Council of Chief State School Officers and the National Governors Association, 2010).

In responding to the time-travel novel *Kindred* (Butler, 2004), students experienced an African American woman, Dana, moving between the identity of a slave on an 1820s plantation and the identity of a contemporary woman in the world of Los Angeles in 1973, shifts that highlighted how these different worlds constituted her identity (Beach, Thein, & Parks, 2008). The literary depiction of Dana's experience as an outsider moving in and out of the bonds of slavery helped White and Asian working-class students in this class to understand the "other", as well as how characters and themselves are positioned in another world, positionality that they can accept or reject in terms of how they construct their identities in a certain world. Through responding to this and other texts, students began to recognize how identities are constituted based on adherence to practices, norms, and values operating in a particular culture, what Ladson-Billings (1994) defined as "cultural competence"—the ability to recognize how one is shaped by cultural forces.

In responding to *The Absolutely True Diary of a Part-Time Indian* (Alexie, 2007), the SBH students were introduced to the lives of Native Americans living on a reservation—a cultural world distinct from their own worlds, which shaped Arnold's identity. In adopting Arnold's perspective in *The Absolutely True Diary of a Part-Time Indian*, students can begin to understand a Native American's experience in ways that echo and differ from their own: the systemic racism and oppression that has real, significant effects on the ability of any given person to gain economic or social agency.

Adopting this perspective entails students stepping out of their familiar world to perceive that world from an outsider stance so that they are making the familiar strange and the strange familiar (Erickson, 2004), or "unlearning" one's familiar ways of operating in a world (Pennycook, 2010), something that can be a challenge, particularly for students who are "fish in water" within their own culture. By adopting historical/institutional perspectives, students gain an understanding of "history in persons" and "persons in history" (Holland & Lave, 2001). For example, in studying *To Kill a Mockingbird* (Lee, 1960), students apply historical and institutional perspectives that emerged during the civil rights movement, perspectives that critique forms of systemic racial inequality inherent in segregation, and draw on those perspectives to interpret how characters' identities were shaped by the kinds of segregation and inequality found in daily life and in the legal justice system during the 1930s (Beach, Haertling-Thein, & Webb, 2012).

Adopting a cultural perspective entails recognizing how events or practices constituting identities are shaped by norms and values within a particular culture or "figured world" (Holland et al., 1998)—a concept discussed in greater detail in Chapter 5. However, like fish in water, adolescents often have difficulty recognizing that their own perspectives are constituted by their experiences within a particular culture. Because most adolescents are socialized within a particular, single cultural community, they have not been exposed to other cultures in ways that help them recognize their own school or community as shaped by certain cultural beliefs and norms. While JHS students could identify how Bloomington was constituted by certain racial or class demographics, most did not perceive Bloomington as a world with certain cultural beliefs and norms that distinguished it from other cultures.

In responding to literature, students are entering into cultural worlds distinct from their own worlds. Their instinct is typically to contextualize the characters' actions in terms of their own cultural contexts. Rather than imposing their predispositions, they gain from adopting characters' perspectives constituted by the cultural beliefs and norms operating in the text. For example, in responding to *The Absolutely True Diary of a Part-Time Indian*, the SBH students were introduced to the lives of Native Americans living on a reservation, an environment completely new to them. They contrasted the practices and norms between the "White world" where Arnold attends school and the world of the reservation where Arnold has lived his whole life, based on the prompt:

> In what ways is life on the rez harder than life in the white town? In what ways is life on the rez better than life in the white town? When you think about your own community, how is it like a stereotypical white community and how is it like Arnold's world on the reservation?

These questions allowed students to consider the world of the text, their life, the social world at large, and the similarities and differences throughout. Students admired the way the reservation community came together during funerals in the context of the book and likened it to the sense of pride and connection they knew in their own communities. A number of others saw their own neighborhoods as complex—that an outsider might see a dangerous neighborhood but the students felt safe, and in other areas where some students lived, tree-lined streets with single-family residences might look welcoming, but crime was a problem.

It is also the case that in moving between these two worlds, Arnold "always felt like a stranger" (Alexie, 2007, p. 118) in that he was operating according to different norms or rules. Students could discuss the official and unofficial norms or rules shaping their everyday experiences, how they know which norms or rules are operating in certain spaces, and whether they adhere to these norms and rules (Bruce, Baldwin, & Umphrey, 2008)—a topic we describe in more detail in Chapter 5 on negotiating identities across different social worlds.

Activity: Adopting Contrarian Ways of Believing and Knowing

An ability to live in the gray area is a mark of maturity, humility, and wisdom. Asking students to take on viewpoints different from their own, and defend those viewpoints, is an approach to teaching rhetoric as well as an opportunity to "try on" alternative perspectives. There are a number of activities that invite students to adopt these contrarian perspectives:

- Holding debates on topics of genuine interest to the students and then flipping a coin to establish pro or con sides is one activity that supports this practice.
- Holding mock trials for characters who are morally ambivalent, such as Meursault in *The Stranger* (Camus, 1993) or Edna Pontellier in *The Awakening* (Chopin, 2012).
- Asking students to rewrite stories from the perspective of the antagonist is another way one can adopt contrarian perspectives. Reading Gregory Maguire's (2009) book, *Wicked: The Life and Times of the Wicked Witch of the West*, where the "Wicked Witch of the West" shares her perspective is a great model for adopting the antagonist's view.
- Rewriting history. Rather than accepting that history is written by the victors, encourage students to retell common frameworks of historical events, such as 9/11 or the Civil War, from the perspectives of the "losers."

Activity: Adopting Alternative Perspectives in Response to Literature

To foster students' adoption of different perspectives in responding to literature, teachers can employ the following activities—activities employed by teacher Daryl Parks (Beach, Thein, & Parks, 2008, pp. 127–137; Thein, Beach, & Parks, 2007):

- *Monologues.* Students search through a text to identify certain consistent patterns in a character's actions, beliefs, and attitudes, as well as how those actions, beliefs, and attitudes may vary across different contexts (Vinz et al., 2000). They then write monologues that challenge their peers' presuppositions about their assigned character's identity with the statement, "You think you know me, but you don't!" They then read aloud their monologues, which serve as the basis for a discussion about that character.
- *Role-play.* Students adopt roles of characters, as well as characters outside the text, to address an issue or challenge in the text (Edmiston, 2014). For example, in Parks's multicultural literature class, students assumed the roles of characters and counselors. In response to *Their Eyes Were Watching God* (Hurston, 2006), they adopted the roles of Janie and her grandmother meeting with a family counselor to address reasons for their conflicts, conflicts stemming from the grandmother's experience of sexual abuse, poverty, and slavery.
- *Contrasting characters' narrator perspectives.* Students can read texts in which different characters serve as narrators adopting totally different perspectives

to create different versions of the same events. For example, in our study, students read *A Yellow Raft in Blue Water* (Dorris, 2003), a text in which a Native American grandmother, mother, and daughter—the three main characters—each tell the story from their own perspective.

- *Writing prompts.* Teachers can provide students with specific writing prompts based on quotes or statements from characters about their identities to elicit students' responses. For example, for responding to the character of Lulu in *Love Medicine* (Erdrich, 1993), Daryl gave students this statement:

> Everybody around me keeps calling me a "slut" based on the actions that happened in Chapter 5. They don't see all of the other parts of my life that you guys have read about. Will you explain to them that there is more to me than just that behavior?
>
> *(Thein, Beach, & Parks, 2007, p. 58)*

In doing so, he asked students to consider the need to recognize the limitations of their own and other characters' perceptions of Lulu that were influencing her self-perceptions.

He also took anonymous quotes regarding perceptions of characters' identities from the students' journals to hand out to students in order to spark further discussion about those quotes. For example, note the following quote regarding perceptions of Native Americans:

> On the reservation Indians are well-to-do with free money. Somehow in *Love Medicine* they tend to portray our government as cheap but I don't see it. Indians see us as unfair, but I don't believe it is true in real life.
>
> *(Thein, Beach, & Parks, 2007, p. 59)*

Activity: Adopting Perspectives Through Voicing Characters' Language

Students can also assume the perspectives and voices of characters by engaging in a conversation in the role of the characters or by writing letters or text messages between the characters. In studying *Cyrano de Bergerac* (Rostand, 2012), Elizabeth had her students write love letters—two from each of the two males, Christian and Cyrano, each of whom are wooing Roxane:

> In this assignment, you will take on the perspectives of both Christian and Cyrano to write love letters in a traditional format and a modern day text message. You will write a total of four love messages, two messages from Christian and two messages from Cyrano. For each gentleman, you will write one traditional love letter (a minimum of 150 words) and one text message (a minimum of 100 characters and no more than 160 characters) to Roxane.

As you are writing these messages, keep in mind how Cyrano and Christian talk. Cyrano uses vivid details, witty lines, and usually has much to say. In contrast, Christian tends to use shorter sentences and less descriptive words. Refer back to scenes and lines where they describe Roxane and their feelings towards her. You will be assessed on how well you can effectively portray each character's perspective in how they view and express love for Roxane.

Activity: Parodying Language Use for Constructing Identities

To examine how people adopt the identities of others through "double-voicing" or mimicking others' social language use, students can study examples of parody in *The Onion*, *Saturday Night Live*, *The Daily Show*, or instances of literary parodies. They could note how different features of language were being used to portray a person's identity, for example, how use of informal language is used to parody someone who normally uses more formal language.

Students could then create their own parodies by writing scripts for skits related to actual people or to characters in a text they are reading. In studying *Hamlet*, Kristen Varpness had her students rewrite the scene where Gertrude and Claudius interact with Hamlet for the first time: "I had them rewrite it in slang. And they had to perform it in their groups. It forces them to look at it and translate it into a way they can understand and to make it funny."

GERTRUDE: What up, Hamlet, why you still sad? I'm not sad, I'm fine. I'm glad you fine. People die; it happens. Yep.

HAMLET: What's up, it's so common, bro. I know that it's common but it still sucks that he died.

CLAUDIUS: Hamlet, you're a nice guy, you should mourn, but everyone loses a father, so suck it up.

GERTRUDE: Yeah, Hamlet, stay with us; don't go back to school. Fiiiiiiine.

CLAUDIUS: Off to Kinko's. Let's go party.

Gertrude and Claudius leave.

HAMLET: This sucks. My mother's a loser for marrying my uncle a month after my dad dies. But, I'm going to try to keep my anger to myself.

Kristen noted, "They had to act it out. When they get to perform for each other, there's a different level of engagement. They all look at each other because they want to see each other. And, they ham it up."

When and Where Am I?

The "when" in the title of this section is about supporting students as they gain perspective about how their experience of the present is realized. It supports developing a consciousness about the past and an ability to imagine a future. In almost all of the indicators of identity that Gee references as falling under his four categories, the issue of context matters significantly. What did it mean to be a woman a hundred years ago? What will it mean to be unable to read well in a hundred years—will it matter?

Beyond gaining perspective, thinking about the "when" supports a consideration about the relative nature of time itself. For example, in an elective philosophy course Anthony taught, students read different chapters from the book *Einstein's Dreams* by physicist Alan Lightman (2011). In this small collection of short stories, the author envisages the nocturnal imaginings of Einstein's dreams in the weeks leading up to his theory of relativity. Each chapter presents a plausible, if fantastical, theory about the relationship between time, space, and reality. Students were asked to create artistic representations of different chapters and then asked to devise their own theoretical imagining of our existence and the laws that govern it.

The question of "Where am I?" offers a host of micro to macro entry points. In large part, our "where" is as much a product of our beliefs about the sociocultural and historically produced norms, values, roles, scripts, and purposes of a particular place as "figured world" (Holland et al., 1998). Part of a larger theory of identity, a figured world is described as "a socially and culturally constructed realm of interpretation in which particular characters and actors are recognized, significance is assigned to certain acts, and particular outcomes are valued over others" (p. 52).

Figured worlds are also discussed as being populated by a set of agents (teacher and students) involved in a series of meaningful activities (reading, taking notes, arguing) as moved by a specific set of forces (mandatory attendance, interest in learning, school rules). In figured worlds, people come to produce or reproduce subjective roles (being the "teacher's pet") that they recognize and are recognized by others as constituting their identity. Figured worlds also involve "scripts," "frames," and "schema" that allow individuals to participate within them. It is always useful to be mindful that all of the above components of a figured world would look different in the past and will look different in the future.

Activity: Adopting Alternative Literary Critical Perspectives

Another aspect of perspective taking that helps one consider the spatial and temporal factors shaping identity involves adopting different literary critical perspectives or approaches for responding to texts—biographical, New Critical, historical, psychological/psychoanalytic, archetypal/mythic, deconstruction/poststructuralist, reader-response, feminist, Marxist/class, and so forth (Appleman, 2013; Vinz et al., 2000). In adopting these different perspectives, students are experimenting with assuming the roles and identities of critics applying a particular critical perspective, for example, that of an archetypal or Marxist critic.

After she reviewed the strategies of the different critical approaches, Elizabeth asked students, working collaboratively in groups of three, to select one approach for analyzing *Beloved* (Morrison, 1987). Students then shared their analyses using different perspectives, which helped students appreciate how different critics generate alternative interpretations of the same text, enhancing their sense of alternative ways of interpreting texts. By having the students themselves adopt and share multiple interpretations, Elizabeth was addressing the Minnesota CCSS:

> Analyze multiple interpretations of a story, drama, or poem (e.g., recorded or live production of a play or recorded novel or poetry), evaluating how each version interprets the source text. (Include at least one play by Shakespeare and one play by an American dramatist.)
> *(Minnesota State Department of Education, 2010, pp. 61–62)*

In their New Critical analysis of *Beloved*, Brian noted that the image of red in *Beloved* functions as a

> prominent symbol of death and mortality . . . used numerous times throughout *Beloved*, and it helps give the reader a better sense of the deep rooted anger, sorrow, and despair throughout the book. . . . [Sethe's] memories are full of blood, pain, and despair, all of which relate back to the color red. The blood of her child and the pain of being whipped surely visit her thoughts every day. Sethe's memory is awash with symbolically red things, such as pain and blood.

Igor applied a Marxist critical perspective to their analysis of *Beloved* to examine how different characters were shaped by a class hierarchy of

> wealthy, middle class, poor, and African Americans. . . . In society, the rules are usually set by those who are rich and/or in power. Whether the people who are in power are elected by the people or establish themselves through force, they ultimately end up making the rules. Oftentimes those rules that are established end up benefiting a few at the expense of the many.

Students can also adopt a historical critical perspective that involves framing characters or events in literature in terms of past historical contexts, a perspective that is a key focus of the ELA CCSS related to reading and writing social studies texts. For example, in their unit on *The Scarlet Letter* (Hawthorne, 1994) for their 11th-grade AP English classes at Jefferson High School, Susan Bianchi and David Johnson asked their students to analyze how the larger institutions of the church and marriage influenced each character's actions or decisions. This included, for example, how the Puritan rules about marriage fidelity influenced characters' actions across the spaces of events in their homes, church, and community. Susan noted that her students have difficulty analyzing the influences of institutions on characters' identities.

> This concept is difficult for the students because they can't see that there is an influence. They don't understand the powerful underlying influences at play in the world. When they look at how influenced the SL characters are by the Puritan lifestyle, they begin to understand how one is influenced by their "time." They do not readily accept that they are also influenced by their time.

To model this process of analyzing the influences of institutions on identity, Bianchi and Johnson decided to first have students identify how their own institutional contexts influenced norms operating within certain spaces/places, which in turn influenced actions within specific events. To scaffold this activity, they had students create circle maps based on the categories of characters' actions, spaces, and institutions.

In their maps, students first described how the larger institutional rules operating in their suburb of Bloomington influenced their actions in spaces/places within the suburb and events within those spaces/places, for example, rules about behavior in the Mall of America located in Bloomington associated with surveillance of adolescents in the mall. Students then applied the same analysis to identify characters' actions/decisions in *The Scarlet Letter* in terms of the characters' actions/decisions, space/place in which the actions/decisions occurred, the larger institutions shaping the actions/decisions, and students' judgments about their actions/decisions.

Students also discussed how Hester, Dimmesdale, and Pearl changed over time in their use of language, actions, and appearance across different locations as shaped by the institutions of the church and family. Based on their analysis of how location influenced these characters' changes, students then wrote in response to the following prompts:

- Consider how location affects you. Write a page on a location/space where you behave differently than you would in another space. How do you behave differently?
- What about the space allows/influences you to act differently?
- Do you feel you are less you, or just showing a different side of you, either inside or outside of this space?

In this activity, students were adopting an institutional/historical perspective to reflect on the influence of the church and family spaces positioning the characters, as well as how they themselves are influenced by certain spaces.

Summary

In this chapter, we described activities for helping students adopt alternative perspectives to analyze how characters' and their own identities are positioned by participation in certain social worlds. By doing so, students gained an understanding of how institutions position identities and how identities position institutions, enhancing their ability to define ways to navigate the institutions in their own lives. (For additional resources, activities, and further reading, see http://tinyurl.com/lq438by.)

References

Alexander, M. (2012). *The new Jim Crow: Mass incarceration in the age of colorblindness.* New York: The New Press.

Alexie, S. (2007). *The absolutely true diary of a part-time Indian.* Boston: Little Brown.

Allison, D. (2012). *Bastard out of Carolina.* New York: Plume.

Alvermann, D. (2012). Entrepreneurship education and gendered discursive practices. In B. J. Guzzetti & T. Bean (Eds.), *Adolescent literacies and the gendered self: (Re)constructing identities through multimodal literacy practices* (pp. 74–82). New York: Routledge.

Alvermann, D., Marshall, J.D., McLean, C.A., Huddleston, A.P., Joaquin, J., & Bishop, J. (2012). Adolescents' web-based literacies, identity construction, and skill development. *Literacy Research and Instruction, 51,* 1–17.

Appleman, D. (2013). *Critical encounters in high school English: Teaching literary theory to adolescents* (2nd ed.). New York: Teachers College Press.

Athanases, S.Z. (1999). Building cultural diversity into the literature curriculum. In E.R. Hollins & E.I. Oliver (Eds.), *Pathways to success: Culturally responsive teaching* (pp. 139–155). Mahwah, NJ: Lawrence Erlbaum.

Bachman, J.G., O'Malley, P.M., Freedman-Doan, P., Trzesniewski, K.H., & Donnellan, M.B. (2011). Adolescent self-esteem: Differences by race/ethnicity, gender, and age. *Self and Identity, 10*(4), 445–473.

Beach, R., Haertling-Thein, A., & Webb, A. (2012). *Teaching to exceed the English language arts Common Core State Standards: A literacy practices approach for 6–12 classrooms.* New York: Routledge Press.

Beach, R., Thein, A.H., & Parks, D.L. (2008). *High school students' competing social worlds: Negotiating identities and allegiances in response to multicultural literature.* New York: Routledge.

Beckman, J. (2014, July 12). All children should be delinquents. *The New York Times.* Retrieved from http://tinyurl.com/mpcb8bh

Bonilla-Silva, E. (2001). *White supremacy and racism in the post-civil rights era.* Boulder, CO: Lynne Rienner.

Bruce, H.E., Baldwin, A.E., & Umphrey, C. (2008). *Sherman Alexie in the classroom.* Urbana, IL: National Council of Teachers of English.

Butler, O. (2004). *Kindred.* New York: Beacon Press.

Camus, A. (1993). *The stranger.* New York: Everyman's Library.

Chbosky, S. (1999). *The perks of being a wallflower.* New York: Simon & Schuster.

Chopin, K. (2012). *The awakening.* New York: Dover.

Conley, A. (2014, July 14). Nurturing intrinsic motivation and growth mindset in writing. *Edutopia.* Retrieved from http://tinyurl.com/o38bo5v

Council of Chief State School Officers and the National Governors Association. (2010). Common Core State Standards from English Language Arts. Authors. Retrieved from http://www.corestandards.org/ELA-Literacy

Delgado, R., & Stefancic, J. (2013). *Critical race theory: An introduction* (2nd ed.). New York: New York University Press.

Dorris, M. (2003). *A yellow raft in blue water.* New York: Picador.

Drabinski, K. (2011). Identity matters: Teaching transgender in the women's studies classroom. *Radical Teacher, 92*(1), 10–20.

Dweck, C. (2012). *Mindset: The new psychology of success.* New York: Random House.

Edmiston, B. (2014). *Transforming teaching and learning with active and dramatic approaches: Engaging students across the curriculum.* New York: Routledge.

Erdrich, L. (1993). *Love medicine.* New York: Harper.

Erickson, F. (2004). *Talk and social theory.* Cambridge, UK: Polity Press.

Gee, J. P. (2000). Identity as an analytic lens for research in education. *Review of Research in Education, 25,* 99–125.

Gee, J. P. (2013). *The anti-education era: Creating smarter students through digital learning.* New York: Palgrave Macmillan.

Gee, J. P., Allen, A., & Clinton, K. (2001). Language, class, and identity: Teenagers fashioning themselves through language. *Linguistics & Education, 12*(2), 175–194.

Gibson-Graham, J. K., Resnick, S., & Wolff, R. D. (Eds.). (2000). *Class and its others.* Minneapolis: University of Minnesota Press.

Guzzetti, B. J., & Bean, T. (Eds.) (2012). *Adolescent literacies and the gendered self: (Re)constructing identities through multimodal literacy practices.* New York: Routledge.

Hall, S. (Ed.). (1997). *Representation: Cultural representations and signifying practices.* Los Angeles: Sage.

Hawthorne, N. (1994). *The scarlet letter.* New York: Dover Press.

Holland, D., Lachicotte, W., Skinner, D., & Cain, C. (1998). *Identity and agency in cultural worlds.* Cambridge, MA: Harvard University Press.

Holland, D., & Lave, J. (2001). *History in person: Enduring struggles, contentious practice, intimate identities.* Albuquerque, NM: School of American Research Publications.

Hosseini, K. (2004). *The kite runner.* New York: Riverhead.

Huie, W. Y. (2012). Using photography to study people's identities. Presentation at the meeting of the Minnesota Council of Teachers of English, Rochester, MN.

Hurston, Z. N. (2006). *Their eyes were watching God.* New York: Perennial Library.

Jenkins, H. (2011, March 21). How learners can be on top of their game: An interview with James Paul Gee (part one) [web log post]. Retrieved from http://tinyurl.com/4cpv578

Joaquin, J. (2010). Digital literacies and hip hop texts. In D. E. Alvermann (Ed.), *Adolescents' online literacies: Connecting classrooms, digital media, & popular culture* (pp. 109–124). New York: Peter Lang.

Kay, K., & Shipman, C. (2014, May). The confidence gap. *The Atlantic.* Retrieved from http://tinyurl.com/kel4xfz

Kidd, D. C., & Castano, E. (2013). Reading literary fiction improves theory of mind. *Science 342,* 377–380. DOI:10.1126/science.1239918.

Ladson-Billings, G. (1994). *The dreamkeepers: Successful teachers of African American children.* San Francisco: Jossey-Bass.

Lee, H. (1960). *To kill a mockingbird.* New York: Lippincott.

Lightman, A. (2011). *Einstein's dreams.* New York: Vintage.

Maguire, G. (2009). *Wicked: The life and times of the wicked witch of the west.* New York: William Morrow.

Minnesota State Department of Education. (2010). Minnesota K-12 Academic Standards in English Language Arts. St. Paul, MN: Author. Retrieved from http://tinyurl.com/72fzzr9

Moje, E. B., Overby, M., Tysvaer, N., & Morris, K. (2008). The complex world of adolescent literacy: Myths, motivations, and mysteries. *Harvard Educational Review, 78,* 107–154.

Morrison, T. (1987). *Beloved: A novel.* New York: Knopf.

Moya, P. M. L. (2006). What's identity got to do with it? Mobilizing identities in the multicultural classroom. In L. M. Alcoff, M. Hames-Garcia, S. P. Mohanty, & P.M.L. Moya (Eds.), *Identity politics reconsidered* (pp. 96–117). New York: Palgrave Macmillan.

Pennycook, A. (2010). *Language as a local practice.* New York: Routledge Press.

Rostand, E. (2012). *Cyrano de Bergerac.* New York: Signet.

Scollon, R., & Scollon, S. (2003). *Discourses in place: Language in the material world.* New York: Routledge.

Shohat, E., & Stam, R. (2013). *Unthinking Eurocentrism: Multiculturalism and the media.* New York: Routledge.

Silva, J. M. (2013). *Coming up short: Working-class adulthood in an age of uncertainty.* New York: Oxford University Press.

Smith, C. (2011). *What is a person?: Rethinking humanity, social life, and the moral good from the person up.* Chicago: University of Chicago Press.

Smith, S. L., & Choueiti, M. (2010). *Gender inequality in cinematic content? A look at females on screen & behind-the-camera in top-grossing 2008 films.* Los Angeles: Annenberg School for Communication & Journalism, University of Southern California.

Thein, A. H., Beach, R., & Parks, D. L. (2007). Perspective-taking as transformative practice in teaching multicultural literature to White students. *English Journal, 97*(2), 54–60.

Tutu, D., & Tutu, N. (1989). *The words of Desmond Tutu.* London: Hodder.

Vagle, M. D., & Jones, S. (2012). The precarious nature of social class-sensitivity in literacy: A social, autobiographic, and pedagogical project. *Curriculum Inquiry, 42*(3), 318–339.

Vinz, R., Gordon, E., Hamilton, G., LaMontagne, J., & Lundgren, B. (2000). *Becoming (other)wise: Enhancing critical reading perspectives.* Portland, ME: Calendar Islands.

Young, S. B. (2013, November 8). The middle class: An American tragedy, in numbers. *Minneapolis Star Tribune.* Retrieved from http://www.startribune.com/opinion/commentaries/231223651.html

Zunshine, L. (2006). *Why we read fiction: Theory of mind and the novel.* Columbus: Ohio State University Press.

4

MAKING CONNECTIONS ACROSS PEOPLE AND TEXTS

We don't, after all, make sense of our complex world as individuals. We make sense through connections . . . and these connections create our identity and help us to find our sense of belonging and our sense of humanity.

George Siemens, Connectivism (2010)

My role as a teacher is to relate the things that are real in the world to the things that are fictional in the text so we can see what things in the text happened in a place and time in history . . . supplying students with more available ways to make connections to things that aren't just, now I'm going to ask you about your feelings about this story, instead, I want them to tell me about the difference between the Shiites and Muslims in the story so that when they are out in the real world they have context for what is actually happening in the world.

Elizabeth Erdmann

The capacity to compare and contrast—to note the often subtle but potentially pivotal effects of even minor discrepancies or similarities between various texts, contexts, people, situations, or dilemmas—is an invaluable ability in the process of identity construction. Through the social process of mediating meaning from texts, ELA is especially suited to the task of examining connections. When students wonder, "What does this remind me of?" the question facilitates the building of rich mental models of the texts associated with connections to experiences with other people or to other texts.

From the standpoint of identity construction, the self can serve as a text. We often think about our life with literary metaphors—the "story of my life," or "I began a new chapter." In reading the narrative of our own lives, what references and examples might one call upon for comprehending the self? Naming the connections between the self and others is how we come to see the self—looking a bit like Suzie in Chemistry class, being a Catholic like Aunt Janice, having a short temper like the old lady in the bakery, always being curious like the protagonist from *Sophie's World* (Gaarder, 1995). This can be useful both in finding models from which to better view the self and in providing road maps for lives both desirable and otherwise.

In this chapter, we discuss how students construct their identities through creating connections with others through various identity-focused ELA activities. In responding to literature or engaging in drama activities, students create connections with characters or roles. They momentarily adopt the perspective of a character or role as a new, alternative lens for experiencing the world. Drama is an embodying activity, and as such, the characters that students "perform" leave traces, or imprints, that the student can add as yet another aspect of their identity.

They also draw on their knowledge of narrative patterns to infer connections between characters' actions, patterns they may then apply to defining scenarios for their own identity development. When writing about their past, and imagined futures, they begin to define connections between their past and present identities to reflect on how events shape their beliefs and attitudes serving to inform their identities. The writerly self can differ from the public personas students adopt in social contexts; and through writing, students can adopt tones, viewpoints, personalities, and other literary voices they may not have other spaces to explore. As adolescents work to define themselves, the connections made between their private writerly selves and their public social face can be integral for crafting the self.

Beyond reading, writing, and drama, the ELA spaces provide opportunities to explore language use. In reflecting on their own and others' usage of language, students infer connections reflecting consistent language styles that constitute their own or others' identities as members of certain groups. Additionally, because we think in language, the language we have to consider the self is limited by the linguistic resources we can access. Developing a consciousness of this limitation, as well as its social and culturally determined context, is an important part of exploring connections across languages and in practicing new languages from which to author the self.

These activities serve as a bridge across people and texts in classrooms where students' identities are welcomed, valued, and accessed as learning resources. In our rush to standardize and make common curricula, students as socially, historically, and culturally produced people increasingly become decentered in the classroom and alienated from learning. Drawing on students' connections to people and texts serves to validate the importance of their experiences shaping their classroom literacy learning.

Fostering Connections Between Texts for Engagement

In planning instruction, teachers can devise activities where students make connections between people and texts. Students then perceive how their prior experiences with people and texts apply to their current experiences with texts—learning consistent with the identity practice of *making connections between texts.* To foster these intertextual links in responding to *Diary*, Rose had students explore similarities between the Alexie novel with other, personal texts they brought to class in the partner text activity. And Elizabeth Erdmann had her 12th-grade students write about similar thematic and topical connections between three of the texts they read during a semester course.

When students have a high level of interest in their work, they are more willing to assume responsibility for successfully completing that work. Rose's classroom exhibited a significant increase in work completed during the Alexie unit in comparison to previous units. Connections generate student interest that serves to support working collaboratively on projects with peers and mentors to foster development of those interests. For example, in a study that Amanda conducted in a working-class high school in St. Paul, Minnesota, she found that one student, Molly, began to notice that across her various social worlds (for instance, her participation in Big Brothers Big Sisters, her work in a nursing home, her role as a mediator in her peer group), she enjoyed helping others negotiate struggles and hardships. Molly therefore began entertaining careers in fields such as psychology and nursing that would allow her to continue to build this element of her identity (Thein, 2009). By noting certain consistent connections or patterns in their interests, talents, or abilities across different social worlds, students can begin to define themselves as people with particular salient traits, beliefs, or practices that move with them across their various identities.

Students are motivated to make connections for social purposes to build relationships with others (Bloome et al., 2004). Students share an online post with a friend because they know that this friend has an interest in the topic addressed in that post, and sharing that bolsters their relationship. As members of a peer group, students share a common interest in a certain type of music, movies, sports, video games, and so forth, sharing that brings them together around that common interest.

Given the importance of these shared peer-group interests, it is therefore useful to build connections between student participation in non-school activities with academic work in schools so that students draw on their non-school participation to support their in-school work. For the rest of this chapter, we discuss activities present in the ELA classroom and consider how these activities can be used to foster connections in ways that support identity work.

Responding to Literature

The increased focus on the use of nonfiction/"informational" texts associated with the Common Core standards has led teachers to consider ways of pairing these texts with fiction texts around shared topics or themes that address a number of different standards (Heitin, 2013), a focus consistent with our identity practice of defining connections between texts and people.

For example, high school English teacher Sarah Brown Wessling, 2010 National Teacher of the Year, describes her focus on making connections:

> I[I]nstead of thinking about teaching *To Kill a Mockingbird*, I'm teaching the concept of courage. *To Kill a Mockingbird* is one text I use. So is a [PBS] *Frontline* piece, a speech, an article. Putting those texts together in a bundle helps us to work toward conceptual understanding. That's the spirit of the core.
>
> *(Heitin, 2013, p. 8)*

Based on their syntheses of texts, students make connections between a diverse range of literary, informational, and multimedia texts in an English class. As they make intertextual connections, students can consider thematic relationships between different texts. They also use hyperlinks in digital texts to connect to other resources, media, and texts.

Activity: Selecting Partner Texts for Making Connections

One activity in Rose's class at South Bay High that can be applied to any ELA class engaging a work of literature is the use of partner texts. About two-thirds of the way into reading *The Absolutely True Diary of a Part-time Indian* (Alexie, 2007), students were asked to bring in a text that they saw as "in conversation" with the Alexie novel. Students selected a theme or concept they found appealing in the book and considered other works that also addressed the theme or concept and brought an example of it to the class. Sitting in a circle, students shared everything from comic books to poems to songs to nonfiction texts, and they justified their view on how the partner text related to the Alexie novel. Some students were moved by the friendships in the novel and brought in other texts that addressed friendships; others focused on Native American issues, or having to cross different borders and boundaries, or issues involving class and race relations. In the end, the class not only benefitted from being exposed to related texts, but they began to learn more about their peers and collectively built a greater understanding of the Alexie novel itself.

Activity: Making Connections Based on Themes Associated With Identities

By making connections based on thematic links related to identity construction, students can begin to see the relationship between issues that pertain both to their personal development and larger, social concerns. For example, in teaching *To Kill a Mockingbird* (Lee, 1994), a 10th-grade teacher, Mr. Johnson, posed the question, "Why is growing up so difficult?" associated with issues of abuse, unfairness, injustice, bullying, and peer pressure (Elish-Piper, Wold, & Schwingendorf, 2014, p. 571).

Johnson had students listen to the song "Unfair," regarding unfairness in social relationships, by Josh Kelley, to pose questions: "What's unfair in your life?" and "What's unfair in our school?" and "What's unfair in our community?" Students next read the story "Epiphany," in which two friends deal with peer pressure and prejudice, and then the students posted tweets on Twitter about these issues. The students then read the young adult novel *Staying Fat for Sarah Byrnes* (Crutcher, 2003) for small-group discussions of characters' coping with issues and conflicts associated with body image issues. These discussions served as resources for the writing of short essays in the "This I Believe" (http://www.thisibelieve.org) format. Later, they read the short story "A Brief Moment in the Life of Angus Bethune" (Crutcher, 1991) to address the question, "Why might growing up be so difficult for Angus?"

Johnson's students also shared their responses to a Poll Everywhere (http://www.polleverywhere.com) survey to respond to the question "Have you ever known someone who stood up against injustice and unfairness?" related to *To Kill a Mockingbird* (Lee, 1994). To help his students understand the unfair, racist nature of Jim Crow laws and segregation, he had his students read "Jim Crow and the Detested Number Ten" in *Claudette Colvin: Twice Toward Justice* (Hoose, 2010). And, to respond to the attempted lynching of Tom Robinson, students read the poem "Incident" by Countee Cullen (1925) and a story about Emmett Till. Students were therefore continually defining connections between these texts to address questions regarding the difficulty of growing up.

Constructing Identities Through Responding to Literature

In responding to literature, students enter a fictional world in which they are vicariously experiencing characters' own narratives as ways of knowing and being. In doing so, they are acquiring ways of reflecting on their own experiences by drawing connections to the characters' textual narrative—a road map of sorts. Additionally, because literary fictions tend to deal in universal themes, students can consider how they would respond to various contexts and situations, and thus draw connections to the characters' choices and what they imagine would be their own. Elizabeth describes her goal of fostering students' empathy through their responses to literature:

> As a person who really liked reading stories, and my family is kind of a storytelling kind of family too, I really enjoyed learning about other people through their stories, so my primary goal is that through reading about other people's experience—whether it's memoir or fiction—we can better understand a person; that's better than when you're reading just a history book, like the *Tale of Two Cities*, which gets you in the mind of characters and gives you a real person's experience.

Empathy, you can feel what they feel. And then being able to relate those experiences to our own lives—that while I'm not in that situation, I can relate to that situation, and then teach students to articulate their thoughts about that situation in a way that's more productive than just "I hate those people." They can then articulate why they feel like they do so that they can support their arguments about their feelings about something.

She also noted that through empathizing with characters' perspectives, students are learning how characters' identities are constituted by specific historical and cultural contexts:

When we read a story like *Night*, they have background knowledge about the Holocaust. So then when we read *Persepolis*, and examine here's this thing that's being vilified or looked at that media shows us about the Arab or Muslim threat and they can see it from a perspective from a person that was there who wasn't even complicit in the crimes that happened in that situation or wasn't even a Muslim. When we look at a girl like Margie, we get to see the world from a little girl's perspective versus what the news media is telling us about something.

At South Bay High, students responded to Arnold's experiences of moving between his Native American reservation world and the world of a White high school in *The Absolutely True Diary of a Part-Time Indian* (Alexie, 2007). In doing so, they are experiencing Arnold's negotiating competing demands of two different worlds, which is the focus of Chapter 5 on negotiating identities across different worlds.

While considering how Arnold challenged his position on both the reservation and in the White high school world, SBH students explored the various ways they are labeled and categorized in both in-school and out-of-school contexts. Andrea, for example, noted that she could understand why Arnold was constantly resisting the labels others assigned to him. Her strategy for coping with others' need to label her was to turn the tables on them. Andrea is a popular and strong-willed Latina who made a concerted effort to dress in a fashion that seemed to vary from one day to the next. At times she looked as if she was going to work in an office and at other times she seemed to be going for a night on the town; at times she seemed like she was off to play sports, and at times she looked as if she was still in her pajamas. Asked about this variety, Andrea stressed that "I'm always gonna be me. But I don't want no one trying to just define me—so I gotta keep them guessing."

Noticing consistencies—as well as inconsistencies—in Arnold's character might subsequently lead students to make connections to their own resistances (and acquiescences) to identity categories. By making these connections to one's own experiences, a student may then infer the beliefs, attitudes, or ideas that shape experiences, inferences that can then be funneled back into a deeper inter-pretation of the text. If that student believes that a resistance to being categorized or labeled is justified, the student may then apply that belief back to Arnold's justification for his resistance.

Activity: Reflecting on How Identity Shapes One's Responses

To foster students' awareness of how their identities shape their responses, stu-dents could step back and reflect on how they are responding to literature *as* certain identities based on their own culturally and socially produced meanings tied to gender, sexuality, race, class, age, personality preferences, or nationality. In responding to the gender portrayals of women in *The Kite Runner* (Hosseini, 2004), Jackie reiterates, as noted on page 72, the problem of the lack of gender equality in Afghanistan shaped her responses to the novel:

> Gender has always played a very big role in how people should act. Women have always felt like they needed to fit into society more than men. Women for a long time were consider property to men; if they made a mistake they would be treated harshly, and they all have to have a husband. Men were always considered superior to women in every way. Thankfully times have changed, where women in our society have a little more freedom. Hope-fully in the future women's freedom will continue to grow.

A case-study analysis of three students' identities found that their self-perceived identities influence their blog responses to literature (West, 2008). One student, Katherine, who described herself as a "relationship-savvy teen" (West, 2008, p. 591), responded to the portrayal of Abigail Williams and John Proctor in *The Crucible* (Miller, 1976/2003) by adopting the discourse of romance to focus on Abigail's "out of control" (p. 590) obsessive actions associated with her relation-ship with Proctor: "I also see this play as more of a love story than anything, and love stories = good" (p. 591). A second student, Evan, who described himself as a "tempered rebel" and someone who often resists school, adopted a critical stance in responding to Reuben, narrator of *Peace Like a River* (Enger, 2000), noting that "I think that Reuben needs a slap of reality sent to him, I'm like wtf, do you really think that you got by the police that easily? I really don't get this book, but what's there to get?" (p. 592). A third student, Lucy, who defined herself as a "pop-cultured humorist," drew on popular-culture celebrities to rate her responses to *Huckleberry Finn* (Twain, 1994):

> So far, on a scale of 1–10, with 1 being Christy Brown [lead character in *My Left Foot* (Sheridan, 1989)] and 10 being The Illest Diva [reference to

Missy Elliot's (2001) hip-hop record "4 My People."], I would give it a 5.5 . . . I think after a few more chapters my rating will be around a Celine (9) [reference to the singer, Celine Dion], because I will have gotten used to the writing more.

(West, 2008, p. 594)

Lucy was therefore defining her engagement with the novel through making connections to popular culture in ways that reflected her affinity identity with the common popular trope of rankings and "top-ten lists."

Activity: Inferring Autobiographical Connections With Literary Texts

These student case studies illustrate how students' own identities influence how they interpret texts in ways unique to their identities as constituted by their autobiographical experiences. One resource that literary fictions provide is the opportunity to live inside the minds of the authors and their protagonists. The sensation of being "lost in a book" is often the feeling of taking a temporary departure from the thoughts, language, and rhetorical tendencies one normally employs and instead thinking in ways that are new, differently organized, and often foreign. At the same time, students make meaning of the character's story by inferring connections between their autobiographical experiences and character's experiences. For example, at SBH, Jeffrey developed a strong sense of familiarity and feelings of connection to Arnold. Jeffrey repeatedly referred to Arnold as if he was a friend and a real person, and this connection was rooted in the similarities and differences between Arnold and Jeffrey.

> The Alexie book? I feel like it showed, who I AM. Like, I want to be a person that gets seen by people and seen by colleges and seen for doing stuff—just by being me and keeping that positive attitude. Like, uh, Arnold did. Cause he kept a positive attitude even though he struggled a lot. He went through a lot of struggles. With his family, he did a lot of struggling with, um, with everything, basketball, not having his friends there—I understand how that feels, cause I lost a lot of friends. And I think the book is a type of motivation to me too because, um, it motivates me because even though I am having a kid, I could still do what I gotta do so I could make it in life.

Jeffrey leveraged the book to support his own identity construction. The novel and the protagonist served as resources for motivating Jeffrey to do well in school and provided support for reflecting on his own life and circumstances. Jeffrey's reflection reveals a strong interest in and identification with Arnold that stemmed from a number of similar and divergent experiences and characteristics.

Like Arnold, Jeffrey played basketball, expressed affection for his family, found and lost friendships, eagerly hoped to have a better life, and maintained a positive attitude despite encounters with racism and poverty. Jeffrey found their differences intriguing as well, such as Arnold's Native American background, his crush on a White girl in school, and life on the reservation. Jeffrey does not read at grade level, and is not especially interested in reading, but his engagement with the Alexie novel was less a school assignment and more a chance to spend time with his friend Arnold.

Often teachers look to match books with students based on similar identities and experiences between the characters in the text and the students in their class. However, as Jeffrey's experience suggests, providing books that include both foreign and familiar elements are ideal. When Anthony taught *The Joy Luck Club* (Tan, 1989) to students, he assumed his Chinese American students would both feel part of the class community and appreciate seeing their culture represented. However, after seeing his Chinese American students express resistance to reading the book, he followed up with them and learned that they viewed the book as being their "parents' story" and that they were eager for the voices of their own generation. Interestingly, it was Anthony's students who were African American girls that enjoyed Tan's book the most—because they were drawn to the mother/daughter themes throughout the book. The familiar elements may be useful for motivation and encouraging reading, but the unfamiliar aspects are salient for providing what literature offers—bridges across difference, an emphasis on what makes us similar, and a chance to revisit the self with new narratives.

Using Drama Activities to Make Connections

Drama, both the in-class reading of dramatic pieces and the activity of staging a work, is an excellent resource for making connections across people. One lesson drama offers is the opportunity to learn that character is defined by what one does and how one does it. In addition, it illustrates that emotional lives are universal; both students and characters experience sorrow, joy, anger, excitement, envy, and regret.

However, character (and identities) teaches us that while we may all have the same human emotions, how we express these emotions is funneled through one's identity (Micciche, 2007). For example, imagine you witness two different fathers dropping off their sons at the airport so the boys can head off to college. The first father warmly hugs his son, tussles his hair, laughs with him, and sends him on his way with the advice of reminding him to call his parents every once in a while and to have fun. The second father offers his son a firm handshake, gives him an envelope with one hundred dollars in it, and offers a brief lecture about staying out of trouble and doing his best academically. On the surface, one might imagine that the first father is more loving and caring than the second, but with drama one recognizes that character is shown through what one does and how one does it, and a case can be made that neither father loves their son any more or less than the other.

How Drama Activities Support Identity Construction

When we ask students to enact roles in either a play or the staging of a literary text, and we support and encourage them to fully inhabit the characters they are playing, they learn to make connections between people because they discover that the actions they take on are rooted in shared human themes and emotional lives. Elizabeth stresses the value of adopting different roles through drama that allow students to express emotions associated with empathizing with characters' identities. She described an activity in which students adopted roles in responding to *Cyrano de Bergerac*:

> We were reading *Cyrano de Bergerac* and the girl threw the book against the wall, like "I can't believe what I'm doing to this guy right now," like in acting it out, she was trying to get into the mind of that woman who didn't know that she was breaking that guy's heart, but the girl while she was saying that to the other boy in the class, they could feel then how hard it was for Cyrano de Bergerac to look at this woman and have her tell him that she likes somebody else. So they like yell that "This sucks so bad" or they will complain about the literature we are reading, "Why can't we read anything that's happy?" I really like it when they get upset about it and they can say that out loud.

Professional actors asked to play reprehensible characters often note that they cannot abhor the characters they are playing. Instead, they look to learn what makes the "monster" human; they search for a small kernel of humanity to offer an entry point for the actor to empathize with so that he might begin to inhabit the character truthfully.

In performing a part in a play or staged reading, the practice of deep immersion into language, the deliberate practice involved in the rehearsal process, and the human connections between actors in an ensemble are all resources that help one make connections across people and inform one's identity development.

Another important skill that acting helps develop is listening. As students play parts and interact with others, students are learning how listen to the other actors in the other roles so that they become fully engaged in the emotional connection between their objective and the other characters. Learning to listen deeply often involves employing empathy, noting connections, and being fully present and engaged with others.

Using Language to Portray Emotions of Relationships

Playwright, performer, and professor Anna Deavere Smith has often said that "if you say a word often enough, it becomes you" (Clines, 1992). Smith inhabits real-life characters in her one-woman shows and performs them to tell stories about historical events; her works are excellent examples of using drama to illustrate making connections across people. Her quote essentially hinges on the idea that through inhabiting the language and the speech patterns and voice of a character over and over, the public persona of the self becomes replaced by the character being performed. These performances then leave a trace on one's identity, adding a layer in a sense to the multiple identities one carries.

In a way, acting has a deliberate practice aspect to it as well. Through rehearsing a scene multiple times, trying it out in different ways, identifying "beats" and moments, players can get closer to the heart of what they imagine the playwright's vision was. Simply doing the scene once and then repeating the process the same way each time defeats the purpose of rehearsal. However, if one is motivated by a possible upcoming public performance, gets immediate feedback from a director or teacher, recognizes the journey from simply saying the lines to inhabiting the scene, and repeats the scene (albeit with the intention of improving it) multiple times, then the four elements of deliberate practice are realized.

Benjamin, as an active member of the Jefferson drama club for four years, describes his experience of adopting roles distinct from his own role, along with the importance of reading others' emotions while on stage:

> You have to stop thinking like yourself and how you'd react and think about what that character would do, and if you do it right, by opening night, you step out on that stage, you become that character. It's less about how you'd react and more about how your character would react.
>
> Once you get closer to showtime and your practice becomes more intense, it requires more time of you; you start to become more like that character. It's harder to, with my other friends, to read people's emotions because they are so used to hiding them or channeling them to do what they do. Like with my friends, I can tell if they are happy or sad, or if something is going on. With theater, if they want to hide it, they can, but a lot of them are emotional, which it's easy to see. I'm not quite as emotional as most of them.

Benjamin also noted that some of his actor peers were capable of adopting totally different roles distinct from their own lived-world identity:

> One of my friends plays Gaston in *Beauty and the Beast*, and he is one of the most polite, self-effacing kids that you're going to meet, but when he's on stage, I can start to hate him—he's like arrogant. It's funny, but it's so different from how he normally is.

Beyond plays and dramatizing literary works, the performance of poetry can also be an opportunity to create connections across people and texts. Cat, who was a very shy student at SBH, used poetry, both the writing and performing of it, as a way to exercise and make public her multiple identities. As part of her final project, Cat wrote a series of poems inspired by both the Alexie novel and her own evolving stance on matters of the heart. She read two poems to the class, "clock in, clock out," which addressed feelings of being an outcast, and one called "untitled," a piece clearly written about the boy in the class whom she was in love with but who did not return the feeling. She received respectful applause when she finished her readings and seemed, for the first time in a month, happy about being in class.

In her final interview with Anthony, seven weeks after that day, Cat reported improvements to her academics, better attendance, and that she had matured since reading her poems aloud. Cat cited sharing her poems for her final project as being instrumental in her improved performance. While writing the poems themselves was not too challenging, she admitted to feelings of terror when she read them aloud. "This one (pointing at the untitled piece) was hard because he was, like, in the room. That was like the first time, I um, I can still remember the feeling, and like, um, my chest jumps." She added that sharing the poem publicly helped her to realize that she "had to move on, that it would be hard but it would be a step towards moving on from my love for him."

Cat had relied on her relationship with literacy to distinguish herself from her peers, to provide her with some sense of power when her daily life was a series of repeated reminders of her powerlessness. She spoke about books, authors, and characters in books as if they were friends, as kindred spirits, and people she loved. She spoke about her peers in school as strangers, as regarding her as invisible, and as less intelligent and cultured than she was. In part, this was because Cat had been identified as different and "weird" early in her school experience and she had since embraced her "outcast" identity and found strength in the label.

At the end of the study, when she made the courageous choice to write and read poems about her feelings for the boy in the class and sense of alienation she knew so well, she was making public a very private practice she'd taken refuge in. While she was comfortable with using literacy as a resource for identity work outside of the classroom, this move suggests that she was open to engaging with literacy for the same purpose in the ELA classroom.

Cat's poetry reading reflected a boundary crossing of sorts, where she brought her private use of literacy activities into the classroom, a domain she had not thought was suitable, nor safe enough, for such engagements. The bridges crossed, or connections made, were less between Cat and a character in a book, but between the multiple identities Cat carries. Taking the steps to cross this bridge allowed for needed healing and personal growth. Signs of the growth included improved academic engagement and performance in class (based on both Cat and Rose's assessment) and a continued interest in reading poetry in public, including participating in a spoken-word event at a café in the following summer.

Activity: Interacting with Your Students

One set of drama activities involves imaginative ways of interacting with your students. Julie Blaha, a teacher in the Anoka-Hennepin Minnesota School

District, employs comedy improvisation in her classroom to enhance her interactions with students (Hawkins, 2014). In one "spacewalk" activity, students walked around in the classroom practicing connecting with students nonverbally. So, "The next day at school walking down the hallway I noticed students smiling at me," she says. "I was communicating that I noticed them." She also recognizes that when students insult each other, they are actually attempting to fit in with their peers. "It's giving people the ability to be funny with you versus against you," she explains. "Not everyone has to laugh but no one can cry. Think about that in the classroom. If we could make people feel comfortable and feel welcomed?"

In his use of informal "dramatic inquiry" activities, Brian Edmiston (2014) engages students in addressing challenges, for example, setting up an organization to assist homeless people on the street to find food or shelter. As the activity unfolds, he then poses further complications requiring students to revise and adopt alternative strategies. For example, as members of this organization interacting with a homeless person, what do they do when they find that a homeless person who is mentally ill has difficulty understanding the student offering assistance. Edmiston notes that:

> Over time, inquiry opens up meaning to new possibilities as inquirers learn from and with one another in ongoing, authentic, substantive, polyphonic, dialogic conversations focused on implicit or explicit inquiry questions.
>
> *(p. 40)*

Students could also participate in "cyberdrama" activities based on uses of texting, email, online discussion, websites, or digital videos for communicating before, during, or after a drama activity (Davis, 2011). For example, groups of students in one activity receive an email indicating that they were selected to be immortal, requiring that they collaboratively create a response using a blog post and video to create a character who must decide as to whether to accept the invitation to be immortal. The groups then were asked to create a news or current affairs story involving their character or other related characters followed by a large-group role-play that is videotaped in which the teacher and another adult interview students to request assistance in locating the immortal characters, who themselves are posting video clips about their experiences of being immortal.

Writing

Writing is not only about the production and communication of written content, but also a representation of the self. As such, students construct identities through writing in that they are bound by certain conventions (e.g., not using "I" in an academic paper). How they accept or reject these conventions reflects how they display their identities as writers (Ivanič, 1998).

Writing can also serve as a mediating or buffering source, allowing students to adopt identities they may not have spaces to "try on" elsewhere. Asking students to write rap lyrics, poems, noir thriller short stories, and theatrical plays provides opportunities for students to make connections across differences by attempting various writer identities. This work needs to be intentional, however, and while the following sections review various types of writing used in ELA settings, underlying each is a call to treat each writing activity as an explicit learning opportunity for considering how writing is a chance to present the self.

Gaining an Awareness of One's Writer Identity

Students often engage in writing without much consideration of the extent to which their writing is an identity act. Perceiving one's writing identity entails distinguishing between simply producing written texts versus recognizing how one creates a persona or ethos with particular stances, knowledge, and attitudes constituting one's identity through writing; for example, adopting the identity as "vocal critic" or "gardening expert." Or, in creating a narrative, students portray themselves as someone with certain traits, beliefs, or attitudes—someone who is admirable, proud, boastful, insightful, and so forth.

Through their writing, students are projecting a certain persona or ethos, which leads to readers constructing what Burgess and Ivanič (2010) define as their "discoursal self" or "the impression she creates of herself as a person," for example, the fact that the student's persona is perceived as someone who is knowledgeable about the topics she is addressing. Robert Yagelski (2012) notes that:

> Understanding the experience of writing requires making a key distinction between writing as textual production and writing as a way to experience ourselves in the world; it requires distinguishing between the writer's writing and the *writer writing*—that is, between the text and the act of writing.
>
> *(p. 191)*

Through writing about their experiences, students gain an awareness of using their writing to construct their writing identities. As Yagelski notes:

> In this way, writing has the capacity to intensify our sense of being. We do not exist because of writing, but writing can bring our being more sharply into focus; it can make us more aware *that* we exist. . . . The act of writing, in other words, is an ontological act, an act of being.
>
> *(pp. 192–193)*

Yagelski cites the example of a teacher who had her 12th-grade students, based on reading *The Things They Carried* (O'Brien, 2009) and other texts, write their own "true war stories" about experiences in their own lives, as a way "to learn about life, to live . . . about being human, about confronting life in all its terrible pain and magnificent joy" (p. 201).

Central to these self-perceptions of writing identities is an awareness of students' relationships with their audiences—how they perceive their readers and how their readers perceive them. If a student is writing for someone she knows well, a close peer or teacher, she may then predict how that peer or teacher may react to her writing. If she knows that her teacher likes her use of a formal academic writing style, then she may adopt that style in writing for that teacher.

Activity: Creating Written Narratives

In creating narratives, students are dramatizing the fact that something unusual or extraordinary has occurred that is worth telling—that a story has some point, what Labov (1972) described as "tellability." The stories one tells about the self are deemed worthy to share in that they demonstrate or depict events or activities that the author views as instrumental in shaping the self. As such, the extent to which they served to "shape" the self is in some ways less salient than the perceived importance given to the event when reliving it as one writes a narrative.

For example, in SBH students were asked to write a literacy autobiography, in which they reflected on the ways that engaging in various literacy practices has come to shape them and how they imagine they will engage literacy in the future. Among the varied responses, some wrote about a parent reading a favorite childhood book to them, others noted the importance of poetry or the lyrics from musical artists, and others discussed the practice of drawing as a literacy act they saw as meaningful.

Both the activity itself, thinking about how literacy shapes identity, and the events they recalled were important activities for using writing to make connections between the earlier and present self, between various texts, and between more expansive definitions for what counts as literacy. The writing of and sharing of narratives can be a generative activity for bringing identities out in the class as a resource for learning, for building community within the class, and for supporting a culture of collective meaning makers. (We discuss reading and writing of autobiographical narratives in more detail in Chapter 7, a chapter on the identity practice of *reflecting on identity development over time*.)

Activity: Writing Across Genres

One challenge for many students is that they have difficulties assuming the kinds of identities associated with writing academic essays. Depending on the kinds of assignments, such writing entails employing "essayist literacies" associated with adopting an impersonal persona. Students then experience a tension between their familiar, personal, everyday use of language versus the less familiar, impersonal use of language employed in writing academic essays, reducing the extent of these students' engagement in academic writing (Hyland, 2012). Students may also assume that given their lack of knowledge about a certain topic that they are not experts and so they lack the authority to voice their own personal opinions. Additionally, they may be uncomfortable adopting the disciplinary discourses of social studies, science, or math associated with academic writing in their own subject-matter classes.

Writing across various genres provides students with an awareness of the connections between actions and language use in terms of the use of certain speech or social genres. How one writes as a scientist, a poet, or a lawyer involves understanding the norms and language specific to a particular genre. Similarly, genres such as debating, interviewing, issuing invitations, proposing plans, telling jokes, performing songs/poetry, or ridiculing all involve different discourses, conventions, and norms for communication. The fact that a student can effectively employ a certain genre serves to define the student's identity. The fact that a student knows how to effectively tell jokes serves to define her identity as a "jokester," or to create rap poetry, as a "rapper."

JHS student Sabrina drew on her experience with science fiction novels and movies to write a narrative entitled "Spores":

> I called it "Spores" because it is a plant from the Jurassic period where it technically started out with diseases, it contained the common cold; it would open up and release spores with the common cold after it died and then the DNA would mix with other plants, make other deadly diseases, which is how we got our diseases now. That plant was supposed to have died off with the dinosaurs, but a scientist found it deep-sea diving in a cave and he brought it back and he ran all these tests on it and it mutated and it died, but then it released its spores and he breathed it and he ended up dying but then the spores took over his nervous system so it made him live again almost like a zombie but not exactly because they don't eat people—they just keep spreading like they want to multiply like a disease. They want to multiply like cancer and it's kind of another science fiction with the end of the world with these people trying to stop it or live through it.

Sabrina's foray into science fiction writing reveals not only a creative writing bent but also an awareness of genetic and biological science. Her evident skill and experience writing science fiction indicates that Sabrina sees writing in the genre as part of her identity.

Often, writing across genres offers students a chance to explore authentic questions they carry but do not always feel safe sharing in a classroom space. At SBH, Alejandra was someone who identified as bisexual, but she was not "out" to most of her peers in school. She did a project in which she researched, interviewed her family and others, and then wrote and presented her findings on the history and issues around interracial relationships. In addition to adopting the identity of a researcher, she used the opportunity to gauge her family and friends' reactions to nontraditional relationships and gained some insights about how "safe" it would be to be more open about her sexuality with others in her life.

Roberto, also a student in Rose's class, lived in poverty and was an immigrant from Mexico, living in a small apartment with multiple family members. Not comfortable discussing the many struggles that came with his circumstances, Roberto took a similar approach as Alejandra when he did research and later a presentation on poverty, where he examined its causes, its prevalence, and possible ways to end it. Roberto was able to present his findings to the class and, in doing so, examine his own realities and discover connections to many of his peers who also struggled with being poor. With guidance from Rose, both students took on the identity of being a researcher and wrote their papers in the genre of research writing, providing them a safe and mediating stance with which to consider questions of a highly personal nature.

By reading and writing across the genres, students can grow into seeing their identities as ones in which writing academically has a place. Knowing more about our students, allowing their identities to become centered in the classroom, can provide teachers with more resources to spark interest and learning. Consider JHS student Sabrina's "Spores" piece discussed above in which she used her knowledge about science to help her craft a work of fiction. Her identity as a science fiction writer opens up the possibility that she might also be capable of writing academic science-related works, thus providing her with an additional identity she can access. However, without first allowing the science fiction to be validated and included as part of the class, her teacher would not be aware of this possible bridge to academic writing. Similarly, at SBH, Roberto's use of the research paper genre allows him to develop a connection to being a researcher, and while future topics may not be as personal as his writing about poverty was, the genre will be less of an unknown if he is asked to do another research paper in the future.

Activity: Writing About Emotions

Students can also use narratives to write about emotions constituting their identity construction. English teacher Greg Graham (2013) finds that when he gives permission for students to engage in such writing about their emotions,

> the words come gushing out. Last semester I heard about the heartbreak of a student sitting in her car in an empty parking lot, waiting for her absent father. He did not show up—then or ever. There was the story of a 10-year-old boy whose punishment for bad grades was dancing around in his sister's panties and bra, then getting "whooped." Something inside him

broke while his mom and stepdad mocked him and howled in laughter. And I read the story of the teenage girl who left home to live with her boyfriend at the age of 16. It turned out to be a bad decision, but she was too proud to tell her friends or family that she was going to bed hungry every night. No one noticed as she lost 30 pounds and her hair and skin became brittle.

He posits that "the primary objective of our education system is to pass on knowledge and values while developing cognitive and social skills, but to think those goals can be reached without addressing students' interior confusion is unrealistic."

Given the personal and private risk taking that can occur in classrooms where students' identities are integrated into their learning and made public, emotional lives often come to the surface. Through writing, students can explore how different emotions serve to shape perceptions of self and others. They may note that they experience certain "outlaw emotions" of discomfort or anger when their beliefs or ideas are challenged, discomfort or anger that can lead to recognizing the limitations of one's own beliefs or ideas (Boler, 1999; Thein, Sloan, & Guise, 2015). For example, students reading Nomy Lamm's "It's a Big Fat Revolution" (2001) responded with discomfort over her descriptions of how someone who is gay, disabled, and fat copes with oppression about others' deficit perceptions of her identity. One student, who was disturbed by Lamm's anger, at the same time was able to recognize how Lamm's pride in and confidence about her own body serves as the basis for rejecting societal prejudices about gay people.

In their narratives, students also shared instances of empathizing with others in ways that served to challenge identity stereotypes. For example, JHS student Ashley wrote about serving as a volunteer with a group of her friends at the Twin Cities Marathon along with others who were providing bananas to runners at the end of the race. Because one of the other adult volunteers was behaving in an unusual manner, her friends quickly inferred that he was mentally disabled and refused to interact with him. However, as Ashley observed his use of successful strategies for providing reluctant runners with bananas, for example, holding bananas next to his ear and pretending that they were phones, as well as his use of witty conversations, she recognized the need to challenge

> the mistreatment of people with mental disabilities; if you don't respect them and treat them like the human beings they are, then don't expect them, anyone else, and especially not me, to treat you with respect and dignity.

Activity: Writing About Perceptions of Self and Others

One key aspect of identity construction is how students self-identify or identify others according to certain features of race, ethnicity, nationality, class, gender, sexuality, ability, religious affiliation, interests, and so forth. Some of these features are biological, while others are socially or culturally constituted. Regardless of the origin, the meanings of these features depend on how members of a certain social group or culture define their meanings. For example, in British culture, uses of different dialects are particularly important markers for identifying people's class status.

Students' self-perceptions are influenced by assumptions they may have about how others perceive them. They may assume that others focus initially on certain features as particularly salient in determining their identities. For example, students may assume that others will initially identify them relative to their dress or appearance. In an effort to illustrate the connections between place and identity, SBH students wrote about and discussed three regional places, two from the Alexie novel (the reservation Arnold lived on and the White community he went to school in) and one from their urban Bay Area communities. Students explored the ways in which their communities were more (or less) like the reservation or the White community. They also wrote about and discussed the ways that each of the communities shaped the residents living there. As Andrea stated,

> basically, on my block, it's more like the reservation because everybody knows everybody. You know who is cool, who to avoid, and who is a stranger. But, in the White communities, people just shut their door and don't really, like, know each other.

In the Alexie novel, the whole town seemed to mourn the death of the protagonist's grandmother. The SBH students were very touched by the funeral scene and also somewhat impressed and surprised that the whole town would be affected, especially because death was all too common on the reservation. In a way, death was not uncommon to the students of SBH, some of whom lived in neighborhoods with high rates of crime and poverty. During the tenure of Anthony's study, a student who was a senior died under somewhat bizarre circumstances, and the students in Rose's class were deeply affected. However, unlike the reservation, the school did not have the norms, traditions, experience, and culture to mourn her loss in ways that seemed sufficient. In this way, as one student who was friends with the young woman who passed away noted, they were more like the White community.

To reflect on which features students consider in defining themselves as well as how they believe others perceive them, students can write about their perceptions of self and others using the Social Identity Wheel (http://www.odec.umd.edu/CD/ACTIVITI/SOCIAL.PDF) (Intergroup Relations Center, Arizona State University, 1998). In completing this figure, students first identify those categories they use to identify themselves to put in the outer ring on the wheel. They then respond to the question, "Who am I as a group member?" by noting those three salient features according to "What Others See First."

Activity: Writing About the Experience of Difference

Students can also share stories about interacting with others who differ from them in terms of race, class, or gender, in ways that support empathizing with others' perspectives. Students at University Heights High School in the South Bronx, the poorest congressional district in America, interacted with students from a nearby private school, the Ethical Culture Fieldston School, through letters and field trips (Lovell, 2014). Through this exchange, the students from University Heights High School recognized the class disparities between the students in their own school in contrast to the students in Fieldston School. Students from the two schools then paired up and shared stories about experiences that defined their identity. Then, based on what the organization Narrative 4 (http://narrative4.com) defines as "radical empathy" (Lovell, 2014), students retold their partner's story by adopting a first person point of view assuming that student's persona. In doing so, they learned how to adopt their partner's perspective, which may differ from their own perspective. Lovell cites the example of one student who benefitted from adopting his partner's emotional perspective:

> David Fishman told the story of Angie Ramirez, whose father had died and whose mother had been sick. "I'm afraid of her going away," David-as-Angie said. ("I shared a story about my Outward Bound trip last year," David later wrote to me, as a way of talking about his awareness of the different kinds of strain in their lives, "and how I had to overcome peer pressure and stand up for what I believed in. My partner talked about her father's death and an illness her mother had. She expressed fears about having to take care of her little siblings if her mother died.")

Students can also write about recognizing certain aspects of their identities given experiences in events or sites where they sensed that they were different from others. The fact that students tend to perceive themselves (often in limiting ways) according to certain racial, class, gender/sexuality, or institutional affiliations means that they apply those indicators of identity when perceiving others.

As previously noted, SBH students completed a survey in which they were asked to consider their identities. Students were given ample space with which to describe the multiple and complex factors that made up who they were. He found that, on average, students defined themselves using only three identity markers (e.g., "I am black, chill, and funny"). He found that students struggled, even when given support to do so, to come up with multiple identity markers. In discussing the identities of peers, students used even fewer indicators for perceiving someone (e.g., "he's a nerd"). The students at SBH, like students in many schools, often find themselves in contexts where the benefits of labeling and categorizing others trumps what might be gained in seeing others as fluid, multiple, and in-process. In such settings, students who have been defined as "lazy" or "difficult" struggle to see themselves as otherwise, come to see these labels as "fixed," and are given few opportunities or spaces to present the multiple and contrasting aspects of themselves.

It is relatively normative for the students at SBH, who are 98% non-White, to experience race-based reminders of their identities in most of the social spaces they traverse. In contrast, given that 77% of the student population is White, the students at JHS operate in a more homogeneous context where race is less visible. As a result, the JHS students are less exposed to diverse racial and class perspectives that serve to challenge their recognition of how their racial and class identities are privileged in American society. Given this lack of exposure to cultural diversity in their school and community, JHS students may then not be aware of how institutionalized privilege influences identity construction and opportunities, awareness that requires that they make the familiar strange (Erickson, 2004).

To help students reflect on how their experience with difference could serve to challenge their status quo perspectives, Elizabeth had her students write about their specific experiences of exposure to or interactions with others related to race, class, gender, and/or religion.

Jonah describes how his friends' perceptions of racial identities reflects their existence in the largely all-White schools he has attended:

> I could have just had all White friends and stayed in that little "White bubble." But instead I decided to make friends with anyone starting in elementary school; it didn't matter what race. I can still faintly see racism in our society today. I can see it in the racist jokes that are still told, but rarely hear jokes about White people. I see racism in some of my friends too. It isn't extreme but you can see it in their eyes, they start to get uncomfortable or quiet when a person who is of another race starts talking to them. As a White person I haven't really experienced much discrimination from people, but for other races it is just the opposite. I want to try to end the racism and discrimination, but some people just do not want to change.

And Jordana wrote about experiencing a different perception of class during her upbringing in Brazil in which she perceived herself as better off financially than her friends, but then when she moved to Bloomington, she recognized that she was less well off than others in Bloomington:

> I grew up in one of the poorest areas of Sao Paulo, Brazil. Until I was five years old, I lived in a city where many people lived in shacks. Being one of the wealthier families in this community, I realized that my life was always different than others' lives. For example, I went to a private school further away from the city and my family owned two very nice houses. My friends that I would play with in the streets lived in poor houses and attended the nearby public school or didn't attend school at all. This gave

me the mindset that I was very wealthy. This mindset changed when I moved to the United States in kindergarten. When my mom and I moved to the United States, I noticed that we no longer lived in the nicest houses around.

In asking your students to write about their experience with difference, you can have students describe how becoming aware of difference led them to change their perspectives on how institutional forces operate in society, as did Jonah in recognizing the influence of race and Jordana in recognizing class difference.

Language

One often overlooked benefit to reading various types of literary works, and writing in various voices and genres, is that the practice immerses one into new discourses. By adding additional discourses to the ones we carry, we enrich our reserves from which to draw upon in thinking about not only the world we inhabit but also in considering the self. Students benefit from developing metacognition about the discourses they draw upon and are exposed to, and yet this practical and applied usage of considering language is rarely tapped in ELA settings. Connections between the discourses students bring into the classroom and the discourses found in literary texts, if elicited from the instructional methods, can help mitigate the oftentimes alienating feelings students have toward schoolwork.

Activity: Using Unfamiliar Words

Anthony found that students in the AP English level courses at South Bay High were often intimidated or felt excluded from the language used in AP courses discussing literature. Terms such as "hubris" and "hyperbole" were unfamiliar ones, and those such as "cinquain" and "anthropomorphism" may have well been lifted from the Dead Sea Scrolls. To combat those feelings of being marginalized by language, the teacher asked students to call out words or phrases that were common in urban and youth culture and then charted these on the board. While a few of the terms may have been known to the teacher, most were unknown. The teacher then told a fictional story using the terms (all incorrectly), much to the delight of the students. The display pointed out to students that language serves to identify one as part of a particular group and, importantly, distinguish those who do not belong. The terms associated with discussions of poetry and literature allow speakers of those discourses to feel kinship with others using the same language.

By adopting new languages, identities are further expanded because it allows one access to other social practices and communities. The class then created "literary slang" posters that were hung around the room and served as reminders.

Each poster had a particular literary term or rhetorical device, followed by definitions and examples of the term's usage. By taking ownership of the terms and connecting them to students' own discourses, the students were less intimidated by the terms and language that AP English employed.

The ability to express oneself in language is central to how one is known and perceived. In moving from Brazil to Bloomington when she was five, Jordana describes how being able to speak English changed her identity in first grade:

> I first moved here and I didn't know a word of English so for two years I went through kindergarten and first grade, I didn't speak a word of English. Throughout those two years, I picked up a lot of English and people did not know that I was fluent. I picked it up really fast—remarkably is what my teachers told me—and by a year later I was fluent but I still didn't speak a single word; I was too embarrassed to talk. One day in ESL one of my teachers gave me a book and she caught me reading a book by myself and they kicked me out of ESL and put me in honors English. That was first grade.
>
> I was really quiet and really reserved; I didn't have any friends. And I kind of kept to myself and I thought I was different and now I have achieved a lot. They thought I was weird, that this girl doesn't talk, and now they said, this girl can talk. I finally could express myself. People found out that I was funny and smart; I wasn't just this quiet girl.

Jordana's experience reflects the centrality of language use in constructing identities. The fact that she didn't speak meant that no one knew her as a person. The role of language is particularly salient for ELL students, who often struggle with their use of English in ESL classrooms.

Students enact different identities through the use of language. The languages used are often shaped by the activity or event context. As they develop proficiency in using language, students begin to employ certain types of language or dialects that mark them as a member of a certain group. And they then shift their language as they move across different contexts as different "communicative repertoires" (Rymes, 2013). Betsy Rymes cites the example of Alex:

> Alex shifts between languages virtually from activity to activity. He chats in Spanish on the way to school, gets silent in technology class, socializes in English in his ELL class, and uses Spanish to explain problems to a friend in an otherwise English-speaking math class. On the way home, he uses Spanish with his friends and to call out greetings to adults. Once home, he uses Spanish with his mother as they make dinner, but effortlessly moves in and out of English with his little brother, who has had all his schooling in the United States, as he helps him with his homework.
>
> (p. 288)

Students could reflect on how these shifts in their language use across different contexts represent adoption of different identities. They may note that the informal language use they adopt in interacting with peers differs from the more formal language they employ in the classroom.

Activity: Studying Dialects/Usage and Identities

Students could study how people are marked according to their uses of certain dialects or language usage. Given that formal Standard English represents the norm for what it means to be educated and middle class, alternative dialects or language usage are often perceived as inferior, particularly for written texts.

The notion of Standard English as a static code defining the norm for acceptable language use in the classroom ignores the ways in which English is continually evolving in unstable ways. A translingual model of language use for writing recognizes how English is continually evolving through the remix of different dialects and language usage (Horner et al., 2010).

By 2030, if not sooner, the majority of students in schools will be students of color. Many of them will be ELL students whose identities are shaped by their language use. Teachers can focus on ways to help all students acquire an open, tolerant understanding of language differences so that peers will perceive these students' language use in a positive rather than deficit manner (Lorimer Leonard, 2013).

Language therefore serves as markers of group identification. In writing about being a member of her school's orchestra as an "orch dork," referred to in Chapter 3, Colleen notes that "Orch dorks have their own unique style, have their own way of talking to, and greeting, each other, and have concerts in which they connect." And Tim noted that members of his peer group employ the practice of "being ignant," defined in the urban dictionary as "the person knew damn well but chose to act foolishly anyway," so that

> when you talk to people, it doesn't matter what you say or do, you just have to be ignorant. Most of the time it requires screaming or yelling and most of the time this happens when you're in public. Sometimes it gets very loud and outrageous but after it all, there is usually a laugh or two. The purpose of doing this is to show everyone else that we are ignorant and don't care what other people think. . . . It also shows that we are confident with who we are and that other people's opinions of us don't matter. . . . If you are confident in yourself, you can do anything because you believe in yourself.

As did these students, students could describe what they perceive to be certain unique uses of language associated with being a member of a certain group or organization. In doing so, they can reflect on how and why a group adopts a certain use of language, for example, why the Obscuritans deliberately employ language that no one else employs.

Use of Language Categories

In thinking about these groups, students are drawing on certain language categories such as "geeks," "emo girls," "burnouts," "jocks," "stoners," and so forth, based on assumptions about popularity, status, power, or deviation from academic or social norms operating in a school. "Geeks" may be perceived as conforming to certain academic norms, but lacking the social practices associated with popularity. Students also apply categories based on difference in race, class, gender, and sexuality, categories based on opposition to "the other." These perceptions reflect the need to be defined as *not* a member of another group, for example, students defining themselves as "White" relative to what they consider to be "non-White."

These categories create divisions in groups between the "us" versus the "them." Groups perceived to be "inferior" may resist these representations by challenging the superior group's representations, can change their own practices, or can compare themselves to other "low-status" groups.

Activity: Identifying Use of Categories to Label Identities

Students can identify some of the categories employed in their school to label students, noting how these categories are perceived as positive or negative in terms of popularity, power, status, or deviation from the norm. They can also discuss how they define these categories by using certain markers—dress, tattoos, behaviors, language, common activities, shared interests, and so forth—that identify or label someone based on these categories, for example, labeling students as "preps" for wearing "brand-name" clothing.

Using these criteria of popularity, power, status, or deviation from the norm, they can then create a graph—for example, charting groups perceived to be high versus low in popularity and in power/status. Then, they reflect on the assumptions as to why these groups are perceived to be high versus low in popularity and power/status. How do these categories influence members of these different groups? Do students take them seriously or ignore them? Why or why not?

Students could also examine the limitations of certain binary categories such as "male/female," "White/Black," or "advanced/regular" tracked students; for example, defining how one's identity as "feminine" or "female" or "masculine" or "male" reifies the either/or binary of "male/female" based on certain gender stereotypes.

Use of Speech Acts and Power/Agency Constituting Identities

Students' use of language in the form of speech acts reflects differences in their sense of power/agency constituting who has the ability or authority to perform certain speech acts of requesting, asserting, ordering, questioning, decreeing, commending, complaining, criticizing, and so forth. Whether or not these acts succeed in achieving a positive effect or uptake—whether someone making a request actually receives a response—depends on whether the speaker performing the act is perceived to have the ability or status to perform a certain speech act.

Based on speakers' successful use of these speech acts, students then infer certain traits, beliefs, status, and abilities constituting speakers' identities. Students know that their teachers have the authority to perform certain acts, for example, requesting students to complete an assignment, although if they assume the role of peer instructors, they then could perform similar requests.

Activity: Analyzing How Use of Speech Acts Constitutes Identities

Students could record people's dialogue in conversations or respond to characters' dialogue by identifying the use of certain speech acts. They can then infer traits, beliefs, status, and abilities associated with use of these speech acts, as well as how differences in the power or ability to perform certain speech acts are operating in certain contexts. In describing his experience of working in a Marine recruiting center, Benjamin describes how a sergeant's use of highly laconic, directive speech acts reflects the power hierarchy operating in the setting. In the recruiting center, his peers are saying,

> "yes, sir," "no, sir," using that kind of tone. Orders are given, orders are carried out. . . . From the differences in scouting versus Marine Corps, in scouting sometimes it takes a while to quiet down the group or we have trouble staying focused, but we can be joking in the Marine Corps when the gunnery sergeant walks in, it's like straighten up and he's a very focused, dedicated guy, but at the same time, he's not mean. . . . In the Marine Corps, it's also very brief like in our wording.

In this context, Benjamin identifies how within the Marines, as contrasted to scouting, the Marine sergeant has the authority to issue orders that must be obeyed. Additionally, Benjamin's comments reveal an awareness of the connections and contrasts between language use among the Marines and the Scouts, as well as how these languages come to constitute identities in each context.

Summary

In this chapter, we posit the importance of students making connections between people and texts so that they can compare and contrast their perceived identities with those of their peers as well as characters, connections that help them acquire a sense of stability and feelings of self-confidence. Students can make these connections through their literary responses, drama activities, writing, and analysis of language use, for example, by writing about their experience of difference related to race, class, or gender. Through making these connections as an identity practice, students perceive how English language arts is related to their everyday lives in ways that provide support for constructing stable identities. (For additional resources, activities, and further reading, see http://tinyurl.com/m8k57qz.)

References

Alexie, S. (2007). *The absolutely true diary of a part-time Indian.* Boston: Little Brown.

Bloome, D., Carter, S. P., Christian, B. N., & Otto, S. (2004). *Discourse analysis & the study of classroom language & literacy events: A microethnographic perspective.* New York: Routledge.

Boler, M. (1999). *Feeling power: Emotions and education.* New York: Routledge.

Burgess, A., & Ivanič, R. (2010). Writing and being written: Issues of identity across time-scales. *Written Communication, 27*(2), 228–255.

Clines, F. X. (1992, June 10). At work with: Anna Deavere Smith; The 29 voices of one woman in search of Crown Heights. *The New York Times.* Retrieved from http://tinyurl.com/nw97kno

Crutcher, C. (1991). A brief moment in the life of Angus Bethune. In C. Crutcher, *Athletic shorts: Six short stories* (pp. 8–12). New York: Greenwillow.

Crutcher, C. (2003). *Staying fat for Sarah Byrnes.* New York: Greenwillow.

Cullen, C. (1925). Incident. In C. Cullen, *Color.* New York: Harper and Brothers.

Davis, S. (2011). Digital drama—Toolkits, dilemmas, and preferences. *Youth Theatre Journal, 25*(2), 134–145.

Edmiston, B. (2014). *Transforming teaching and learning with active and dramatic approaches: Engaging students across the curriculum.* New York: Routledge.

Elish-Piper, L., Wold, L. S., & Schwingendorf, K. (2014). Scaffolding high school students' reading of complex texts using linked text sets. *Journal of Adolescent and Adult Literacy, 57*(7), 565–574.

Enger, L. (2000). *Peace like a river.* New York: Atlantic Monthly Press.

Erickson, F. (2004). *Talk and social theory.* Cambridge, UK: Polity Press.

Gaarder, J. (1995). *Sophie's world.* New York: Farrar, Straus & Giroux.

Graham, G. (2013, January 29). Bringing students to life with memoir writing [web log post]. Retrieved from http://tinyurl.com/akxwazh

Hawkins, B. (2014, July 11). Exiting teachers-union leader Julie Blaha talks of tenure, retention, change—and improv [web log post]. Retrieved from http://tinyurl.com/nmj6x75

Heitin, L. (2013, March 13). In Common Core, teachers see interdisciplinary opportunities [web log post]. Retrieved from http://tinyurl.com/c8v3xtk

Hoose, P. M. (2010). *Claudette Colvin: Twice toward justice.* New York: Square Fish Press.

Horner, B., Lu, M., Royster, J. J., & Trimbur, J. (2010). Language difference in writing: Toward a translingual approach. *College English, 73*(3), 303–321.

Hosseini, K. (2004). *The kite runner.* New York: Riverhead.

Hyland, K. (2012). *Disciplinary identities: Individuality and community in academic discourse.* New York: Cambridge University Press.

Intergroup Relations Center, Arizona State University. (1998). Social Identity Wheel. Author. Retrieved from http://www.odec.umd.edu/CD/ACTIVITI/SOCIAL.PDF

Ivanič, R. (1998). *Writing and identity: The discoursal construction of identity in academic writing.* Baltimore: John Benjamins Publishing.

Labov, W. (1972). *The language of the inner city.* Philadelphia: University of Pennsylvania Press.

Lamm, N. (2001). It's a big fat revolution. In J. Ritchie & K. Ronald (Eds.), *Available means: An anthology of women's rhetoric(s)* (pp. 545–61). Pittsburgh: University of Pittsburgh Press.

Lee, H. (1994). *To kill a mockingbird.* New York: Grand Central Publishing.

Lorimer Leonard, R. (2013). Traveling literacies: Multilingual writing on the move. *Research in the Teaching of English, 48*(1), 13–39.

Lovell, J. (2014, May 4). The tale of two schools. *The New York Times Magazine.* Retrieved from http://tinyurl.com/l7gyabw

Micciche, L. R. (2007). *Doing emotion: Rhetoric, writing, teaching.* Portsmouth, NH: Boynton/Cook-Heinemann.

Miller, A. (1976/2003). *The crucible.* New York: Viking Penguin.

O'Brien, T. (2009). *The things they carried.* Boston: Mariner Press.

Rymes, B. (2013). *Communicating beyond language: Everyday encounters with diversity.* New York: Routledge.

Siemens, G. (2010, March 9). Connectivism [web log post]. Retrieved from http://www.connectivism.ca/?p=234

Tan, A. (1989). *Joy Luck Club.* New York: Penguin Books.

Thein, A. H. (2009). Identifying the history and logic of negative, ambivalent, and positive responses to literature: A case-study analysis of cultural models. *Journal of Literacy Research, 41*(3), 273–316.

Thein, A. H., Sloan, D. L., & Guise, M. (2015). Examining emotional rules in the English classroom: A critical discourse analysis of one student's literary responses in two classroom contexts. *Research in the Teaching of English, 49*(3), 200–223.

Twain, M. (1994). *Huckleberry Finn.* New York: Dover.

West, K. C. (2008). Weblogs and literacy response: Socially situated identities and hybrid social languages in English class blogs. *Journal of Adolescent and Adult Literacy, 51*(7), 588–598.

Yagelski, R. (2012). Writing as praxis. *English Education, 44*(2), 188–204.

5

NEGOTIATING IDENTITIES ACROSS DIFFERENT SOCIAL WORLDS

Ideology influences our social practices that, in turn, reproduce the ideology. Through institutions (schools, churches, media, clubs, sports, and others), we are to learn the appropriate social practices as "common sense" in order to affirm the ideas, values, and beliefs that are defined as the "common good." That is why different ideological groups compete for control over schooling in general and reading education in particular.

Patrick Shannon (2014, p. 6)

Identity matters in ways that are not simply based on idiosyncratic differences among people who have largely the same inherent positions of power in society . . . identity, agency, and language are negotiated across boundaries created by systems of difference that have real consequences.

David Wallace (2014, p. 553)

Alejandra Inhabits Many Worlds

Unlike her peers in her classroom at South Bay High School, Alejandra carried herself as having already "grown up" despite only being 16. Alejandra excelled at being the person she believed others wanted her to be. She carried a quiet confidence and evident assurance about her ability to be successful. These traits marked her as arrogant in the eyes of some of her peers but struck Anthony as signs of maturity.

In the various worlds she inhabited, she was adept at presenting herself in the ways she deemed the context asked of her. She played the role of the high-achieving student in school, managed to avoid drama with girls in the school who clearly did not like her, and approached each learning task as an item to mark off her to-do list. She worked at a taqueria on a college campus, where she excelled at customer service. Even in interviews with Anthony, she seemed eager to say what she imagined that he hoped to hear, as opposed to being completely candid to the extent that her peers were. At home, she played the princess role, went to church, and sang in the choir. However, her bisexuality and identification with many of her friends from diverse backgrounds also defined her.

At the time of the study, Alejandra explained that she was in a "good place now" and that she had experienced a difficult past that "sobered" her up in terms of behavior and priorities. She viewed her family as being prejudiced and narrow-minded about race, gender, and sexuality. When she was in 9th grade, she ran away from home. She left what she saw as a close-minded and traditional family and spent several months living on the streets. These months were hectic and at times dangerous; she was couch surfing, doing drugs, and she considered suicide, all to avoid an oppressive home life. She credits a former boyfriend and her decision to return to church with turning her life around. Now, she is eager for life after high school, and she stated a refusal to get caught up in the school drama.

Constructing Identities in "Figured Worlds"

As discussed in Chapter 3, constructing identities in "figured worlds" involves drawing upon generic or prototypical versions of those worlds derived from historical understanding, culture, media, and literature. Students and teachers construct classroom social worlds based in part on what they've read in books, seen on TV and in movies, and experienced in their past participation in schools. For instance, to construct a figured world of romance and to enact identities associated with romantic relationships, students draw on popular culture representations of romance in movies, TV shows, or romance novels, as well as countless other cultural narratives constituting practices and roles associated with romance as a "figured world" (Holland et al., 1998).

Functioning, as a figured world, Rose's SBH classroom tends to be populated with predetermined roles that students to varying degrees adopt or are forced to occupy—the good student, the class clown, the chronically late student, and so forth. At the same time, the class is a highly social one, where "off-task" behavior, humor, a strong sense of community, and moments of tension all seem like daily norms and events. The teacher's role is also a social construct, one that this teacher actively embraces and often resists given the context. Next, the class is part of a school and is nested in a Humanities department, has its own history, and is constantly being (re)defined in the present. Finally, the figured world of an 11th-grade English class is a frame that all participants carry in varying ways—in some cases this means resistance to, or excitement about, academic work, for others it means feeling anxious or eager about debating ideas or issues in a book, and for some it is seen as nap time.

At the same time, participants in any social world also "improvise" upon these common narratives given the particular social and historical moments in which they find themselves as "persons in history" (Holland & Lave, 2001). For instance, a couple today might view older films in which couples write letters to one another or talk late into the night on the phone, while in their own contemporary relationship they text each other or communicate via email. Further, as people improvise within figured worlds, they often resist problematic elements of prior prototypical narratives and models. Although the vast majority of mainstream books and media once featured straight couples performing normative gender roles in romantic relationships, contemporary couples might break with these gender roles or with heterosexuality more broadly.

In thinking about students moving into new social worlds with different norms and expectations, it's important to recognize that worlds are not pre-established, static entities but rather are constructed by their members given their particular knowledge, interests, beliefs, and goals. These worlds are therefore continually shifting as membership changes across time and, subsequently, as the practices and values of that social world change. Holland and her colleagues (1998) refer to this concept as participation in "figured worlds." For example, as described above, Rose's classroom is a "figured world" with its own unique norms and expectations that were constructed by Rose and her students as a relatively safe space for engaging in identity experimentation.

Students construct their identities according to the practices and norms operating within certain "figured worlds" (Holland et al., 1998). However, as they move across figured worlds, the boundaries between them can be blurred and difficult to discern. For example, the boundaries between school work and online play or between formal and informal learning activities are not always clear, so students sometimes have difficulty in knowing how and when to enact different identities (Arnseth & Silseth, 2012).

Influence of Positionings in Figured Worlds

Students need to recognize how their own identities position their perceptions of figured worlds as well as how these worlds position them to adopt certain perceptions (Beach, Thein, & Parks, 2007), what Sanchez (2006) refers to as "positionality." For instance, recognizing how she is positioned as a "struggling reader" shapes a student's perception of the kinds of agency (or lack thereof) she has in her English class.

If students perceive others as positioning them through accepting, supporting, or respecting them, they may perceive themselves as valued members of a peer group, family, school, team, community, or organization, creating a sense of self-worth. In contrast, if students perceive others as positioning them through rejecting, subordinating, or disrespecting them, they may then define themselves as outsiders or deviant within a peer group, family, school, team, community, or organization—as not "fitting in" (Crosnoe, 2011). As JHS student Josh noted:

> Most people think that I'm weird because I don't really talk much so that they don't really know me, but when they get to know me they know that I'm the same as them. Most people have their own friends so they don't have any reasons to come talk to me.

Knowing that they are perceived as having certain identities serves as a means for students to escape uncertainty and anxiety about their identities—they "know where they stand" in a group or family. However, the students we've worked with often express a desire to move beyond the identities that others perceive them as performing. As JHS student Nicole explained:

> It was weird not knowing where to go and not fitting in with anybody. Throughout the years, I've been in different groups; there are a lot of different groups. I would say that there are not a lot of popular kids—you have the theater groups, the show choir group, the band group, the sports groups. I've been lucky to have friends in all of the different groups, so I've been able to do a whole bunch of different things like go to a play with my play friends, but the hockey friends don't want to see the play, because they don't support that, but then I've been able to go to the hockey games with my hockey friends.

Interrogating the limitations of categories or labels helps students to gain an openness toward adopting multiple, alternative perspectives and supports the complexity of identity construction. In an interview, Ellie, who noted that "I've been openly gay since 8th grade," described how she resists external labels:

> It's more or less that Jefferson likes to put you in a little box depending on what you are and if you don't like that box then you have to go out and find your own. I'm floating around between a few of the boxes, but that's just how I like to be. I don't want to be put into a certain clique. I don't want to be just a popular person or just a geek. I don't want people to know me as that; I want people to know me as playing sports or playing band and being gay and being in the Navy and being smart. I don't want to be labeled like everyone else is; I don't like those labels.

Recognizing How Identities Are Constituted by Figured Worlds

Like fish in water, students often have difficulty recognizing their own worlds as shaped by larger cultural or institutional practices, beliefs, and values, assuming that their own figured worlds are driven by practices that are simply "normal."

Elizabeth noted the importance of having students recognize how their social worlds shape their identities:

> The thing that I think is the saddest is the kids that lose hope, you see where the system starts breaking them down and you see that something is going wrong. Kids lose their houses; or kids get pregnant. But, one of them wrote, "Nothing shapes me." That's like saying, "Nothing gives me my identity." But the institutions, the country we live in shapes me. If I lived in Iran this is normal, they just think that it doesn't affect them in any way. My neighborhood is normal or regular, like what does that mean? They don't see beyond right here.

She also defines her role as helping students to go beyond their own insular social worlds assumed to be "normal," to experience alternative cultures through world literature:

> World literature is my favorite class to teach because no matter whose story it is, like *The Boy's Soldier Story* or *Cry, the Beloved Country* or even *Things Fall Apart* or any stories from around the world, the story becomes [something more than] these stereotypes and archetypes—when we watch something on the news, [I] don't see people as people; they don't seem real to me, but when I'm reading a story, even if it's fiction, they seem more real to me than the people we see on TV.
>
> In an English class, you are learning about what it means to be a human and how different it is for all of us—like how can you have the same thoughts about things that other people have—we are inundated with water and other people don't have any—so how couldn't you be different? When you're reading these stories from around the world, you realize that what you're doing isn't normal—it's really different from a lot of other people's experience.

By stepping outside of their figured worlds and studying the norms, values, roles, and practices operating in those worlds, students can begin to make the familiar unfamiliar and notice the culturally specific rather than "normal" aspects of their figured worlds (Erickson, 2004).

Different Worlds Inhabited by Students

Students inhabit peer-group, family, classroom, sports, neighborhood, workplace, digital, and media worlds, "figured worlds" requiring them to negotiate their identities as they move within and across these different worlds. In this chapter we describe these different worlds. We then provide some activities you can use to help students reflect on how their identities are constituted through participation in these different worlds and how they can effectively negotiate the competing demands associated with moving across these different worlds.

Peer-Group Worlds

Students' relationships with peers serve to provide support for dealing with and addressing challenges in their lives. Those peer relationships, in turn, are shaped by their own and their peers' memberships in and allegiances to certain groups (Crosnoe, 2011). Students are continually perceiving and assessing each other according to the norms operating within these social groups, noticing their own and their peers' status or popularity. When Tre was being silenced in the Socratic Seminar, the other participants relied on Tre to be an outsider within this group in order to validate their positions as legitimate contributors to the discussion. Tre's effort to genuinely participate in the group challenged the integrity of the group itself and the fragile academic identities of those within the group.

Students construct their identities based on self-perceptions derived from peer-group alignments. Members of these groups assess each other based on their perceptions of norms or beliefs operating in these groups. For example, a student might be perceived by her peer group as not dressing according to what they perceive to be appropriate or fashionable. Students then draw on these peers' perceptions to define their own self-perceptions. Alternatively, they may choose to ignore their peers' perceptions. Students with a strong internal locus of control or self-efficacy are more likely to resist the pressures to conform to group norms than students with a more external locus of control who fear disapproval for their actions (Kosten, Scheier, & Grenard, 2012).

Based on ethnographic analysis of these peer-group alignments in a Texas high school, Robert Crosnoe (2011) identified two types of peer-group alignments: alignments within the school world constituted by hierarchies of groups (geeks, jocks, druggies, preps, etc.) and alignments to close friends. He found that these alignments with school-wide groups often result in students receiving positive or negative feedback regarding their actions, appearance, or attitudes.

At the same time, having close friends serves to buffer these peer-group perceptions, allowing students to challenge stereotypes of their peer groups. These group alignments and close friendships strongly influence students' engagement with and success in school. Students who experience alienation from not fitting in based on peer-group affiliations often internalize negative judgments, which can lead them to not participating in school activities or dropping out of school (Crosnoe, 2011).

Family Worlds

Students also construct their identities in family worlds as daughters, sons, grand-daughters, grandsons, sisters, or brothers. In doing so, they define their identities based on the nature of their relationships with parents, grandparents, or siblings. Parents, grandparents, or older siblings often serve as role models for students in constructing their own identities. In her analysis of the influence of "power parents" on characters in *1984* (Orwell, 1969), *Ordinary People* (Guest, 1982), and *Beloved* (Morrison, 2007), Nicole noted that "parents are a huge role model to their children and if they act in a certain way around them, their children will catch on and in some cases behave in the same manner." She perceived the government as assuming a parental role in *1984* by controlling its citizens; Beth as controlling her son, Conrad, in *Ordinary People*; and Sethe as engaging in a contentious relationship with her daughter, Denver, who believed that Sethe cared more for Beloved than herself in *Beloved*.

Without these role models, students may then assume different family roles. JHS student Ellie noted that, living without a father, she had to assume the role of being her own parent:

> Since my parents got divorced and I grew up without a father, I had to create my own second parent so I needed to grow up really quickly and I can't be so naïve to things. I needed to learn how to be smarter and make better choices and not make dumb choices and get hurt; I needed to grow up and see what's wrong in life and be able to choose the good and bad.

Ellie's experience is not unique given shifts in the makeup of families. In 1970, 40% of households consisted of a married couple with children, while in 2013, only 19% of families consisted of the same makeup. This demographic shift is due to increases in the number of unmarried adults, birth rates among unmarried women (from 5% in 1960 to 41% in 2012), and divorce rates in the boomer generation (Jensen, 2014).

Classroom Worlds

Students also adopt different identities within and across classroom worlds. Within their classroom world, students align with certain peer groups relative to their degree of engagement or compliance with a classroom's expectations as well as differences in race, class, and/or gender alignments. Within the classroom at SBH that Anthony studied, he analyzed multiple social clusters that made up Rose's classroom. Important for identity development was the students' understanding of the norms and practices that were both expected and created by participants within these social clusters.

Rose's Fourth Period: A Network of Social Clusters

Four clearly marked clusters, or "cliques," of social peer groups inhabited Rose's classroom of twenty-two students. Two individuals (Benny and Jessica) enjoyed the freedom to traverse multiple clusters, but most students inhabited only one cluster. Beyond the clusters, a number of students showed no affiliation to any groupings, but at times paired off among themselves. These clusters were relatively consistent throughout the course of the study and informed Anthony's understanding of the collective academic identity of the class. Rose, in a post-study interview, remarked on the various groupings: "They had been disjointed; there were factions of the class that were at war with each other before the project. They had a really big vibe of NOT participating, not being into school, like, 'Don't let people from that group see you slipping up and doing English!' You know? Almost like an aggressive refusal."

As Table 5.1 illustrates, the clusters possessed various levels of social and academic status in the classroom. Analysis of each cluster considered the *positional* identities (Davies & Harré, 1990) of each grouping and its participants. Social and academic status here is measured based on *perceived* (by the participants and myself) levels, perceptions not always correctly surmised. For example, Jeffrey's actual academic status would be construed as low in most classroom contexts, but because his peers viewed him as assiduous about doing well in school, he possessed a higher level of academic status than he might in another context. In contrast, Andrea, while in possession of strong academic skills, consistently undermined them with her public displays of resistance to schoolwork, and this relegated her, in the eyes of her peers, to having little academic status—enjoying instead a high level of social status.

Andrea, Amari, Johnny, Jessica, Sandra, and Jeffrey made up the cluster referred to here as "the Disruptors." Of all the groups, "the Disruptors" tended to dictate how each class went with regard to time spent engaging academically, time spent socializing, and times during which Rose's teaching efforts were taken off track or undermined. Of the group's members, three managed to both disrupt others and get their work done (Jeffrey, Amari, and Jessica), but the others struggled to regain their academic focus. Generally, Andrea served as the ringleader. Other than the teacher's actions and behavior, Andrea's unpredictable

TABLE 5.1 Student Membership in the Five Groups

Name	Members	Social Status	Academic Status
"The Disruptors"	Andrea, Amari, Johnny, Jessica, Sandra, Jeffrey	HIGH	LOW
"The Fellas"	Carlos, Benny, Joseph	HIGH	LOW
"The Shockers"	Minerva, Alicia, Benny, Jessica	HIGH	MEDIUM
"The Quiet Kids"	Mia, Jasmin, Isabella, Maria, Roberto	MEDIUM	HIGH
Outsiders (not grouped)	Cat, Tre, Alejandra, Jet, Sosa, Arturo	MIXED	MIXED

emotions and her disposition toward school and the class itself played the largest role in determining the likelihood that the class would engage (or not) in the day's lessons. When she seemed upset, or as she puts it "irritated," by something in class or otherwise, her misery loved company. Ironically, when feeling very positive, she came to class with lots of energy and created equal distraction. She laughed very loudly, sang or rapped or danced in her seat, and she was quite good at getting others, such as Jeffrey and Jessica, to join in the fun.

Carlos, Benny, and Joseph made up another group, referred to here as "the Fellas," and this cluster also played a disruptive role. These longtime friends often sat together, and as they joked and talked among themselves they drew in others. Carlos and Benny were cousins, and Joseph had been a friend of the pair since elementary school. They were often seen together at lunch and socialized in the hallways between classes as well. Of the three, Joseph was academically the strongest, and he could usually get his work done while joking around with the other two. Benny instigated off-task behavior by joking with the other two or inviting other students, often Minerva and Alicia, to join him in behaviors that distracted from the lesson. Carlos also found ways to make those around him laugh, but usually did so by teasing the teacher or making fun of himself. On rare occasions, this group would talk together in Spanish so that Rose and other non-Spanish speakers didn't understand them. Given a pedagogical stance of welcoming students to feel that their classroom was "their space" in which an array of discourses were appropriate, Rose never elected to interrupt or dissuade students from speaking Spanish.

Minerva, Alicia, Jessica, and Benny made up the group referred to here as "the Shockers." Led by Minerva, this cluster served a role similar to "the Disruptors," and the two groups often socialized. A strategy "the Shockers" employed involved making off-color statements (often sexual in nature) that invited comments and laughter from other students as well as Rose, who made allowances for such behavior because it was rooted in humor rather than defiance. This cluster tended to be more productive academically than "the Disruptors" and "the Fellas," and they were also quite adept at completing work for other classes rather than doing the English assignments. This group often spoke in Spanish when talking about their lives outside of school, suggesting that they viewed Spanish as a nonacademic language and appreciated having spaces to hold private conversations during class time.

"The Quiet Kids," made up of Mia, Jasmin, Isabella, Maria, and Roberto, were the fourth and final cluster of students. Adept at engaging in clandestine nonacademic behaviors (putting on makeup, passing notes, using their cell phones, copying homework for other classes), "the Quiet Kids" also found ways to complete most of the day's assigned work, albeit often to a minimal standard. The four Latinas of the group were close friends. They adopted Roberto by virtue of his seating placement and his quiet demeanor.

This group was often ignored because they generally completed the work, rarely distracted other students, and socialized only within their cluster. As a group, they possessed a low or medium level of social status and a high level of academic status. Rose often spoke of the group as students she "did not have to worry about." However, as is often the case, while the members of the Quiet Kids rarely distracted from the class, their lack of vocal presence did not necessarily mean they did not need academic support.

One indicator of a durable academic identity is displaying the grit and determination necessary to solve academic problems when they become difficult (Tough, 2012). The quickness with which students asked Rose for help, often before reading directions or making any effort, reflected their fragile academic identities. Rather than rely on the teacher for help, the Quiet Kids tended to assist one another, either by explaining or simply copying one another's work. Jasmin, who was shy, and Roberto, who had immigrated to America within the last five years, both struggled academically. Yet, because of their membership in this group and their quiet demeanors, they did not always get the support they needed.

Not belonging to a specific cluster, the six outsiders in the classroom included Alejandra, Tre, Cat, Sosa, Arturo, and Jet. Of the six, Alejandra and Tre often paired up, as did Arturo and Jet. While not associated with any of the other groupings, to varying levels they would interact with people from the clusters as a result of simply sitting near them or because the academic or social activities supported or required interaction. Popular and handsome, Sosa was a Samoan student who often interacted with multiple groups, but as a newer student to the class, he did not specifically align with any one cluster. Jet and Arturo, both quiet and somewhat introverted students, were friends who often paired off and rarely engaged others in the class. Alejandra and Tre made an odd pair, the strongest student and the most resistant. Their pairing seemed to stem from a few sources. They enjoyed flirting with one another, she liked playing the role of caretaker for him, and he enjoyed the attention. Cat rarely engaged with anyone, but she did talk to Jet and Johnny at times.

As a teacher, Rose recognized and leveraged these various social clusters in the classroom to reach academic goals, develop academic identities, and support learning. Such clusters of students might be treated as insular and possibly undermining of the teacher. Rose's choice to allow for these clusters at times made getting daily work done difficult, but it also helped the students feel a sense of community in the class, ownership over their learning, and safety to exhibit their diverse identities, and—because many students viewed school as a dehumanizing and oppressive space—it served to alter their relationship with school and academic learning.

Negotiating Identity Across Classroom Worlds

Students also adopt different identities in classroom worlds based on the acquisition of different disciplinary discourses (Draper et al., 2010) as ways of thinking and knowing associated with their math, social studies, science, art, or music classes (Gee, 2008). For instance, students might see themselves as "math whizzes," "history buffs," "science geeks," "artists," "musicians," or "creative writers." In their science classes, students employ the language of science inquiry constituting the identity of "scientist," while in their social studies class, they employ the language of historical, sociological, or psychological analysis constituting the identities of "historian," "sociologist," or "psychologist."

Students who effectively acquire a certain disciplinary discourse may then experience more agency constituting their identities in one classroom world than in other classroom worlds. At the same time, students may experience transfer of certain practices across these different disciplinary classroom worlds. For example, they may use what they learn about descriptive writing in your ELA class when writing up their lab reports in their Chemistry class.

Sports Worlds

Students also construct their identities through participation in the figured world of sports, either as sports fans or through playing sports (Vegneskumar, 2014). Sports events and television broadcasting represent a trillion dollar enterprise designed to socialize students to construct their identities as sports fans. Sports stars assume the roles of popular culture celebrities who are framed as role models for students to emulate, often creating false hopes that they can become future football, basketball, or baseball "stars."

In playing sports, students can display physical competence to their peers and adults in ways that may compensate for lack of competence in other worlds. Through membership on a sports team, students experience support and friendship from other team members in ways that enhance their sense of self-worth. JHS student Zach described how being on his swim team bolstered his self-perceptions:

> This year when I joined the swim team, it really changed my outlook on things and about other people because there are some other members of the swim team that I had written off—that kid is weird because of the way he dressed. When I got on the swim team I got to know the people better so it's like a new family. I seem to be more open to other people now. . . . Everybody treats everybody like they are part of the family—like they love them—like we're all best friends.

And Alexis Dunlop notes how participation in her karate group served to enhance her self-confidence:

> I had low self-confidence for most of my life until I joined a Tae Kwon Do group the summer before I started high school. It gave me a lot more self-confidence with who I am; I became less self-conscious and it raised

my self-esteem because it was such a good experience. . . . I'm a black belt now. . . . It made me like myself more and just embrace my own identity instead of trying to be different people.

Neighborhood Worlds

Students also construct their identities as members of neighborhood worlds. These worlds are more than simply physical residential spaces. They are also spaces that can support positive social interactions and relationships contributing to identity development (Ralston, 2012). In his research on students' adoption of prosocial or "niceness" attitudes and their neighborhoods in Binghamton, New York, David Wilson (2011) asked high school students to respond to question-naire items having to do with their level of prosocial, civic contributions such as "I am serving others in my community" as well as items related to the level of social support in their neighborhoods such as "I have neighbors who help watch out for me"; their school: "I have a school that cares about kids and encourages them"; their families: "I have parents/guardians who help me succeed"; and extracurricular activities: "I am involved in a sport or creative things such as music" (p. 149). He found that the students receiving more support were also the students who were more likely to contribute to their communities. Stu-dents receiving less support in neighborhoods with higher crime rates and fewer resources were focused primarily on protecting themselves simply to survive and were less likely to acquire prosocial skills.

These neighborhood worlds impact school worlds, as evident in data on the rel-atively large number of students who still do not graduate from high school. While the national graduation rate has increased to 80%, only 68% of African Ameri-cans and 76% of Hispanic students are graduating, with one-quarter of all African Americans attending "dropout factory" high schools located in low-income neigh-borhoods that graduate less than 60% of students (Balfanz et al., 2014). The largest study of its kind on reasons for two hundred students dropping out of high school, "Don't Call Them Dropouts" (Center for Promise, 2014), found that students often drop out not due to lack of motivation or interest in school but because they are coping with homelessness, crime, violence, neglect, abuse, family health issues, or lack of parental support—conditions that often mean that they have to drop out to cope with these issues. Thirty percent reported being abused, 22% experienced homelessness, and 18% spent time in juvenile detention.

Workplace Worlds

Many of the JHS students held jobs after school and on weekends. They noted that in these workplaces they adopted different identities constituted by norms, expectations, and roles required by their employers in terms of their behavior, language, demeanor, and dress. In describing his work as a driver delivering pizza, Brian described how he adopted a more impersonal manner of interacting with his co-workers than with interacting with his close friends:

> I'm more open with a closer group of friends—there are only certain jokes that we would understand since we've been together and other people haven't experienced the same things. I can jab other people in the close group and they understand that I'm not serious. As I get further away from that, I have to be more polite, but I usually maintain the same disposition. At work, I probably speak the least out of all of my co-workers.

Brian's workplace experience shows how working with their coworkers created relationships that differed from their relationships with their peers; in workplace worlds, students explained that it was essential that they engaged in the identity practice of collaboration. In his ethnography about working at a local Dairy Queen restaurant, JHS student Jacob noted that his job

> [h]elped me figure out who I really am. The trust that I bestow on the people that I work with has built an indestructible bond of friendship that surpasses even many of my friendships at school. I care for them and they care for me.

In his interview, he noted how he shifted his identity as he moved between his school and workplace worlds, elaborating on why these work friendships were important to him:

> At school, you hang out with your friends but you'll never be with them like you are at work, and interacting with them and building strong relationships with them is important. I love all of the people I work with so much and being able to be myself more. At school, things are so cliquey and you have to do things in a certain way or be a follower in a certain way. At work, everyone is wearing the same uniform; it's like you have the same level; it's equal playing ground because it's a lot easier to make friends and be close to these people and keep friends for a longer time.

Digital Worlds

Students are also engaged in online digital worlds. Ninety-five percent use the Internet; 93% have computer access; 74% access the Internet through mobile devices; 37% own a smartphone; 23% own a tablet; and 63% text daily (Lenhart, 2014). Further, in one study 73% of teachers indicated that they and/or their students used mobile phones for classroom work, 45% used e-readers, and 43% used tablet computers (Purcell et al., 2013). While students may still prefer to interact with their peers face-to-face, they often have difficulty doing so given restrictions placed on them by loitering or curfew laws, and by a lack of safe, public spaces for such interaction (Boyd, 2014). Instead, students turn to online social networking that allows them to readily move across boundaries between home, school, peer-group, and workplace contexts (Vasudevan, Schultz & Bateman, 2010).

While critics posit that on these sites students represent inauthentic versions of themselves, others note that participation on these sites allows users to adopt more authentic identities. For instance, young gay people sometimes first come out in the supportive communities these sites offer prior to coming out in face-to-face communities (Avance, 2014). And, contrary to the notion that spending more time online displaces face-to-face relationships, use of online networking serves to strengthen the quality of relationships with friends by providing increased opportunities to interact with those friends (Davis, 2013; Sosik & Bazarova, 2014).

Students also adopt different identities as avatars in playing online video games. Creating avatars allows students to draw on their lived-world identities while simultaneously developing "projective identities" that reflect attributes, beliefs, and agendas they want to perform for their audiences or other players (Gee, 2008).

Media Worlds

Finally, students also construct their identities through participation as fans of popular culture media or music, movies, television, radio, magazines, news, as well as video games and literary texts; for example, as readers of the *Hunger Games* novels (Collins, 2014), manga fans, or World of Warcraft players. Through sharing their responses to media or literary texts as members of certain "affinity groups" (Gee, 2013), students build relationships with peers based on common interests in the same media or texts.

However, the media represents adolescents in often problematic, simplistic ways. For example, adolescent females are often portrayed in sexist, deficit ways, for example, as either "good" or "immoral"; as mindless celebrity fans, reflected in female responses to Elvis in the 1950s; or as helpless victims of predators on social media (Thiel-Stern, 2014).

Activity: Responding to Characters' Negotiations of Identities Across Different Social Worlds

How then do students learn to negotiate the competing demands of these different social worlds? In their ELA classrooms students can begin by studying the ways in which characters negotiate the boundaries, norms, and practices among their competing social worlds. Tim O'Brien's (2009) *The Things They Carried* offers a useful example.

In this novel the protagonist, O'Brien, fresh out of college at age 21, has been drafted into the U.S. Army to go fight in Vietnam, "a war I hated . . . [that] seemed to me wrong" (p. 38). When he receives his draft letter after his graduation, he initially assumes that there was some mistake, given his current identity as someone who graduated sum cum laude from college.

After he receives his draft letter, he's not sure about what to do—whether to report to his draft board or attempt to escape to Canada. He therefore considers the option of escaping to Canada, leading him to imagine how his parents or people in his town who he believed supported the war out of ignorance would construct his identity as "the damned sissy [who] had taken off for Canada" (p. 43).

He then quits his summer job at a meatpacking plant and heads north to the Rainy River that divides Minnesota from Canada, where he works at a lodge for six days, operating in a "neutral zone" (Bridges, 2009), reflecting on whether or not to go across the river into Canada.

In this novel, O'Brien therefore negotiates his identity and his choices based on how he is positioned in different worlds. He was highly successful in college, resulting in his being admitted to graduate school at Columbia University, and is strongly opposed to the Vietnam War. At the same time, because he's from a small town, he remains concerned about how his family and other townspeople would perceive his action of "draft dodging."

So, O'Brien constructs some imagined identities. First, he considers the identity of a draft dodger: "the law closing in on all sides—my hometown draft board and the FBI and the Royal Canadian Mounted Police" (p. 48). As he considers this identity, he imagines how his family and community would position him negatively: "I did not want people to think badly of me" (p. 49). He also imagines the identity of a protester and how opponents of the Vietnam War want him to express his opposition to the war by avoiding the draft. In this imaginary inner debate, O'Brien evokes multiple voices representing different competing perspectives, what's called "double-voicing" (Bakhtin, 1982). Being open to entertaining these different voices is more likely to lead to awareness of a momentary truth than is adopting one singular voice:

> The truth about myself requires both the multiplicity of inner voices and giving equal rights to the inner and outer voices . . . every self has a multitude of inner voices, some of which represent, to some degrees, voices of other individuals . . . some voices may merge, some wither, and some further split into yet more voices. But if my internal chorus is reduced to just one voice, there is no more self, and what remains is but a sterile dogma.
> *(Sidorkin, 1999, pp. 43–44)*

In responding to *The Things They Carried*, students could discuss O'Brien's identity construction in the book by describing the different worlds O'Brien occupies and/or imagines: his "hometown," Vietnam, college, the Tip Top Inn,

Rainy River, and Canada. Students might consider how O'Brien perceives himself as being positioned in these different worlds:

- What imagined or actual narratives does he draw on to define these spaces?
- How does he perceive the Rainy River space as a neutral, transitional space for him to consider an escape to Canada?
- How do his perceptions of how others view him influence his decision about going to Vietnam?
- Have you had to make a difficult decision related to a transition in your life? What were the factors that you took into account to make that decision? How did others' perceptions of you shape the decision?

Activity: Conducting Mini-Ethnographies for Studying Figured Worlds

Understanding figured worlds as cultural constructions requires the ability to infer the cultural norms and roles shaping participants' identities in these worlds. Doing so entails the ability to adopt an outsider perspective through perceiving the "familiar as strange" (Erickson, 2004) or what Pennycook (2010) describes as "a process of unlearning, of questioning the familiarity of one's own location" (p. 45).

Stepping out of their familiar cultural lenses can be difficult for students who, like fish in water, may not perceive their worlds as shaping their actions. To help students learn to perceive the "familiar as strange," students can conduct mini-ethnographies of specific events or activities associated with participation in certain social worlds (Sunstein & Chiseri-Strater, 2012). In doing so, students collect data about a certain site by taking field notes, interviewing participants, and/or taking photos/video. And they find insider "cultural broker" informants who have familiarity with the social world in question and can provide insights into the unique norms and roles operating in that world. Students then identify consistent patterns and practices that suggest participants' adherence to particular cultural norms or beliefs.

Elizabeth gave her 12th-grade students an ethnography assignment that asked them to study a place or site that required them to adopt a cultural perspective:

> Choose a place where you would like to observe people and identify a human trait. Focus on a place and on how a place dictates behavior. You must go to this place and take notes on what you see happening there in order to begin the research. Visit your place's website and take notes on your location's web presence.
>
> You must also conduct an interview with someone who is a patron/ works at this place. What does the place/behavior say about society? How does the place reflect identity? What quality is most prevalent in the people

who work, attend, frequent, join, participate in your place? What does research say about this quality? What do religion, philosophy and science have to say about this quality?

Develop a thesis statement based on your observations of people. Based on your observations, you must come up with your own thesis statement regarding human behavior and show, through research/documentation, that humans have this quality.

For this assignment, Elizabeth stressed the importance of inductively deriving their thesis *from* their observations as opposed to letting their thesis deductively shape their observations. She cited the example of Nicole's ethnography in which she observed parents and children waiting in line at a department store to talk with Santa, observations that led her to a thesis that parents perpetuate falsehoods in interacting with their children:

And from that, her conclusion was parents lie to their kids because they want their children to have this idea that there is something magic. So then she went and explored why parents lie to their children. She never thought about that we make up these myths and stories, whatever, that parents don't call things as they are—that they are always trying to shelter children, so looking at the psychology behind that.

In conducting this research project, students were addressing the Minnesota Common Core State Writing Standard:

Conduct short as well as more sustained research projects to answer a question (including a self-generated question) or solve a problem; narrow or broaden the inquiry when appropriate; synthesize multiple sources on the subject, demonstrating understanding of the subject under investigation.

(Minnesota State Department of Education, 2010, p. 76)

For their final ethnography reports, students had to present their results not only as a written report, but also with an image of their site/event, a video interview with a participant, and a map showing the site or event's location. This multimodal presentation addressed the Minnesota Common Core Writing Standard:

Use technology, including the Internet, to produce, publish, and update individual or shared writing products in response to ongoing feedback, including new arguments or information.

(Minnesota State Department of Education, 2010, p. 76).

FIGURE 5.1 Abbey's Photo of the Walmart Strike

For example, for her analysis of a local Walmart store, Abbey included photos of the store as well as of employees on a picket line outside of the store, as illustrated in Figure 5.1.

Based on her analysis, she noted that:

> Walmart runs its business in a way that increases the government welfare spending, contributes to suburban sprawl, drives companies out of business, decreases employment in both retail and manufacturing while reducing the wages in both companies, and increases our drive to consume natural resources that we don't necessarily need.

Abbey was therefore focusing on how the culture of Walmart's corporate workplace world shapes certain norms and attitudes operating in that world.

Activity: Conducting Mini-Ethnographies of Media/Sports Fan Identities

For studying identity construction in sports or media worlds, students could conduct mini-media ethnography studies of how being a fan of a particular sports team, television show, video game, literary genre, or musical group/singer serves to define people's identities (Beach, 2009; Jenkins, 2006). They can:

- go to online television shows, movies, or music fan sites and conduct a content analysis of the most prevalent responses to topics, story lines, or actors/actresses that serve to define their identities.
- study fan participation on teen magazine, commercial, or merchandizing sites and then ask peers how and why they respond to these sites as fans, particularly in terms of how their consumption of certain products serves to define their identities.
- "lurk" on fan websites for certain television programs (for soap operas, http://www.soapoperafan.com) or Facebook fan groups, as well as the Fan-Fiction (http://fanfiction.net) site for members who create fiction based on certain shows. They can then interview their participants about how they constructed their identities through adoption of particular viewing/game social interactions, language use, or rituals, as well as what aspects of the team, show, game, book(s), or music appeal to them.

Activity: Studying Portrayals of Figured Worlds in Literature, Films, and Television Programs Shaping Identities

Students could also respond to figured worlds portrayed in literature, films, or television programs in terms of how those worlds shape characters' identities. For example, they can examine demographic shifts influencing how family roles are portrayed in literature, films, and television programs. Elizabeth's students responded to the portrayals of the suburban, middle-class family in the novel *Ordinary People* (Guest, 1982), set in the 1970s. To help her students gain a historical understanding of how the family as an institution was defined during that period, Jackie Van Geest, Elizabeth's student teacher, as part of the *Ordinary People* unit described in Chapter 2, had her students examine the cultural and historical contexts of the 1970s shaping the character's identities—in this case, the prevailing beliefs about what constituted the "ordinary" family in the 1970s and how those beliefs shaped the Jarrett family's actions. To do so, she created a PowerPoint presentation on media portrayals of families in the 1970s in popular television programs such as *Family Guy, That '70s Show, Gilmore Girls,* and *The Cosby Show.* She then asked students to discuss:

> How do family members influence each other? What roles and dynamics do you see in these media depictions? Are these roles typical of mothers, fathers, children? What is typical/ordinary?

Students applied their understanding of what were often idealized popular cultural portrayals of 1970s families to examine why, for example, the Jarrett family members, one of the families shown in the PowerPoint, were so concerned about maintaining their own public image. As Nicole noted in her final paper about the mother, Beth's, obsession with her public image:

> Beth was only thinking about her own appearance and how she looked in front of her friends. Since she only cared about herself and what others thought of her, Conrad withdrew and didn't share anything with her.

Students also critiqued how Beth fails to provide emotional support for her son, Conrad. Brian describes how Beth ignores Conrad's report of success in his swim team's practice:

> It is clear at this point that Beth doesn't want to make the effort to talk to Conrad about even the most commonplace of topics. It may not seem vital to her, but incidents like these are what lead Conrad to feel that he doesn't matter. From then on, Conrad struggles in forming his identity because he doesn't have the support of a loving mother. He is unsure about his decisions because he lacks moral points of reference that someone with a proper mother might have. Conrad's battle with self-worth is largely internal until Christmas rolls around. . . . Many of Conrad's identity struggles are due to a mother incapable of taking on her expected emotional roles. A lack of sincere conversation and the notion that she is the only one whom her decisions affect exacerbate Conrad's already low self-esteem. Beth's disdain for even the smallest events in Conrad's life result in incalculable detriment to Conrad's search for an identity.

Students can also respond to examples of characters adopting positive family roles in ways that support positive identity development. In responding to *The Catcher in the Rye* (Salinger, 1991), Elizabeth's students consistently noted how Holden's sister, Phoebe, provides positive support for Holden. Katelyn noted that:

> He describes her as mature, understanding, smart, and a beautiful girl. . . . Being with Phoebe forces Holden into reality. She allows him to see himself in a new light and brings out the kindness in him. Their ability to get along and be so open together acts as an escape from Holden's negative mind set.

South Bay High student Carlos examined the figured worlds of families in his previously discussed Touchstone Text final paper. Carlos held a view of families that reflected binary and simplistic portrayals often shown in media. His research question for his final, "Why were some families healthy and happy and others were not?" exemplified this perspective. For Carlos, the portrayals of happy families on television, where all the problems were neatly solved in a half-hour sitcom, seemed in stark contrast to his home life and that of many of his peers. However, after doing research on families, considering Alexie's (2007) depiction of families in *The Absolutely True Diary of a Part-Time Indian*, and pushing his own thinking on the topic, he eventually reached a more nuanced and complex understanding of families. His final analysis, that all families have problems but healthy ones try to address the problems and find ways to still enjoy one another, was a sophisticated response that revealed a more expansive view of the family as a figured world.

Students could respond to literary portrayals of family relationships in poetry. In her high school English class, Kelly O'Brien had students read the following poems that portray both parental and adolescent perspectives on family relationships: "Sentimental Moment or Why Did the Baguette Cross the Road" (Hershon), "For Julia, in Deep Water" (Morris), "The Pomegranate" (Boland), "You're" (Plath), "This Happened" (Williams), "The Sacred" (Dunn), "Ground Swell" (Jarman), "Deer Hit" (Loomis), "Sticks" (Ellis), "Oranges" (Sato), "Adolescence" (Andrews), "Bike Ride With Older Boys" (Kasischke), "To a Daughter Leaving Home" (Pastan), "My Papa's Waltz" (Roethke), and "Mother to Son" (Hughes).

Students can also draw on how media positions people's identities to create videos portraying their experiences coping with the challenges of identity construction. For instance, in a study by Rogers and colleagues, two Canadian First Nation students created a video entitled "Peer Pressure," which employed photos of their social lives along with voice-over narrative to portray their lives in an urban setting related to peer pressure for "partying" with alcohol. Additionally, they included commentary describing their resistance to this peer pressure and explaining their understanding of stereotypical media positioning of First Nation people as alcoholics (Rogers et al., 2010). Other students created a PSA video adaptation of "Hills Like White Elephants" (Hemingway, 2003), a story about a couple deciding on whether the woman should have an abortion. This video included ultrasound images of a fetus and hotlinks to youth clinic and pregnancy crisis centers set to a recording of Beethoven's "Moonlight Sonata." The students' goal in this video was to portray issues of adolescents coping with teen pregnancy (to view that film, see http://www.theresarogers.ca) (Rogers et al., 2010). Through these video productions, students inserted media representation images of identity practices to then interrogate those images with counter-images.

A related activity involves analysis of generational family differences based on how younger generations adopt different beliefs and attitudes from previous generations by studying literary texts that portray multiple generations of families. Novels portraying immigrant experiences such as *How the Garcia Girls Lost Their Accents* (Alvarez, 2010), *Crossing the Wire* (Hobbs, 2007), *American Born Chinese* (Yang, 2008), *Downtown Boy* (Herrera, 2005), *Interpreter of Maladies: Stories* (Lahiri, 1999), and *First Crossing: Stories About Teen Immigrants* (Gallo, 2007) are particularly compelling in their exploration of tensions among generational worlds.

In responding to these and other texts, students could critically examine how discourses of illegality, racism, colonialism, and class disparities influence representations of immigrants in these texts and media coverage of immigration issues (Bejarano, 2005; Honeyford, 2014). Based on the notion of "transcultural repositioning" of identities (Guerra, 2007) in which immigrant people draw on hybrid practices from their previous and new cultures, middle school immigrant students in one study, largely from Mexico, created photo essays for their school's open house entitled "I am from *aquí* and *allá*" to portray their experiences with transnational identities and conflicted allegiances across their previous and new cultural spaces (Honeyford, 2014), adopting a cosmopolitan stance (Appiah, 2006).

Studying Neighborhood Worlds

By examining their neighborhood worlds, students can recognize their impact on their identities. For example, students might consider how patterns of immigration have shaped their neighborhood's demographics over the years and how those changing demographics have determined what it means to be from their neighborhood. As John Foreman, commenting on a *New York Times* story on immigration (Cave & Heisler, 2014), noted about his Oklahoma City neighborhood:

> Immigration has changed my neighborhood and my city significantly over the last 20 years. Demographically my neighborhood has gone from a majority white working class area with a unique sense of identity, to a majority Hispanic area with a unique sense of identity. There has also been an exodus of whites from south Oklahoma City to the suburbs further hindering any attempts at integration.
>
> *(for other related perceptions from the same story,*
> *see http://tinyurl.com/plpgkbs)*

These differences in neighborhoods often reflect and shape differences in students' schools. Schools in lower-income neighborhoods with high populations of students of color do not provide students with the same quality of schooling as do schools in higher-income neighborhoods (Rich, 2014).

Activity: Conducting Mini-Ethnographies of Neighborhoods

Students could conduct mini-ethnographic analyses of their own neighborhoods through observing certain neighborhood interactions and events, obtaining demographic data from their city or county databases, taking photos and creating maps, and interviewing neighbors regarding their perceptions of what they value in the neighborhood and the neighborhood's historical evolution, resulting in multimodal online or face-to-face presentations. In doing so, students may determine the level of what Wilson (2011) described as prosocial practices that serve to support their own and their neighbors' positive identity development.

Steph's Curriculum for *The House on Mango Street*

These analyses can include how certain racial, ethnic, class, and/or cultural elements of a neighborhood influence the practices and norms operating in their own neighborhood, as well as neighborhoods portrayed in literature or film, as did students in Steph's 9th-grade class at Linden Junior/Senior High School in Eastern Iowa, in response to *The House on Mango Street* (Cisneros, 1991). In a series of vignettes in the novel, Esperanza, a young girl living in a working poor neighborhood in Chicago, explores the joys and challenges of her life and the lives of those around her, determining ultimately that she must leave Mango Street in order to come back. Consistent with the identity practice of *negotiating identities across different social worlds*, the novella seemed to Steph a perfect fit for her goal of engaging her students in thinking about how their identities are shaped by their environment and how they might choose to position themselves in the future.

A second goal of Steph's was to encourage her students to explore use of simile and metaphor in descriptive writing to address the CCSS 9th- and 10th-grade writing standard: "Use precise language to develop a picture of how the events, experiences, and ideas emerge and unfold" (Council of Chief State School Officers and the National Governors Association, 2010, p. 42).

Steph believed that her 9th graders had little experience with descriptive writing and hoped to show them how descriptive writing might serve as a means for literary exploration and identity work consistent with the identity practices of *making connections between texts and people* as well as *reflecting on changes in identities over time*. Steph constructed an assignment in the spirit of *The House on Mango Street* in which students wrote their own novellas that consisted of ten vignettes. Students were free to write nine of these vignettes about anything they noticed in their lived worlds and how the things they noticed reflected aspects of their own identities. Students were asked to focus their tenth vignette on the American Dream and how it was reflected or failed to be reflected in their previous vignettes and life experiences.

Because Steph anticipated that this work would be highly personal for students, she provided several opportunities for students to workshop their writing and share ideas in small groups. At the culmination of the writing project, Steph led students in a larger dialogic discussion in which they reflected on their own vignettes and synthesized these with interpretations related to *The House on Mango Street*.

Students' Identity Work Around *The House on Mango Street*

Students' final writing projects and their discussion around these projects illustrate how this assignment guided students in identity work that involved a careful examination of their own worlds, drawing on the vignette style of *The House on Mango Street* to help them construct short, focused narratives reflecting their specific identity practices.

Some students, for instance, were inspired by Esperanza's honest, detailed depictions of her home and neighborhood in *The House on Mango Street* and began writing about their lives and identities by *engaging in critical analysis* of their own homes and their imagined dream houses, using these as identity texts. Daniel began his project by writing contrasting vignettes about his "dream house" and his "real house":

> My real house looks old and scary. It has a white layer of paint over many other colors all over the house. It has a fence around three quarters of the house, wood and metal fences.
>
> The house has four apartments in it. They are all boring looking, white walls all around. And then there's old carpet on the ground. There is a dusty smell in it even after it has been cleaned. I think it's because of all the dust flying around.
>
> My dream house is a huge white building. I imagine it to have glass doors all around. I would have a small garden in the front yard, next to the front door. My yard would have green grass that's really soft and tickles your feet when you walk on it. And inside, I would have it all nice and clean.

Other students described small, detailed moments from their everyday lives, noticing and reflecting upon how they *negotiate identities across different social worlds*. Several students wrote about their experiences as members of families with their own businesses, questioning whether work on a family farm or in a family bar was part of their identities as members of their families, or whether that work positioned them as teenagers with part-time jobs.

Students also noticed and considered *alternative perspectives* as they wrote about their lived experiences. Katy wrote a vignette that focused on a dinner out with her family in New Orleans, noticing through her depiction of that dinner not only that the cuisine was different from what she experienced as a farmer's daughter in Iowa, but also that portions in the restaurant were much bigger than those in her small town's restaurants and service was different. She said, "Someone is always greeting you and asking if you need anything, and there's always someone willing to help you."

The unit that Steph planned and the writing students completed in this unit served to help students notice, appreciate, and critique the sometimes invisible identity practices they participated in every day. And this writing aided students in imagining their identities in different social worlds and thinking about alternative practices and perspectives that inform the identities of others.

Activity: Studying Construction of Online Identities

For studying their construction of online identities, students could reflect on how they adopt different identities across different social networking sites, Twitter, Flickr, blogs, video games, or posting to curation sites. Ian O'Byrne (2014) describes how he varies his identities across different sites depending on his purposes for using those sites and the audiences for those sites:

> I'm currently on Twitter, Google+, Facebook, Scribd, Academia.edu, Foursquare, numerous Google Sites pages, and about 45 NINGs around the planet. I view my identity on each of these as different than one another, and sometimes they intersect or support one another. What I mean is that I see myself as being more like "me" on Google+ and Twitter, than I am on Facebook. On Google+ and Twitter, I share links about interesting projects I'm working on, or things I read that I find interesting. However on Facebook I share links and ideas, and toss in my fair share of family photos and videos. It's important to understand what the affordances are for each group, or tool . . . and also decide how you chose to use them.

Students are able to identify how they select certain information or images to project their own persona or ethos in these online worlds. For her online college composition course, Laura Ewing (2013) wanted her students to reflect on how creating an online persona functioned rhetorically to create a persona or ethos that others find believable and credible. She asked her students to contrast their identities adopted on a class Tumblr blog with their identities on Facebook, Flickr, and Twitter. She noted that on these social network sites students were aware of their audiences' potential reactions:

> [T]hey were much more personal and afforded them more freedom to post pictures, comments, and videos that may be considered unsuitable in other contexts. I was comforted by the fact that despite my own expectation that first-year college students would post inappropriate material to these social networks, the majority were highly cognizant of parents, relatives, and potential employers seeing their pages, and so they took due diligence in selecting what was posted and, perhaps more important, what was not posted.
>
> (p. 559)

One challenge for students creating online identities or personas in disembodied online discussion contexts is that they can no longer rely on the cues they employ in face-to-face interactions to enact certain identities. Students must therefore rely more on their use of written language to construct "discoursal identities" (Burgess & Ivanič, 2010).

Activity: Reflecting on Identity Positioning in Social Networking Sites

Students are cognizant of how they are positioned to adopt certain identities on social networking sites in ways that may be inconsistent with their own lived-world identities. One critique of Facebook noted that it

> encourages an identity that is extroverted, outgoing and even sometimes narcissistic; most importantly, one that would be approved by their peer group. The pursuit of such an identity made it difficult for the participants to critically engage with the site, as they become immersed in the social reality of Facebook.
>
> *(Pangrazio, 2013, p. 39)*

Given that students may conform to these expectations, students may be reluctant to critique Facebook because doing so entails critiquing their own adherence to use of Facebook to construct their identities.

It is also important to remember that when you employ Facebook in your classroom, students may have difficulty separating out their own personal, informal use of Facebook from any academic, formal uses of Facebook in the classroom. As Allen (2012) notes:

> [A]ny use of Facebook will necessarily confront both teachers and students with the fact that, in an online environment which is so closely entwined with real identities, real places and persistent communication, they are always explicitly negotiating the boundaries between formal and informal. In other words, Facebook does not allow us to separate formal and informal uses in education. Its design and social affordances are all about confusion and overlap, while its computer mediated format also trumps the traditional use of time and place as a means of enforcing the separations between people based on role and function.
>
> *(p. 224)*

Activity: Constructing Online Identities Through Online Role-Play

Through experimenting with adopting different identities through online role-play activities, students can participate in argumentative writing about issues in their own lives or portrayed in texts (Beach & Doerr-Stevens, 2011). In these role-plays, conducted on a class blog or an online discussion forum, you can ask students to adopt pro–con roles related to a particular issue. Students then respond to these posts, refuting or agreeing with the positions espoused and formulating counterarguments.

For example, eighteen students and the instructor in an English methods course adopted different roles based on characters in *To Kill a Mockingbird* (Lee, 1994), to share their responses to the text (White & Hungerford-Kresser, 2014). They created profile pages based on information about the different characters. To model this process, the instructor created an Atticus Finch page based on information from the text about Atticus's hometown; career; political beliefs; taste in music, books, and film; as well as images from the 1962 film adaptation.

In creating their own profile pages, based on their research about the historical and cultural context of the novel, students employed multimodal texts including historical and contemporary photographs; links to popular music, films, and artwork; and newspaper articles from the era. For example, a student assuming the role of Scout posted a Playbill description of her performance in a school play and then used "Events" in Facebook to invite others to the performance. The student assuming the role of the White female Mayella posted a movie poster for *The Birth of a Nation* to justify her racist beliefs.

In Elizabeth's class, in responding to the novel *Montana, 1948* (Watson, 1993), students addressed the issue of institutional racism toward Native Americans relative to the University of North Dakota's Fighting Sioux mascot (http://roleplay mascots.blogspot.com; http://mascotroleplay.blogspot.com) (Beach & Doerr-Stevens, 2011). Students adopted the roles of characters from the novel as well as the roles of actual people such as Russell Means, a leader of the AIM (American Indian Movement); Louise Erdrich, Native American author; or Dan Snyder, owner of the Washington Redskins. In responding to *The Perks of Being a Wallflower* (Chbosky), students addressed issues of teen drug and alcohol abuse that were present both in the book and recent news stories about a school administrator's actions regarding MySpace and Facebook photos (http://wallfloweronline.blogspot.com).

Coping with Tensions and Contradictions Across These Different Worlds

In coming to notice how they are positioned differently by their different worlds, students will also begin to perceive the tensions and contradictions between how they are positioned in their school, community, home, peer-group, and workplace worlds. While a student may assume a leadership role in his peer-group world, he may be positioned in deficit ways as a "struggling reader" in his school world. Or, while a student may acquire certain game-playing skills as a "gamer," those skills may not necessarily transfer to or be exploited in her school world. Finally, while women are encouraged to achieve a career status in the workplace world, they are also encouraged to simultaneously begin having children. All of this suggests the importance of students acquiring the social practice of negotiating alternative positioning of their identities across different worlds.

In the case of Tre, the schism between his world outside of school and the norms and expectation of the school setting was vast. In the out-of-school world, Tre was struggling with many challenges—poverty, a new baby, having to report to a parole officer, violence in his neighborhood, and struggles he faced with his mother. Survival in the out-of-school world often meant utilizing skills and resources not deemed appropriate in a school context. Being viewed as threatening, flirting with people as a form of manipulation, trying to "con" one's way through life might pay dividends in an out-of-school setting. Asking Tre to shed these behaviors might seem appropriate for when he is in school, but in doing so, his teachers were unaware of the danger that might put him in outside of school.

In her ethnographic study of Hmong American students in an urban high school, Ngo (2010) painted a complicated portrait of the tensions and contradictions Hmong American students face, challenging simplistic notions of students' identities. She found that not only did the Hmong American students in her study adopt different identities across different contexts, but they also experienced

> ambivalence—contradictions, uncertainty, fractures—of *individual* identities, where the subject position of a person shifts with each speaking, from one moment to the next. From this perspective, identities are not just "multiple," hybrid," and "situated," but significantly, they are also subdivided, inconsistent, and temporary.
>
> *(p. 24)*

Ngo notes that these shifting positions are shaped by various discourses, such as the discourse of the "model minority," which draws upon stereotyped conceptions of Asian American students. Ngo found that students adopt certain subject positions by drawing on the discourses circulating in their worlds. In the urban high school she studied, Ngo also found students adopted subject positions associated with discourses of urban, immigrant students derived from Hollywood movies such as *Dangerous Minds* (Smith, 1995), which position them as deficient and as needing to be saved by their teachers. Finally, Ngo found that students in her study, as well as in their school at large, were positioned as failing or dysfunctional through discourses of business management associated with political demands for "accountability," "measurable outcomes," and "standards." Students and teachers in this school, however, pushed back against these deficit positionings and defended their school, explaining that they perceived their school as "the most consistent thing in many of these kids' lives" and as "a surrogate family if you will that might not exist at home" (Ngo, 2010, p. 64).

As this example of the Hmong American students in this high school illustrates, the ability to notice tensions across worlds and recognize the discourses that position students within various social worlds allows students agency to resist and push back against those positionings. This ability to notice tensions, then, is a key outcome of the unlearning process and a critical step in acquiring the identity practice of negotiating identities across different social worlds.

Resisting Positioning in Certain Worlds

Given their experiences with these tensions, students may also resist how they are positioned in certain social worlds, particularly when they perceive these worlds as immune to change. When students in a socioeconomically diverse school in Pittsburgh blogged about rules, norms, beliefs, and roles constituting the various social worlds they inhabit, students perceived these social worlds to be insular, pre-established worlds that do not overlap with one another (Thein, Oldakowski, & Sloan, 2010).

Students also perceived their identities as static across their participation in these worlds, foreclosing their ability to negotiate identities across these worlds. Kevin, a White middle-class student, chose to write about the social world of his church for the blogging project. In Kevin's early blogs, he insisted that his identity was consistent across his church, home, and school worlds, causing him no tensions whatsoever. Further, he had trouble imagining that the social world of his church was in any way constructed. However, as he continued on in the project, he began to unlearn this stance and notice how the social world of his church functioned, positioning him in certain ways and conflicting with some of his other beliefs. For example, Kevin wrote:

> My religious belief is challenged almost every day at school. . . . There is a conflict in my brain about evolution theory. . . . On some days the evolution theory actually makes sense then on other days I believe the beliefs of my church which is creationism. The things I am taught in school and the things I am taught in church are very hard because the evolution theory has evidence behind it and the things I learn at church do not have evidence. You have to believe. My beliefs in the church are strong and I will probably never give up my faith even though there are struggles everyday.
>
> *(Thein, Oldakowksi, & Sloan, 2010, p. 30)*

In family, workplace, or neighborhood worlds, females may be positioned to adopt both nurturing, submissive domestic roles versus adopting assertive roles in non-domestic, competitive workplace contexts (Anyon, 2014). Low-income female students of color are often positioned in schools in courses linked to vocational pink-collar work that limits their potential academic development, leading to their resisting such positioning (Bettie, 2003).

Helping Students Transfer Identity Practices Across Different Worlds

How then, as teachers, can you help students learn to negotiate their identities across these different worlds? As students move across these different worlds, they transfer identity practices and "funds of knowledge" (Moll et al., 1992) from familiar worlds to new, less familiar worlds. For example, they may use their experiences engaging in conversations with parents in a family world to engage in conversations with adult customers in a workplace world.

However, given the tensions and contradictions in moving across different worlds, students often experience difficulty in transferring certain practices or knowledge from one world to another world (Russell & Yañez, 2003). For example, in a case study of Molly, an 11th grader from a working-class school in the Midwest (Thein, 2009), Amanda found that although Molly was an avid reader of narrative fiction outside of school, she was disengaged with nearly all of the novels taught in her English classroom. Outside of school Molly read to see examples of characters who experienced difficulties and challenges but still worked hard and held out hope for the future—a narrative or "cultural model" (Gee, 2008) that was important for Molly as a young girl growing up in uncertain times in a working-class neighborhood. In contrast, the books Molly read in her English classroom rarely aligned with this cultural model, causing her to disengage with those books. She continued to read those texts through the same cultural models and for the same purposes that she read texts outside of class, creating dissonance when school-based literature contradicted those cultural models and purposes.

The case of Molly illustrates the importance of helping students learn to transfer their practices or "funds of knowledge" across different worlds. In order for Molly to bridge her home and school worlds toward engagement in the ELA classroom, she would have needed a teacher who could identify, acknowledge, and value the reading resources and knowledge Molly already brought to the classroom. At the same time, that teacher would need to be able to help Molly build upon those practices and knowledge by teaching her to consider the usefulness of other practices, theories, and perspectives for interpreting texts.

You can help students such as Molly engage in transfer of practices and knowledge by asking them to:

- *Identify and reflect on characters' or their own experiences coping with differences between the norms or expectations across different worlds.* Students could note differences between their own or characters' practices and knowledge associated with participation across different neighborhood or community worlds. For example, Rose's students contrasted Arnold's practices and knowledge between his reservation and White high school worlds. Elizabeth's students contrasted their experiences in their workplace and their school worlds.
- *Identify and reflect on characters' or their own use of language, narratives, images/videos, and media to position themselves as adhering to certain identities.* For example, use of narratives serves to position participants as active agents successfully dealing with challenges or as passive victims of forces operating in a figured world. On the one hand, narratives position urban students as helpless victims with little agency, minimizing their ability to contest or dissent

from being positioned as passive victims (Ngo, 2010). On the other hand, urban students are positioned as "comeback kids" who "beat the odds" based on their individual initiative, positioning that presupposes an autonomous identity model that diverts attention to the inequities in the economic system that create urban poverty (Gorski & Landsman, 2013). Both of these narratives reify the false binaries of class differences associated with us/normal (White, middle class) versus them/not normal (low-income people of color).

Or students may employ "racialized narratives" (Nasir & Shah, 2011) or "narrative of exclusion" (López-Bonilla, 2011) as a means of positioning each other in a classroom. For example, one study of Jeremiah, an African American male student, contrasted his actions on the basketball court and in a math classroom (Nasir & Hand, 2008). In playing basketball, Jeremiah assumed the role of a leader who taught his peers through modeling certain actions as well as learning from his peers. He therefore was providing and acquiring a range of resources in that context associated with being a successful, highly active basketball player. In contrast, in his math class, he demonstrated little or no participation, largely because he had difficulty accessing the resources associated with success in math.

One explanation for adopting these opposing identities in these two contexts has to do with the ways in which narratives themselves position African American males in quite different ways related to their actions in both basketball and mathematics. These narratives position African Americans as unintelligent, lazy, inclined toward criminality, and "in danger" (Devine & Elliot, 1995; Nasir & Hand, 2008, Schott Foundation, 2012). As a result, their teachers and/or other students may position African American males as lacking the academic propensities to succeed in school, positioning that African American males may internalize and accept. These deficit narratives may then be compared with "model minority" narratives.

Students may also construct their identities using "narratives of exclusion" that position them as failing to succeed in school, particularly due to the difficulty in acquiring disciplinary literacies or cultural models constituting certain subjects (Moje, 2008). These narratives dramatize people's inabilities to cope with certain challenges based on their presumed lack of certain abilities or competencies—that because a person is of a particular race, class, or gender or lacks certain skills, she lacks the capacity to succeed. For example, students may share narratives of instances when gender influenced a student's inclination to engage in certain academic pursuits/professions, sports, military activities, and so forth.

Analysis of students in Mexican high schools who were having difficulty in school found that many internalized these "narratives of exclusion" voiced by teachers and administrators that positioned them as lacking the knowledge, resources, or motivation to succeed in school—a lack attributed by teachers or administrators to their socioeconomic backgrounds (López-Bonilla, 2011). In some cases, students shared narratives about teachers who adopted monologic, authoritative discourses of failure (Bakhtin, 1982) based on the use of arbitrary testing practices while denying students any input or dialogue about their learning. In other cases, students voiced narratives to challenge these authoritative discourses of failure (Rymes, 2001). In doing so, they challenge deficit, fixed-identity narratives by engaging in "boundary crossing that creates possibilities for the revision of these personal narratives" (Sumara, 2002, p. 58).

- *Identify and reflect on ways characters or they themselves do or could challenge deficit positioning in social worlds.* Students could counter this deficit positioning by collecting or creating counter-narratives portraying instances in which people assumed to be incapable of acting in a certain manner are actually successful in transferring practices and knowledge from one world to another. Through responding to literature, students experience narratives with characters who are successful in coping with and transferring practices and knowledge across different worlds. For example, in responding to *The Absolutely True Diary of a Part-Time Indian*, Carlos, who was a junior but who read at about a 7th-grade level, enjoyed the novel given its appealing blend of cartoons, vivid and witty dialogue, and taboo elements. Carlos, like Arnold in the novel, had important male friendships and also had a challenging home life, and this was yet another entry point for engagement.

Therefore, the novel offered enough intrinsic motivators for Carlos to choose to read it, and his enjoyment of the novel created the conditions for him to acquire new tools and resources to cope with the tensions and contradictions he faced daily. As previously noted, he analyzed the differences between healthy and unhealthy families through creating a comic book as his final project using the models offered in the Alexie novel and his own family as entry points.

As a result of reading the book and then researching this topic, Carlos revised his own narrative about his family. While his family had its share of problems (divorce, substance abuse, etc.), Carlos noted that Arnold's family had many problems as well but, like his own family, their ability to communicate with each other and have a sense of humor helped them still be, in Carlos's opinion, a healthy family. In the end, Carlos reconsidered his own family and decided that "really, all families have problems, what matters is how they deal with it" and that, in his own home, "things be pretty good now, not like before when I stayed locked in my room."

Carlos was able to see beyond the struggles in his family and focus on the positive ways they handled these struggles. While the issue of healthy versus unhealthy families is not the dominant theme in the Alexie novel, this issue mattered to Carlos, suggesting the importance of having students identify those particular challenges faced by characters and/or themselves to address in terms of coping with these challenges.

- *Identify experiences of and strategies for characters or their own successful transfer of practices and knowledge across disparate worlds.* Rose's students noted how Arnold was able to use his display of competence in playing basketball at his reservation school so that he was perceived in a positive manner at the White high school.

Summary

In this chapter, we described how students construct their identities across the peer-group, family, classroom, sports, neighborhood, workplace, digital, and media worlds. To help students understand how these worlds are constructed as "figured worlds" (Holland et al., 1998), students can conduct mini-ethnographies to begin to perceive their familiar worlds as less familiar cultural constructions based on certain norms constituting their identities. Students can also infer connections between their analyses of how characters negotiate different worlds with their own experiences of negotiating lived worlds, as well as reflect on how they construct online identities as distinct from lived-world identities. Given their experience of tensions and contradictions between different worlds, we proposed practices designed to help students transfer practices across worlds associated with acquiring competencies in these different worlds. (For additional resources, activities, and further reading, see http://tinyurl.com/lx7nxl2.)

References

Alexie, S. (2007). *The absolutely true diary of a part-time Indian.* Boston: Little Brown.

Allen, M. (2012). An education in Facebook. *Digital Culture & Education, 4*(3), 213–225. http://www.digitalcultureandeducation.com/cms/wp-content/uploads/2012/12/dce1077_allen_2012.pdf

Alvarez, J. (2010). *How the Garcia girls lost their accents.* Chapel Hill, NC: Algonquin Books.

Anyon, J. (2014). *Radical possibilities: Public policy, urban education, and a new social movement.* New York: Routledge.

Appiah, K. A. (2006). *Cosmopolitanism: Ethics in a world of strangers.* New York: Norton.

Arnseth, H. C., & Silseth, K. (2012). Tracing learning and identity across different sites: Tensions, connections, and transformations in and between everyday and institutional sites. In O. Erstad & J. Sefton-Green (Eds.), *Identity, community and learning lives in the digital age* (pp. 23–38). New York: Cambridge University Press.

Avance, R. (2014). Community: Digital key words project. Tulsa, OK: University of Tulsa. Retrieved from http://orgs.utulsa.edu/dkw

Bakhtin, M. M. (1982). *The dialogic imagination: Four essays.* Trans. M. Holquist. Austin: University of Texas Press.

Balfanz, R., Bridgeland, J. M., Fox, J. H., Paoli, J. L., Ingram, E. S., & Maushard, M. (2014). *Building a grad nation 2013–2014 update.* Everyone Graduates Center at the School of Education at Johns Hopkins University. Retrieved from http://tinyurl.com/nxe7xfn

Beach, R. (2009). Digital tools for media ethnographies of audience use. In R. Hammer & D. Kellner (Eds.), *Media/cultural studies* (pp. 206–228). New York: Peter Lang.

Beach, R., & Doerr-Stevens, C. (2011). Using social networks for online role-play: Play that builds rhetorical capacity. *Journal of Educational Computing Research, 44*(1), 165–181.

Beach, R., Thein, A. H., & Parks, D. (2007). *High school students' competing social worlds: Negotiating identities and allegiances in response to multicultural literature.* Mahwah, NJ: Erlbaum.

Bejarano, C. L. (2005). *Que onda? Urban youth cultures and border identity.* Tucson: University of Arizona Press.

Bettie, J. (2003). *Women without class: Girls, race, and identity.* Berkeley: University of California Press.

Boyd, D. (2014). *It's complicated: The social lives of networked teens.* New Haven, CT: Yale University Press.

Bridges, W. (2009). *Managing transitions: Making the most of change.* Boston: Da Capo Lifelong Books.

Burgess, A., & Ivanič, R. (2010). Writing and being written: Issues of identity across time- scales. *Written Communication, 27,* 228–255.

Cave, J. D., & Heisler, T. (2014, June 8). The changing ethnic landscape. *The New York Times.* Retrieved from http://tinyurl.com/plpgkbs

Center for Promise. (2014). *Don't call them dropouts: Understanding the experiences of young people who leave high school before graduation.* Medford, MA: America's Promise Alliance/Center for Promise, Tufts University.

Cisneros, S. (1991). *The house on Mango Street.* New York: Vintage.

Collins, S. (2014). *The hunger games trilogy box set.* New York: Scholastic Press.

Council of Chief State School Officers and the National Governors Association. (2010). Common Core State Standards for English Language Arts. Authors. Retrieved from http://www.corestandards.org/ELA-Literacy

Crosnoe, R. (2011). *Fitting in, standing out: Navigating the social challenges of high school to get an education.* New York: Cambridge University Press.

Davies, B., & Harré, R. (1990). Positioning: The discursive production of selves. *Journal for the Theory of Social Behaviour, 20*(1), 44–63.

Davis, K. (2013). Young people's digital lives: The impact of interpersonal relationships and digital media use on adolescents' sense of identity. *Computers in Human Behavior, 29*(6), 2281–2293.

Devine, P. G., & Elliot, A. J. (1995). Are racial stereotypes really fading? The Princeton trilogy revisited. *Personality and Social Psychology Bulletin, 11,* 1139–1150.

Draper, B. J., Broomhead, P., Jensen, A. P., Nokes, J. D., & Siebert, D. (Eds.). (2010). *(Re) imagining content-area literacy instruction.* New York: Teachers College Press.

Erickson, R. (2004). *Talk and social theory: Ecologies of speaking and listening in everyday life.* Boston: Polity Press.

Ewing, L. A. (2013). Rhetorically analyzing online composition spaces. *Pedagogy, 13*(3), 554–561.

Gallo, D. R. (Ed.). (2007). *First crossing: Stories about teen immigrants.* Somerville, MA: Candlewick Press.

Gee, J. P. (2008). *Social linguistics and literacies: Ideology in discourses* (3rd ed.). New York: Routledge.

Gee, J. P. (2013). *The anti-education era: Creating smarter students through digital learning.* New York: Palgrave Macmillan.

Gorski, P. C., & Landsman, J. (Eds.). (2013). *The poverty and education reader: A call for equity in many voices.* Sterling, VA: Stylus Publishing.

Guerra, J. (2007). Out of the valley: Transcultural repositioning as a rhetorical practice in ethnographic research and other aspects of everyday life. In C. Lewis, P. Enciso, & E. B. Moje (Eds.), *Reframing sociocultural research on literacy: Identity, agency, and power* (pp. 137–162). Mahwah, NJ: Erlbaum.

Guest, J. (1982). *Ordinary people.* New York: Penguin.

Hemingway, E. (2003). Hills like white elephants. In A. Charters (Ed.), *The story and its writer: An introduction to short fiction* (pp. 475–478). Boston: Bedford/St. Martins.

Herrera, J. F. (2005). *Downtown boy.* New York: Scholastic Press.

Hobbs, W. (2007). *Crossing the wire.* New York: HarperCollins.

Holland, D., Lachicotte, W., Skinner, D., & Cain, C. (1998). *Identity and agency in cultural worlds.* Cambridge, MA: Harvard University Press.

Holland, D., & Lave, J. (2001). *History in person: Enduring struggles, contentious practice, intimate identities.* Albuquerque, NM: School of American Research Publications.

Honeyford, M. A. (2014). From *aquí* and *allá*: Symbolic convergence in the multimodal literacy practices of adolescent immigrant students. *Journal of Literacy Research, 46*(2), 194–233.

Jenkins, H. (2006). *Fans, bloggers, and gamers: Exploring participatory culture.* New York: New York University Press.

Jensen, B. (2014, June/July). The new American family. *AARP Magazine*, 34–40.

Kosten, P. A., Scheier, L. M., & Grenard, J. L. (2012). Latent class analysis of peer conformity: Who is yielding to pressure and why? *Youth & Society 45*(4), 565–590.

Lahiri, J. (1999). *Interpreter of maladies: Stories.* New York: Houghton Mifflin.

Lee, H. (1994). *To kill a mockingbird.* New York: Grand Central Publishing.

Lenhart, A. (2014). *Teens & technology: Understanding the digital landscape.* Washington, DC: Pew Research Center Internet Project. Retrieved from http://tinyurl.com/k2e6qt9

López-Bonilla, G. (2011). "Teamwork": Conflicting cultural models of gender, class, school, and family among high school students. In G. López-Bonilla & K. Englander (Eds.), *Discourses and identities in contexts of educational change: Contributions from the United States and Mexico* (pp. 75–100). New York: Peter Lang.

Minnesota State Department of Education. (2010). English language arts standards. Author. Retrieved from http://tinyurl.com/ow6o6lp

Moje, E. B. (2008). Foregrounding the disciplines in secondary literacy teaching and learning: A call for change. *Journal of Adolescent & Adult Literacy, 52* (2), 96–107.

Moll, L., Amanti, C., Neff, D., & Gonzalez, N. (1992). Funds of knowledge for teaching: Using a qualitative approach to connect homes and classrooms. *Theory Into Practice, 31*(2), 132–141.

Morrison, T. (2007). *Beloved.* New York: Vintage.

Nasir, N.S., & Hand, V. (2008). From the court to the classroom: Opportunities for engagement, learning, and identity in basketball and classroom mathematics. *Journal of the Learning Sciences, 17*(2), 143–179.

Nasir, N., & Shah, N. (2011). On defense: African American males making sense of racialized narratives in mathematics education. *Journal of African American Males in Education, 2*(1), 24–45.

Ngo, B. (2010). *Unresolved identities: Discourse, ambivalence, and urban immigrant students.* Albany, NY: SUNY Press.

O'Brien, T. (2009). *The things they carried.* Boston: Mariner Press.

O'Byrne, I. (2014). Creating and curating your own digital brand [web log post] Retrieved from http://tinyurl.com/l2x55b6

Orwell, G. (1969). *1984.* New York: Signet.

Pangrazio, L. (2013). Young people and Facebook: What are the challenges to adopting a critical engagement? *Digital Culture & Education, 5*(1), 34–47.

Pennycook, A. (2010). *Language as a local practice*. New York: Routledge Press.

Purcell, K., Heaps, A., Buchanan, J., & Friedrich, L. (2013, February 28). *How teachers are using technology at home and in their classrooms*. Washington, DC: Pew Internet Research Project. Retrieved from http://tinyurl.com/laqo2kb

Ralston, D. F. (2012). Where ya at? Composing identity through hyperlocal narratives. In D. Journet, C. E. Ball, & R. Trauman (Eds.), *The new work of composing*. Logan: Computers and Composition Digital Press/Utah State University Press. http://ccdigitalpress.org/nwc/chapters/ralston/

Rich, M. (2014, March 21). School data finds pattern of inequality along racial lines. *The New York Times*. Retrieved from http://tinyurl.com/m73yab6

Rogers, T., Winters, K-L., LaMonde, A-M., & Perry, M. (2010). From image to ideology: Analysing shifting identity positions of marginalized youth across the cultural sites of video production. *Pedagogies: An International Journal, 5*(4), 298–312.

Russell, D. R., & Yañez, A. (2003). "Big picture people rarely become historians": Genre systems and the contradictions of general education. In C. Bazerman & D. R. Russell (Eds.), *Writing selves/writing societies* (pp. 331–362). Fort Collins: Colorado State University Press. Retrieved from http://wac.colostate.edu/books/selves_societies

Rymes, B. (2001). *Conversational borderlands: Language and identity in an alternative suburban high school*. New York: Teachers College Press.

Salinger, J. D. (1991). *The catcher in the rye*. New York: Little Brown and Company.

Sanchez, R. (2006). On critical realist theory of identity. In L. M. Alcoff, M. Hames-Garcia, S. P. Mohanty, & P.M.L. Moya (Eds.), *Identity politics reconsidered* (pp. 31–52). New York: Palgrave MacMillan.

Schott Foundation (2012). *The urgency of now: The Schott 50 state report on public education and Black males*. Author. Retrieved from http://blackboysreport.org/#sthash.9nqDruSb.dpuf

Shannon, P. (2014). *Reading poverty in America*. New York: Routledge.

Sidorkin, A. M. (1999). *Beyond discourse: Education, the self, and dialogue*. Albany: State University of New York Press.

Smith, J. N. (Director). (1995). *Dangerous minds* [motion picture]. United States: Hollywood Pictures.

Sosik, V. S., & Bazarova, N. N. (2014). Relational maintenance on social network sites: How Facebook communication predicts relational escalation. *Computers in Human Behavior, 35*, 124–131.

Sumara, D. J. (2002). *Why reading literature in school still matters: Imagination, interpretation, insight*. Mahwah, NJ: Lawrence Erlbaum.

Sunstein, B. S., & Chiseri-Strater, E. (2012). *Fieldworking: Reading and writing research* (4th ed.). Boston: Bedford/St. Martins.

Thein, A. H. (2009). Identifying the history and logic of negative, ambivalent, and positive responses to literature. *Journal of Literacy Research, 41*(2), 273–316.

Thein, A. H, Oldakowski, T., & Sloan, D. L. (2010). Using blogs to teach strategies for inquiry into the construction of lived and text worlds. *Journal of Media Literacy Education, 2*(1), 23–36.

Thiel-Stern, S. (2014) *From the dance hall to Facebook: Teen girls, mass media, and moral panic in the United States*. Amherst: University of Massachusetts Press.

Tough, P. (2012). *How children succeed: Grit, curiosity, and the hidden power of character*. Boston: Mariner Press.

Vasudevan, L., Schultz, K., & Bateman, J. (2010). Rethinking composing in a digital age: Authoring literate identities through multimodal storytelling. *Written Communication, 27*(4), 442–468.

Vegneskumar, M. (2014). *Sports participation and cultural identity in the experience of young people.* New York: Peter Lang.

Wallace, D. (2014). Unwelcome stories, identity matters, and strategies for engaging in cross-boundary discourses. *College English, 76*(6), 545–561.

Watson, L. (1993). *Montana, 1948.* Minneapolis: Milkwood.

White, J. W., & Hungerford-Kresser, H. (2014). Character journaling through social networks: Exemplifying tenets of the New Literacy Studies. *Journal of Adolescent & Adult Literacy, 57*(8), 642–665.

Wilson, D. S. (2011). *The neighborhood project: Using evolution to improve my city, one block at a time.* New York: Little, Brown, and Company.

Yang, G. L. (2008). *American Born Chinese.* New York: Square Fish Publishing.

6

ENGAGING IN CRITICAL ANALYSIS OF TEXTS AND THE WORLD

(with Samuel Tanner, Primdale High School, Minnesota)

Adopting a Critical Stance: Depends on Where You Stand

Our argument in this book is that students' identities are shaped by the social, cultural, and institutional worlds in which they reside. These worlds have histories that inform participants' understandings of what it means to inhabit these worlds—what roles to adopt, language to use, structures to follow, and norms to either abide by or flaunt. At the same time, participants shape these worlds in new ways; they take up agentive stances that can have lasting effects on the social world that others will later come to inhabit.

One important step in influencing a particular world is having a critical view of it. For example, Jeremy Lin, the NBA star who broke barriers as an Asian American point guard, challenged perceptions about who Asian Americans are and can become, overcame institutional bias in the NBA that did not see him ever becoming a legitimate point guard, and provided Asian American youth with a model of following one's dreams and authoring one's own identity, even if it means ignoring cultural expectations. In order for Jeremy Lin to reach this level of success, he first had to develop a critical stance toward the perception that Asian Americans could not be NBA players, much less stars.

In writing this book, we've been struck by differences in what students across various contexts believe it means to adopt a critical stance. The SBH students were adept at having aesthetic and emotional responses to works of literature, but they struggled to analyze texts with the "close reading" approach encouraged by the Common Core State Standards (Council of Chief State School Officers and the National Governors Association, 2010). In contrast, JHS students tended to reside at an oppositional place on this imagined continuum. They were adept at noting the uses of literacy devices, at analyzing character development and uncovering a perceived understanding of the author's intent, but were less willing to engage the aesthetic and emotional connections to the literary works than the students at SBH.

We believe that both responses (and others) are valid, and that both deserve a place in ELA classrooms. As a teacher faced with a collective of students, it is important to discover what the class is good at and then use those skills to serve as a bridge to engage in texts in new or more challenging ways. While "critical analysis," the primary focus of this chapter, encourages an examination of how a text or a situation is influenced by larger forces such as the historical treatment of people, institutional and corporate entities, and "status quo" ways of being and doing, we'd like to preface this discussion with an important addendum.

In this chapter, we focus on having students discover how they engage in learning and literacy to then encourage them to be critical of their own ways of seeing and understanding. Sometimes students are well versed in supplying the types of critical responses they believe teachers want to hear, but in doing so, they miss opportunities for different kinds of criticism that might not abide by typical "emotional rules" of the ELA classroom. For example, 10th-grader Nina constructed a series of highly academic, politically correct responses to *To Kill a Mockingbird* in the context of her English classroom, where she perceived her teacher as appreciating such rational and distanced responses. By contrast, in a literature circle outside of the earshot of her teacher, Nina responded to literature through expressions of anger and sadness, and through profanity and direct address of characters. Although Nina's more academic responses were certainly valuable, the emotional rules of rationality that often accompany critical analysis limited other kinds of responses she may have constructed related to *To Kill a Mockingbird* (Thein, Guise, & Sloan, 2015). As we discuss methods for critical analysis, then, we encourage you to remember that all classroom contexts and curricula—even those that aim to critique status quo worlds—are laden with emotional rules that require frequent disruption in the interest of encouraging a wide range of ideas, interpretations, and forms of critique.

Because some of the White, middle-class students we've worked with enjoyed the privileges that come with their status, they struggled to see the institutional forces that awarded them privilege based on individualistic beliefs about why some people struggle and others do not. Like fish in water, they needed to be able to step outside their familiar worlds to be able to critique the limitations of those worlds constituted by cultural and institutional norms that privilege some and limit others. As Sam Tanner discusses in this chapter through an example of a play performed by White students about their privilege, ELA can be a space where students can learn to adopt a critical stance on, in his example, how institutionalized White racism shaped a school's culture. We encourage teachers to help students critique those norms in the contexts in which they are teaching. Criticism should lead to some level of dissonance, because this uncomfortable sense of a challenged perception is an important step toward learning.

Motivating Students to Engage in Critical Analysis Through "Critical Engagement"

One challenge in attempting to foster students' engagement in critical analysis is that students sometimes have trouble understanding the value of such work. This is particularly true if they are simply completing an assignment based on a topic or issue that doesn't seem immediately relevant or important. Rather than treating critical analysis as an abstract, analytical process, it is far more effective to use a "critical engagement" approach to critical analysis. In such an approach, teachers lead students in critique by tapping into topics, issues, and concerns that deeply engage students and mobilize emotion in the classroom (Lewis & Tierney, 2011). For example, noticing how they are positioned in limited, deficit ways in their classroom or school might motivate and deeply engage students' emotions, leading them to adopt a critical stance to challenge that positioning (Rymes, 2001).

In a study of students' critical engagement, Lewis and Tierney (2011) examined urban high school students' discussion of an essay that critiqued gender and race representations in Disney's *Pocahontas* (Gabriel & Goldberg, 1995). One of the students in the discussion, Vanessa, expressed her anger about the fact that other students in the discussion did not recognize a reference to a lawn jockey in the essay as itself demeaning for African Americans (Lewis & Tierney, 2011). Vanessa's willingness to publicly critique the lawn jockey reference mobilized emotions like anger in this classroom, leading her peers to critically engage with issues of racial assumptions and discrimination both within the text at hand and beyond.

For Lewis and Tierney (2011), Vanessa's anger is more than simply individual "feeling" or "affect." Instead, it is a socially constructed way of knowing or acting embodied in language, activity, or physical behavior (Micciche, 2007). Wetherell (2012) perceives these emotions as social actions, as "things we *do*, rather than things we *have*," explaining that "emotion, like anger or fear, is not an object inside the self, as basic emotions research assumes, but is a relation to others, a response to a situation and to the world" (p. 24), actions that lead to being perceived as a certain kind of person (Lewis & Tierney, 2011; 2013). These emotions then circulate among people and come to sediment in particular spaces as norms for expression that allow for certain discourses to emerge and others to remain dormant (Thein, Guise, & Sloan, 2015). For example, in the case study of Nina described earlier in this chapter, Thein, Guise, and Sloan found that when Nina and her peers formed a literature circle, they initially responded to literature much as they did in their large group seminar circle. However:

> After the first few sessions the girls began to abandon their literature circle roles, participation patterns, and seating arrangements—often sitting or lying on the floor during discussion. New registers were used and different discourses emerged. Moreover, the emotional rules previously established

for literature discussion became unstuck and unbound and different spaces for interpretation were opened up.

(p. 213)

In other words, within a new learning context, new forms of emotion were embodied, expressed, and circulated, influencing the kinds of discourses that emerged in response to literature.

Rather than think of these emotions as simply expressions of individual dispositions, as with identities, it's important to recognize how they are culturally constructed in social worlds. For example, Boler (1999) makes the case that schools promote and regulate certain kinds of emotion in students—empathy, calmness, kindness, and promptness to name a few. Students who are adept at following these emotional rules are far more likely to succeed in school than those who don't. Students of color can experience emotions of sadness, isolation, and alienation in a predominately White, middle-class school or college classroom, an experience that is shaped by the cultural construction of school. In writing about these students, particularly the Mexican American college students with whom she works, Nancy Barron (2003) notes that:

> I keep meeting students of color who describe classroom and campus experiences in painful glimpses. Their sense of worth takes a beating. Their understanding of who they are no longer stays internal. They begin to believe the external words and behavior instead of seeing Differences. They fight off their emotions and try to intellectualize but usually end up angry and need to leave. . . . They begin to believe that maybe they've done something wrong, or that their ways of seeing need to adjust to the external behaviors from the Anglo mainstream, exclusively.
>
> *(pp. 21–22)*

Barron argues that these students have difficulty sharing these emotions because they do not have sympathetic audiences with whom to share them. As a Mexican American student in graduate school, Barron cites her own classroom experience of discussing "the Other": "I was always so frustrated, irritated, wishing I was anywhere but in the classroom. The confident students took to talk about the Other rather than talk about themselves" (p. 29).

Barron's emotions of frustration and alienation are located in more than simply her individual dispositions. They are constituted by larger discourses and cultural models of race and class that serve to position her identity as one with "the Other"—as marginal within American society. In Rose's class at SBH, Jeffrey's critique of racism in his Touchstone presentation was precipitated by his emotions of being positioned in deficit ways, explaining that racism "make[s] me feel that I can't become someone in this world . . . that other kind of people are better than me," and that it "keep[s] me with low confidence . . . [and] stressed out" as well as how "you think different of yourself."

Spaces are therefore constituted by certain "emotional rules" (Zembylas, 2002) that serve as social glue connecting or distancing individuals from others. For example, students in classrooms position their bodies relative to each other in ways that communicate their support or rejection of peers as a joint, collaborative, social performance whose meaning is understood by all of the students in the classroom (Leander & Rowe, 2006). Other research finds that students, particularly those with histories of abuse, display resistance to attempts to marginalize or "treat" them through actions reflecting "embodied ambivalence," evident in refusal to participate in classroom activities or behaviors perceived to be deliberately deviant (Pyscher & Crampton, 2013).

To foster a link between embodiment of emotion and her students' use of language and writing, Micciche (2007) has students select a text and reflect how a particular emotion constitutes the meaning of that text. Each student in the group then records himself reading aloud the text. Students then listen to each other's recordings and discuss how each performance reflects their reading of the emotions portrayed in the text. Enacting different voices through "deep embodiment" "opens us to experimentation with inhabiting, as much as possible, another's embodied emotions through an intimate relation to words as well as through a bodily based performance of those words" (p. 60).

Resistance to Deficit Positioning

As we noted in the previous chapter, students experience the emotion of resistance to being positioned according to race, class, and gender in ways that vary across different social worlds (Sanchez, 2006). A student might become aware that she is positioned in deficit ways in school while she is simultaneously positioned in positive ways in her neighborhood. Sanchez (2006) defines one's reaction to this awareness of positioning as "positionality"—one's reflexive stance toward certain positionings. She notes that "positionality" helps explain why people positioned in the same or similar roles and identities may respond to or live in quite different ways:

> A working-class Chicano, for example, may see the structural location of people living in his barrio variously: from a bourgeois perspective (disdain in the face of what he considers to be lack of individual effort or merit on the part of those he considers to be lazy and incompetent), a religious perspective (resignation before the will of God who determined their condition of poverty), or a progressive perspective (resentment against capitalist enterprises in collusion with the state to keep his segregated community polluted by industries, fragmented by freeways, underemployed, ill-served by poor schools that lead to a high dropout rate, and faced with conditions that generate violence and drug-dealing).
>
> *(p. 38)*

One aspect of positioning involves identification of a person by certain institutions or the state according to group categories. Such categories can serve to isolate, reject, segregate, or subordinate that group, or to foster bonding between group members, leading to activism. For Sanchez, identity construction involves a reflexive, critical response to such identifications, as well as "non-identity—that is, an acknowledgment of difference, of being one thing and not another (the 'not-I')" (Sanchez, 2006, p. 41). She cites the example of Latino immigrants who, when they are stopped by police as victims of racial profiling or are discriminated against in workplaces, become aware of being identified as members of a certain group. Their positionality in response to this positioning then becomes, as an action, their identity as either a member of that group (as "Latino") or as a "non-identity" (as someone who may no longer want to be a member of that group). At the same time, one can be positioned in different ways in different spaces—a Latino male may be positioned in a different way than a Latina female across various spaces.

Cat's Response to *The Absolutely True Diary of a Part-Time Indian*

Students often express emotions of frustration or alienation due to their positioning in schools or community. Expressing these frustrations or a sense of alienation can lead them to identify tensions and contradictions associated with competing forces in their lives resulting from allegiances to different social worlds as described in Chapter 5. For example, students may express frustration with the fact that if they want to attend a "competitive college," they are told to build up their resume through taking a lot of AP courses and engaging in different extracurricular activities that leave them with little time to pursue their other interests, work, or helping their families. At the same time, they are told to "follow their own passions," which may have little to do with building this resume for college admissions. Tapping into this frustration with this contradictory positioning can lead them to critique the practices or norms associated with the college admissions process that create these tensions and contradictions between idealized "first-space" worlds (gaining admission to a "competitive college") versus the realities of "second-space" worlds (building a resume that may have little to do with their passions) (Soja, 1998).

You can also have students consider and respond to characters' frustrations and alienation as a means of contextualizing their own frustrations and alienation. In responding to *The Absolutely True Diary of a Part-Time Indian* (Alexie, 2007), students experienced Arnold's marginalization as a Native American student in a largely White school, as well as his marginalization on his reservation for attending the White school. Similarly, Cat, described in Chapter 3, struggled with being marginalized in different settings. As a young Latina who dyed her hair red and who believed she was perceived as White by her peers, Cat did not participate in her peers' urban, hip-hop cultural activities. Nor was she particu-larly interested in making connections to her Mexican cultural heritage. Instead, Cat actively positioned herself in opposition to others in her environment. From her fashion sense to her musical tastes, she hoped to display the identity of the romantic, tortured artist. She wrote poems about love, read books about teens feeling alienated by society and their peers, and did not socialize with the other Latinas in the class.

Given her emotions of alienation, Cat was sympathetic to Arnold's plight. During a Socratic Seminar, she described him as "alone in the ethnic depart-ment, he is alone period, he can't open up to anyone, and his family isn't there for him, and he's being made fun of in school. He and his best friend are apart. It is sad that he is standing alone." Then she asked, in her own thoughtful and poetic way, "Do you ever feel alone in a crowded room?" Cat was therefore drawing on her experience, and her poet sensibilities, with Arnold's contradictory position-ing to reflect on similar positioning in her social worlds.

Phases of Critical Analysis

As illustrated in Figure 6.1, tapping into your students' emotions can lead them to engage in critical analysis as "critical engagement" (Lewis & Tierney, 2011) based on three recursive phases: emotions, critique, and entertaining transforma-tion. This means that students can engage in critique by starting with emotions, critique, or entertaining transformation—it not a linear process.

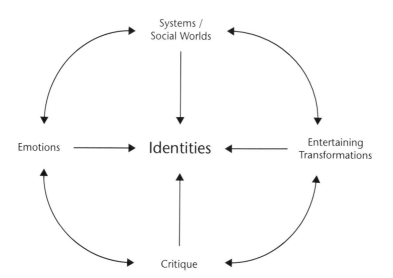

FIGURE 6.1 Relationships Between Emotions, Critique, and Transformations of Systems/Social Worlds Shaping Identity Construction

Emotions Leading to Critique

Students' experience of anger, frustration, joy, envy, grief, elation, curiosity, anxiety, and so forth can lead students to adopt a "critical engagement" stance (Lewis & Tierney, 2011). Experiencing these emotions can motivate students to engage in critique. Cat's frustration with how she and the character Arnold are positioned led her to critique how her own and Arnold's school and community positioned them.

Students frequently experience frustration with practices they perceive as conflicting with their beliefs and attitudes constituting their identities. In creating a Comic Life portrait of her sixteenth birthday party at her house, JHS student Jackie noted that her peers spent time during the party texting and updating their Facebook pages rather than talking to each other; "taking pictures of ourselves when people were being bombed" and "the campaigns for president were being run"; eating food "when others were starving"; and plugging in their phones "when others are without power." She then asked, "Why do people feel like it's necessary to be on their phones all of the time? So that's why I'm boycotting cell phones. I'll be able to live my life in the real world instead of on a mobile device." Jackie's irritation at her peers' obsession with texting and taking photos in ways that ignore problems in the world led her to critique their obsession as well as change her own actions by no longer using smartphones.

Rather than initially asking students to critically analyze an event, experience, or text, we encourage you to listen to your students, noticing events, experiences, and issues in which they are already emotionally engaged. By better understanding what matters to your students, and what engages their emotions, you will be able to plan critical analysis work that begins with what students find truly engaging and important.

Critiquing Social Worlds

In critiquing the kinds of social worlds described in Chapter 5, students can analyze how social worlds operate as systems that serve to limit or enhance positive identity development. In doing so, students can engage in both *critique of* a world or system—for example, how a standardized testing system in schools is based on results that correlate highly with family income—and *critique for* the purpose of changing a system (Diab et al., 2012).

Students experience anger and resentment given their experiences with systemic and institutional forms of racism, class prejudice, and sexism. For example, students might experience racism found in inequalities related to employment, law enforcement, the criminal justice system, health care, schooling, housing, and transportation systems (Bonilla-Silva, 2001). A stark example of institutional racism from *The Absolutely True Diary of a Part-Time Indian* that stood out to Jeffrey was when a White dentist explained, "Indians only felt half as much pain as White people did, so he only gave us half the Novocain" (Alexie, 2007, p. 2). When asked about this scene in the novel and the connections he had to it,

Jeffrey cited an example of institutional racism in his own life. Jeffrey shared that his mother, who worked for his city's major bus company, became active in organizing other employees of the bus company after it became evident that African American employees had been routinely denied requests to be transferred to work in an affluent, largely White section of the city.

Juxtaposing the novel and his life experiences, Jeffrey determined that Whites enjoy privileged lives—"they never have no problems," a reflection of his ability to critique larger institutional systems. In his presentation on race described in Chapter 4, Jeffrey shared his research on ways that white privilege results in "the advantages that White people enjoy in societies beyond those commonly experienced by people of color" given that Whites "are wealthy . . . don't have to suffer like other color people . . . [have] more freedom . . . [and] a better education than most other people."

At the same time, awareness of these institutional forces may not necessarily lead to critique of those forces. Given the familiarity Tre has with institutional racism, particularly related to law enforcement, it is interesting to note that while Tre expressed in interviews a keen awareness of how he has been shaped by such forces, this did not necessarily lend itself to a critical analysis of institutions. In large part, this is because Tre's hectic and unstable life did not offer the opportunity or distance to participate in supported, reflexive activities that might engender a greater self-awareness.

To have students critique systems shaping their own, others', or characters' actions and reflecting beliefs and attitudes constituting their identities, you can ask students:

- What are the systems shaping your own identity or those of the characters/people you are studying?
- What are the goals driving these systems—what are these systems trying to achieve?
- How did these goals influence your own, others', or the characters' decisions about actions within certain systems, spaces, or institutions?
- What are your observations about your own, others', or characters' decisions to take these actions?

For example, in responding to *The Scarlet Letter*, students in Susan Bianchi's and David Johnson's JHS AP literature class completed charts in which they responded to each of four characters, Arthur Dimmesdale, Roger Chillingworth, Hester Prynne, and Pearl, in terms of their "actions/decisions," "what space/place was this decision made," "what larger institutions influenced this decision/action," and "your judgments about the character's choices" as described in Chapter 3. In responding to Hester Prynne, one student, Julia, indicated that:

"actions/decisions": "Married Mr. Prynne/AKA Roger Chillingworth"
"what space/place was this decision made": "She did this in England when life was difficult and she needed to be taken care of financially. Her family could not provide for her any longer."

"what larger institutions influence this decision/action": "Women could not solely support themselves—not appropriate. Marriage was an arranged financial agreement, not necessarily based on love. Life was unbearable for some in England."

"your judgments about the character's choices": "Hester, although strong, was influenced by her time period and culture. She placed physical survival above love and didn't trust that there was another option."

Julia interpreted Hester's actions as motivated by her status as a female given her need to survive within the institutional and ideological forces operating in 17th century England. Interpreting characters' actions and identities as shaped by institutional systems leads students to then critique how these systems and ideologies guide and sometimes limit characters' actions.

Transforming Systems or Worlds

Based on their critiques of systems/ideologies, students can then entertain ways to transform or change these systems/worlds so that they are more supportive of positive identity development. It is often the case that students can do no more than entertain or recommend transformations as opposed to actually implementing such transformations given the realities of students' lack of power to make changes. At the same time, proposing or recommending changes can serve to enhance their sense of themselves as agents seeking to make changes.

As noted in Chapter 5, formulating and proposing changes requires use of argumentative practices highlighted in the Common Core Writing Standard: "Write arguments to support a substantive claim with clear reasons and relevant and sufficient evidence" (Council of Chief State School Officers and National Governors Association, 2010, p. 37). In formulating arguments, students need to create a credible, believable, and knowledgeable persona or ethos perceived by their audiences as convincing them of the seriousness of a problem requiring the need for change. They also need to consider which tools are most likely to engage audiences, for example, employing images or videos to portray the gravity of an issue or problem.

Activity: Using Critique to Engage in Action

Based on their critiques of problems inherent in certain institutional practices, students might propose ways to address these problems. For example, in her first-year composition courses at the University of South Florida, Susan Taylor (2013) engages students in a "Rhetoric in Action" (http://tinyurl.com/myox766) project in which students engage in an activity associated with addressing an issue or problem for the purpose of effecting change. (For examples of students' projects, see http://tinyurl.com/kxdwlgw.) She has four objectives for students:

> 1) educate your audience about an issue that needs changing, 2) invite them to your point of view, 3) acknowledge and refute opposing arguments, and 4) motivate readers to act in specific ways.

To prepare students for taking action, she has students choose issues, then organize and lead flash mobs in an effort to raise awareness on campus about those issues. For example, one student organized a flash mob protest of rape culture to promote the university's Take Back the Night event. She also gives extra credit for participating in the university's counseling center "I'm Stronger Than I Knew" project, in which students videotape themselves describing how they have overcome personal challenges. She then has students determine ways to use their language or communication to influence audiences to make change with the following question and task:

> How can your ideas and passion about an issue translate into a tangible act?
> Your job is to convince your readers of the importance of your chosen topic and motivate them to enact change by offering a well-researched and persuasive argument. It's not enough, however, to argue for a change; this project will also ask you to participate in enacting some sort of change.

She wants her students to "think big" in terms of distributing their work by, for example, putting their videos on YouTube to influence larger audiences. One student organized a sleep-out to raise awareness on campus about homelessness, and generated a YouTube video (http://tinyurl.com/lbwh3ex) that includes interviews with homeless people in Tampa.

Taylor also asked students to reflect on how their use of certain tools or rhetorical strategies served to achieve a certain intended audience.

Activity: Critical Engagement Through Online Role-Play

In her 12th-grade composition class, Elizabeth noted that her students were upset about the fact the school blocked access to certain websites, access they needed to write their research papers. For example, students writing about gun control found that access to the NRA site was blocked. Students seeking information about Diane Hacker's MLA formatting guidelines found that references to "hacker" were blocked. Students therefore noted the contradiction of their being told to access relevant research for their papers but at the same time not being able to access that research given the school's Internet policies.

Based on these frustrations with their school Internet policies and drawing on her previous use of online role-plays for responding to literature (described in Chapter 5), Elizabeth had her students engage in an online role-play in which they debated pros and cons of the school policy of blocking access to websites (Beach & Doerr-Stevens, 2011). Students adopted the roles of administrators (principals, superintendent, technology people), teachers, students, librarians, lawyers, counselors, coaches, parents, businesspeople, computer hackers, and so forth. Some argued for the need to unblock sites to provide access to needed material for their work, while others argued that students should not have access to sites that are problematic or that contain objectionable material.

Using a Ning forum platform, Elizabeth had students create avatar images and fictional profile bios similar to those they create for Facebook. Creating these profiles helped students in adopting a persona or ethos in formulating their arguments—persona or ethos that would be perceived as credible, believable proponents for their pro or con positions.

Students then posted their arguments on the forum and responded to each other's arguments over several days. Students' emotions of frustration and anger led to their need to critique the school's status quo Internet policies. For example, "Judith Rosario," the president of the school's Youth Against War and Racism Club, expressed her anger about adult assumptions that students "are stupid enough to let ourselves be molested by an Internet predator. As if we are that stupid. Just another way that adults are underestimating us" (Beach & Doerr-Stevens, 2011, p. 174). This emotion led her to a critique for the need for change in the policies, explaining that she will

> fight for what I believe in and will take stands against issues, even if the rest of the student body is too afraid to. . . . I don't take anything lying down. That's why I can't let the Internet stalking by our administration continue any longer.
>
> *(Beach & Doerr-Stevens, 2011, p. 174)*

In constructing their roles, students employed certain discourses as ways of knowing and thinking (Gee, 2008) constituting those roles. A student assuming the role of the ACLU lawyer adopted legal discourses of students' rights to access to information, as reflected in the statement:

> Government mandated Internet blocking is censorship. . . . Some content is blocked because it has opposing viewpoints which are contrary to local, political, or religious opinions.
>
> *(Beach & Doerr-Stevens, 2011, p. 174)*

Students assuming the administrator roles adopted discourses of management and protectionism. For example, the school principal, John Smith, noted:

There is an exception to every rule or guideline, in this case, if an administrator suspects a student of wrong doing they should have every right to get to the bottom of it.

(Beach & Doerr-Stevens, 2011, p. 175)

Once students completed the role-play, they then drew on the different arguments from the forum transcripts to write their own position papers on the issue, knowing that they would be using these papers to ask the school administration to change their policy. Students then met with the administration and, based on arguments from the role-play and their papers, noted the contradictions associated with the current policy. As one student noted:

We can't get onto Nazi websites, but *Mein Kampf* is on display in the library. I can understand that you can't go on websites, but we can read this book, but we can't go to a website that might have historical facts.

(Beach & Doerr-Stevens, 2011, p. 177)

Based on the students' arguments, the administration decided to change their policy to unblock the sites, as well as provide teachers with access to YouTube, an example of how students can make changes in their own school through their writing.

Students noted that by being exposed to competing perspectives in the role-play, they sometimes changed their own perspectives. The student who played Judith Rosario, a student activist, noted that she

began the role play believing that administration's monitoring of student access was a good idea, but my opinions changed a little as time progressed. As I continued to write as Judith and research the topic more carefully, I came to see how a person could come to feel so strongly about privacy in the academic setting. At the beginning, I saw the blocking of websites as an educational benefit that would only help students, not hurt them. I thought that blocking websites that are crude or vulgar should simply guard students against features that they would not want or need to access at school, but then I looked further into it. The school blocks sites such as YouTube that can actually be used by teachers as an educational asset.

(Beach & Doerr-Stevens, 2011, p. 176)

Participation in the online role-play led students to recognize that through shared, collective action people acquire the power to make change. As a student who assumed the role of an ACLU lawyer noted:

The school administrators have power. But it's still static—if we could empower or actually give people the ability to change things in the environment, for people to respond to, then they would have more power, but theoretically, it's the principal or especially the superintendent. . . . If I could bring a lawsuit, if I had the ability to change something—you could go to the Supreme Court or have the ACLU challenge the basic law.

(Beach & Doerr-Stevens, 2011, p. 177)

By successfully making changes in a system, students acquire the identity of change agents associated with what Laura VanDerPloeg (2012) defines as "socially just education," in which students

learn to become agents for justice and social good in their own lives and communities. A socially just education helps students to answer, and to live with, larger questions of agency: What does my learning help me to do in the world? And how can I use my learning to make a difference?

(p. 22)

Activity: Critiquing Media Representations of Identities

Students' perceptions of their identities are shaped by stereotypical media representations of identities associated with race, class, gender, and sexuality as "ideal egos" (Dashtipour, 2012). For example, female students may create self-perceptions based on images of females in advertising as Caucasian and thin, while male students may create self-perceptions of themselves relative to advertising images of males as muscular. As one 11th-grade female student at Mount Rainier High School, Seattle, Washington, noted:

I was thinking about all of the movies I watch and the books I love and they all have women that are insecure; they are worried about how they look and all they want is a boyfriend or husband. I began to think about myself and how I'm always worried about being pretty and boys liking me.

(VanDerPloeg, 2012, p. 75)

JHS student Susan attributes students' need to conform to these media images as being due to their insecurities about their own self-perceptions:

That's where the insecurities come from because they want to be that person. . . . I don't understand why people will want to be like that because they are not healthy—they are too skinny, they are not healthy weight. I'm able to see that. I do have some insecurities about myself—but that's every teenage girl. I learn to get past that.

Consistent with an activity in Chapter 3, students can select images or video clips of these different representations of identities in magazine ads, television programs, and/or in online sites in terms of representations according to race, class, gender, age, occupations (teachers, lawyers, doctors, etc.), spaces (neighborhoods, houses, bars, etc.), fan activities (sports, TV, computer games), and/or leisure activities (vacations/hobbies) (Janks, 2014). Students can access examples of media representations from Richard's media literacy resource site (http://tinyurl.com/8u9ho9o), including examples from the Critical Media Project (http://www.criticalmediaproject.org) that contains media representations related to race, class, gender, and sexuality as portrayed in over 250 media artifacts. Students can then import these images or video clips into the Voice-Thread application (http://voicethread.com) or VideoANT (http://ant.umn.edu) for collaboratively sharing annotated responses to these images.

Students can also analyze representations of adolescent identities in literature, magazine articles, and print/television news. Adolescents are often represented in the media in both positive ways (as adventurous, inquisitive, curious, romantic, and caring) or in negative ways (as irresponsible, dangerous, overly emotional, naive, driven by changing hormones, and susceptible to being misled) (Bernier, 2011).

Students could then reflect on how those images and/or characters represent identities in terms of the use of social markers, physical appearance, dress, status symbols, setting, practices portrayed, and so forth, as well as assumptions about the brand names related to race, class, and gender differences and whether, how, and why these images may influence their perceptions.

Students' Critical Engagement With Whiteness in a Suburban High School

For his dissertation research, Sam Tanner (2014) examined students' participation in a project in which they wrote and produced a play in his class at Primdale High School (PHS) (pseudonym), Minnesota, on the effects of a culture of Whiteness in their school. The following is Sam's description of that project.

Community Contexts

Primdale High School (PHS) is located in a Minnesota suburb whose population is predominantly White (83.7%); other groups consist of 8.2% Asian, 7.3% African American, 1.3% American Indian and Alaska Native, 0.1% Native Hawaiian and Other Pacific Islander, and 2.4% from other races. PHS had an enrollment of about 2,250 students in grades 9 through 12 during 2011. It publicly expresses a commitment to equity work in the phrase "Quality teaching and learning for all . . . Equity in all we do."

During the theatrical inquiry into Whiteness that I conducted both as my dissertation project and the spring play, students reflected on the racial systems in the school.

One White student, Sally, shared a story about her participation in the racial politics of PHS in her journal. In reflecting on the story, she became troubled about how her own White identity implicated her in the racial systems in the school. She was both in the process of developing a critical stance as well as describing the school context of PHS in terms of race when she wrote the following:

> I had a story. I can clarify any questions you have about it later. Anyways, this event occurred this last winter. I was walking down the hall during class and I passed a teacher (we'll keep it anonymous for now, but you can ask me later if you're curious). I realized as I walked past her that I didn't have my passbook with me and that she was fully aware of that. I kept walking anyways and she said nothing. Not far behind me, a black student was walking down the hallway, also without a passbook. The teacher proceeded to stop the student and ask them where they were supposed to be and why they didn't have a pass. This story is interesting to me because both me and the black student were in the same situation, but I wasn't questioned.

Another White student displayed her understanding of the school's racial climate by describing the importance of doing research into Whiteness. This student's writing, like Sally's referenced above, occurred at the beginning of the project and both displayed a statement about the student's perception of her high school as well as her burgeoning critical identity.

Planning This Project

I worked in an urban school, north of Minneapolis, for four years. That was my first job as an English and drama teacher. It was also the first time that I stood in front of a room of mostly Black students and realized that my White identity had pedagogical implications. I spent four years learning how to navigate my Whiteness and its implications for my students. I had to reflect on the cultural and racial norms that had been inscribed on me by my own high school experience in an affluent, White suburban high school and by my undergraduate work at the University of Minnesota. By the end of those four years, one of my 9th graders shared something during a discussion of the use of the N-word in *To Kill A Mockingbird* that stuck with me. I always chose to read that word aloud when I taught the book, to honor the author's choice.

"It is okay if you say the word, Mr. Tanner," Chris told me, "you are one of *us*."

Chris was Black. In that moment, he recognized a racial solidarity in our work in the classroom. Whatever that meant to him, it meant a great deal to me. I was trying to work beyond my participation in White identity and use the ELA classroom to make critical disruptions into systems of racial inequity with my students. Chris publicly acknowledged that he saw that in a Socratic Seminar.

The next year I took a job at Primdale High School. This became the site for the project that is described in this book. Though PHS was a first-ring suburban high school experiencing growing diversity, it *felt* more like the school I attended as a student than the school where I cut my teeth as a teacher. I had returned to a White space. The honest discussions I had shared in my first classroom were replaced by anxiety, silence, and preprogrammed responses.

"It is better now, Mr. Tanner," was a typical response from my mostly White, 11th-grade students when we worked through *Black Boy* in American Literature together. "We don't need to talk about this."

After the class would agree that racism was pretty much solved, the bell would ring. White students would congregate near the music and art rooms. Some of them would hang out in my classroom, the drama room. I would overhear disparaging comments about "Compton Corner," the student moniker given to the space near the administrative offices where the Black students hung out. Or I would hear a joke about "Hmong Mountain," the area at the top of the stairs, near the media center where the Asian students hung out.

It was as though the White students were unable or unwilling to see how discourses of White supremacy were reproducing themselves in their social contexts.

This realization became the inspiration for the project described in this book. I wanted to build a critical intervention on a social phenomenon that troubled me. Could I help the White students in the theatre program at PHS become aware of their own Whiteness and its social implications in the same way that I had grown to see it in my first teaching job? Could I make an intervention in how students constructed their racial identity through critical pedagogy?

A Youth Participatory Action Research (YPAR), Theatrical Inquiry Into Whiteness

Racial inequities continue to create disparities in our societies and our schools. As opposed to understanding Whiteness as a number of privileges, it is imperative that we begin to understand the mechanisms of Whiteness as a system of power and the relationship it has with racial identification. In a 1998 interview with Charlie Rose, author Toni Morrison (1998) had this to say: "If you can only be tall because somebody is on their knees, then you have a serious problem. And my feeling is that White people have a very serious problem. And they should start thinking about what they can do about it. Take me out of it."

I set out to gain further understanding of Morrison's serious problem in the summer of 2012 by gathering together with students at PHS to make critical, collective, and artful interventions on participation in White identity and systems of Whiteness. As a veteran English/drama teacher as well as a doctoral student in Critical Literacy, I planned this project as both the spring play at PHS in 2013 and my dissertation research.

As is well documented, racial categorization continues to have profound influence on schooling. Oftentimes this trend is rationalized through deficit models. This approach lends itself to examining why non-White students have problematic experiences in schools. Routinely, this is done in the absence of an inquiry into how Whiteness fits into this categorization, exists outside of it, and reifies the system of categorization itself. As a response, my project interrogated configurations of Whiteness as systems of power in schools through a collaborative, youth participatory action research theatre project. I did this to explore the viability of teachers and students taking up systems of power as sites of inquiry in order to build democratic, epistemological interventions within their identities and communities.

Writing a Play About Whiteness Constituting the School Culture

As a teacher-researcher, I conducted a critical ethnography of a youth participatory action research (YPAR) theatrical inquiry into Whiteness during the 2012–2013 school year. I facilitated and directed this project with 9th- to 12th-grade students involved in the theatre program at PHS. The project was open to any interested student from the outset. Students participated on a voluntary basis. Nearly forty students were involved throughout the year. Twenty of those students participated for the duration of the project. Nearly all of the students involved were White. In that way, this project directly took up Morrison's request for White people to start thinking about race without putting people of color at the center of the conversation.

In September of 2012, I built and facilitated a YPAR collective (Cammarota & Fine, 2008; Morrell, 2004) with students that tasked them with researching Whiteness in their community. In December of 2012, I led a scriptwriting project that turned their findings into a play (Boal, 1979; Mandell & Wolf, 2003). Finally, I directed the production as the spring play, performed for the community in May of 2013.

For writing the play, the students and I employed long-form improvisation that requires players to go off script in order to make discoveries in a scene. As a director of long-form improvisation, its practices have become central to my teaching. Rather than negating my students by imposing my own rigid outcomes on their learning trajectories, I tried to engage them by building a collaborative dialogue with their prior knowledge and motivations, whatever those might be. My job was to help students figure out how to use what they knew about the world to build research agendas, curricular processes, and shared outcomes. This commitment allowed students to take serious stock of their own understandings of White identity and led to the construction of a critical stance.

Lewis and Tierney's (2013) recent work with emotion suggested the necessity for the teacher to see emotional response as a valid part of intellectual discourse. Rather than managing emotion as off-task behavior or disruptive to academic outcomes, they encourage teachers to understand emotion as part and parcel to a growing critical consciousness or the transformation of student identity, in this case, how the emotions of concern and anger about race could lead students to adopt a critical stance on the issue of race in ways that lead to change in the school.

The play that the students ended up writing was entitled *Blanchekreist: A Collaborative Play About Whiteness*. The title was an amalgam of the French and German words for "white" and "circle." The story centered around the fictional community of Blanchekreist. A new family moved to the town and a dormant virus was activated. This was an allusion to the students' claim that White supremacy was a circular phenomenon that was socially reproduced throughout generations by way of societal structures. The symptom of this virus was blindness.

The community spent the duration of the play reacting to the virus. Eventually, a powerful faction in the community decided that the virus was a blessing instead of a curse. After convincing the mayor of the town that those with the blindness have actually been chosen to lead the town, Bedford, the leader of the faction, said the following to the community:

> Hello. Thank you Mayor! I am so honored to be your acting chief of police and I am so pleased that people are finally "seeing" the light about this whole blindness mess. I would have written a speech for this event but I wouldn't be able to read it! (laughs) Now to business. I would like to encourage everyone to return to their former habits and ways of life before this so-called virus. As the mayor has said there's nothing to fear in fact, what has been called a virus is really just the next step for our town. We are changing in a wonderful way. Thank you.
>
> *(Blanchekreist script, p. 65)*

Bedford became a way for the students to characterize White supremacy. While the virus was the potential for humans to formulate and marginalize the Other, Bedford was the students' codification of Whiteness. After Bedford was named the chief of police, the town systematically attempted to rid themselves of those who were not infected with the virus.

Whereas Bedford became the symbol for White supremacy, a little girl in the play, Victoria, became the characterization of critical awareness. She refused to buy into the town's social and discursive realities from the outset of the play. She had been shut away in a shack throughout the play for refusing to conform to her teacher's norms. The town ridiculed her for her beliefs. After becoming friends with Hurston, Victoria asked:

> Do you want to know why they put me here? (Silence). It's because I did what they were too afraid to do. I dared to be different. (darkly) Do you see the world we live in? This is becoming a corrupt place again. The worst is when a person looks different. You see a girl whose skin is a little bit darker, hair's too curly, whose wardrobe isn't plain, and she has to make up for it. As if she owes these people something. She has to talk the same

as the conformers. Dress the same. And if she wants to get anywhere, God knows she can't acknowledge her differences. (Almost at a scream) People are ruined here. (She pauses). They think I'm the dead one. They should take a look at themselves.

(Blanchekreist script, p. 33)

This led to the lynching of Victoria, who was trying to protect her friend Hurston. Hurston was the youngest son of the new family that had moved to the town in the beginning of the play. This led to Bedford's downfall and the community's realization that the virus was a problem.

John, one of the scriptwriters, indicated that the writers wanted audiences to recognize that in the town, conforming to the status quo was a problem. He also noted that, through working on the play, he began to recognize that people are not aware of the phenomenon of White privilege, leading to him perceiving his own school experience from a different perspective in terms of institutional racism:

I see things differently and you notice how much the media impacts perceptions. Even teachers shy away from it. How many people are infected by this virus without being aware of it. I think a lot more about whiteness in general. I was so blind to things that were going on.

The literacy practices involved in the project included dialogical journal writing, constructivist student research, role-playing, storytelling, fiction writing, academic writing, peer review, and so forth. All of the practices I used as a facilitator and director in this project have also shown up in my curricular English and Theatre classrooms.

Students negotiated the script during the month of February. This process was entirely student driven, relying on the youth participatory action research axiom that students should have the space to negotiate power dynamics in the process and project of their work. This went hand in hand with their engagement and ultimate formations of critical identities.

By putting YPAR in conversation with elements of social justice theatre and long-form improvisation (Boal, 1979; Mandell & Wolf, 2003; Sawyer 2003), I built a curricular project that gave students space to construct their own collective curriculum, explore emotional reactions to inquiries into racial identity, and adopt a critical stance in terms of White identity.

Victoria's Identity Construction Through Adopting a Critical Engagement Stance

I am going to trace the emergence of a critical stance in the identities of one student, Victoria, who used her emotional response to her inquiry into systems of Whiteness as a springboard to the writing she did for the script.

Victoria developed a critical stance regarding her own White identity through the year. An 11th grader, Victoria took mostly AP classes, participated in cheerleading and theatre, and had a GPA that ranked near the top of her class. She first became engaged in this project over the summer of 2012. She was a on a trip to Israel with her parents when she emailed her first journal entries about Whiteness to me. Responding to a particular prompt that I assigned to interested students, she wrote the following.

> We were watching a Euro-sport competition in Barcelona from our hotel in Tel Aviv today. A family friend was staying with us, and we watched the US team dominate in the 4×4 women's relay. It was awesome, but as soon as it was done, our friend said, "Of course they're all black." That really pissed me off. I can't pinpoint exactly why.

Victoria was unable to name the White supremacist discourse that stood behind her friend's statement. She was only able to respond with emotion, by being "pissed off." Rather than assuaging or shutting down Victoria's anger, I sent an email a couple of days later with the following response. This was my attempt to foster Victoria's observation in a way that might generate further thinking.

> Just another example of how much race ideology is part of our reality. And again, what does it mean that black people run the 4×4? And that people expect that? Where does it come from? (I would argue from a history where black people were understood by physical prowess. That is a long conversation though, right?)

Victoria spent the next month journaling and thinking about my response to her journal. At the end of August, as the school year was about to start, Victoria sent me another collection of journals. This writing displayed how Victoria moved from emotion to reflection:

> (Regarding both the 4×4 race and the "black people are scary" topic): I think the answer to both of these questions can be, like you said, traced back to a history of black physical prowess. African-Americans have always been associated with physical strength and speed (explaining the automatic association with something like the 4×4 relay). Where this comes from, I'm not sure; maybe the idea of hard manual labor performed during the slavery era? But along with this strength comes fear; I think the reason many people flinch from the black guy is because we've associated the race with physical power for so long. And that idea has developed into the stereotypes we hold today; things like violence, crime, and aggression.

Victoria's response shows that she was trying to make sense of the emotional reaction she had to the statement her family friend had made. She was trying to understand how a White perception of Black stereotypes might operate. Again, rather than trying to give Victoria a clear answer or outcome, I was letting her form her own trajectory as a thinker.

In conducting research for the play, she noted in her journal that:

> The research will be awesome, because I feel like race is kind of an elephant in the room at PHS. We all know that we have a reputation as the "ghetto school" of the area, and it'd be straight up bullshit if you said race wasn't a part of that. Direct quotes from the urban dictionary definition of PHS mention "the black perch" and students of "questionable moral character." And we all know there's the stereotype of the loud, rude black person at school. You know, the "hold my weave" thing. But I've never understood how the color of your skin can effect demeanor/personality. Upbringing and culture, yes. But not skin color. Which brings up the question of what race is, what it encompasses. I've never really bought into stereotypes, considering that they have virtually no value. But I go to Primrose, which means they're everywhere. So I guess I want to use this project to confront the idea of race in the most direct way possible, and see what we find.

In writing the character Victoria's monologue for the play, Victoria articulated the repercussions of adopting a critical stance and disrupting discursive systems. This writing came about after she spent the fall of 2012 setting up a research project in the elementary schools in the district. She examined how children in grades K–8 perceived racial discourses, namely Whiteness, in terms of power dynamics. She experienced many institutional limitations as she proposed and executed her projects in a number of schools. For example, of the six schools that she reached out to, only three allowed her to come in and conduct her research. This only happened after extensive negotiation with district administrators. This gave Victoria a sense of the nature of doing critical scholarship that disturbed the status quo.

Victoria grew frustrated in the fall as her research was limited by people who were afraid that her work might cause problems. In fact, a principal at the local elementary school told her directly that she was not capable of executing her research project by discussing Whiteness with children. This made Victoria angry. The more that Victoria researched institutional racism and systematic Whiteness, the more she saw elements of dehumanization. In part, this inspired her work on the character Victoria. The following is how the character Victoria responded to Hurston when she first met him. He told her that she was strange, and she said this.

VICTORIA: Don't you dare talk down to me. Don't you dare tell me that I made a
          mistake. I have been through things you couldn't dream of, all because

I trusted someone. *(Rises. Begins to walk towards him slowly.)* I am thir-
teen years old, and they've turned me into this half-dead memory
that barely clings onto life. I have been stripped of everything. They
scraped off every piece of dignity I had, every piece of worth and love
I had ever felt. They called me a freak. And they put me here.

(*Blanchekreist* script, p. 33)

This was clearly an instance where Victoria's anger served as a springboard to
critical action, the construction of a character that was meant to show the audience how systematic Whiteness and institutional racism marginalized the Other.

She also recognized the value of the playwriting project as not only addressing
issues of racism but as also fostering change in their own perceptions and identities, as she noted in an interview:

But as it went on I realized it was as much about changing ourselves as it
was about changing our community. And I almost feel as if, we weren't
aware of this in the beginning, but one of the big, one of the main purposes of this project was to make ourselves more aware of what was going
on and I think we almost like tricked ourselves into doing some introspec-
tion. Which I think was the greatest benefit for me personally, was that
I learned so much about myself. Creating awareness more than anything.

Due to Victoria's authentic engagement in her own learning project, she was
able to use her sustained inquiry to move from her emotional response to a family friend's White supremacist comment to the ability to see how her own White
identity implicated her into systems of institutionalized racism. Furthermore,
Victoria actually created strategies to help continue transforming her identity to
be more critical of how she perceived other people. Later in that same interview,
she had this to say about how she was changed by being in this project:

How I see the world outside myself: I told Tanner that as much as we
would all hate to admit this, obviously we go through the hallway every
day and we make snap judgments about people constantly. Although I
strive to be a sort of good person, that still happens. And I just remember
there was this day, and I wrote him this essay called "I Am Beautiful, I Am
You" and that was about how we needed to stop with the power struggle
and stop making these snap judgments and it was more articulate than
that. But I just remember the day after I wrote that I was walking through
the hall and every time I made a snap judgment about somebody I remember reaching into myself and finding an emotion that was really poignant
for me and thinking that person has probably felt that at some point in this
day. And all of a sudden it was like we were just both people, and now I
do that all the time.

By the end of this project, rather than making "snap judgments," Victoria was disrupting her own discursive perception of others and trying to force herself to realize that "we were just both people." Furthermore, Victoria shared that "now I do that all the time." By the end of this project, Victoria had tasked herself to become critical of how she perceived people, namely in light of race. She had developed a critical stance in terms of her White identity.

And while the most obvious attempt at change they made was writing and producing a play for the PHS community, perhaps the clearest evidence for transformation can be found in their own articulations of how they understood their own transformation by the end of the project.

After a report about the play's production appeared in a local newspaper, a former student of mine who graduated in 2008 responded to a negative comment underneath the report on the *Pioneer Press* website with the following post.

> As someone who had Mr. Tanner as a teacher myself I would say that instead of indoctrinating me with his own ideas (as you seem to think he does) I actually developed more of a critical lens about the world. He's encouraging students to think critically about the world around them. He's doing what most teachers don't—he's teaching them to THINK.
>
> *Homer (2013, May 6)*

Sam's project illustrates how students' critical engagement with the ways in which Whiteness shaped students' identities in their school led them to create their play as a means of fostering discussion of how institutional racism shaped their school's culture. In your own classroom, as also illustrated by Elizabeth's use of online role-play to address the issue of sites being blocked at JHS, you could have students identify certain issues facing their school or community and then have them create plays, stories, video documentaries, or exhibits portraying how this issue influences people's attitudes and identities. Through engaging in these actions, as illustrated by Sam's and Elizabeth's students' success in effecting change through their play and online role-play, students acquire a sense of agency constituting their identity as change agents.

Summary

In this chapter we focused on how emotions evoked by institutional and systemic positioning of identities can be harnessed to stimulate critical engagement in the ELA classroom. These emotions of anger, frustration, concern, and confusion—when taken seriously by teachers—can lead students to critique institutional forces and engage in actions to address these forces. In the next chapter we discuss how you might foster positive identity development. (For additional resources, activities, and further reading, see http://tinyurl.com/o29vo88.)

References

Alexie, S. (2007). *The absolutely true diary of a part-time Indian.* New York: Little, Brown Publishers.

Barron, N. G. (2003). Dear saints, dear Stella: Letters examining the messy lines of expectations, stereotypes, and identity in higher education. *College Composition & Communication, 55*(1), 11–37.

Beach, R., & Doerr-Stevens, C. (2011). Using social networking for online role-plays to develop students' argumentative strategies. *Journal of Educational Computing Research, 45*(2) 165–181.

Bernier, A. (2011). Representations of youth in local media: Implications for library service. *Library & Information Science Research, 33,* 158–167.

Boal, A. (1979). *Theatre of the oppressed.* Trans. Charles A. & Maria-Odilia Leal McBride. New York: TCG.

Boler, N. (1999). *Feeling power: Emotions and education.* New York: Routledge.

Bonilla-Silva, E. (2001). *White supremacy and racism in the post-civil rights era.* Boulder, CO: Lynne Rienner.

Cammarota, J., & Fine, M. (2008). *Revolutionizing education: Youth participatory action research in motion.* New York: Routledge.

Council of Chief State School Officers and the National Governors Association. (2010). Common Core State Standards for English Language Arts. Authors. Retrieved from http://www.corestandards.org/ELA-Literacy

Dashtipour, P. (2012). *Social identity in question: Construction, subjectivity, and critique.* New York: Routledge.

Diab, R., Godbee, B., Ferrel, R., & Simpkins, N. (2012). A multi-dimensional pedagogy for racial justice in writing centers. *Praxis: A Writing Center Journal, 10*(1). Retrieved from http://tinyurl.com/omf6a7z

Gabriel, M., & Goldberg, E. (Directors). (1995). *Pocahontas* [Motion picture]. United States: Disney Productions.

Gee, G. P. (2008). *Sociolinguistics and literacy: Ideology in discourse.* New York: Routledge.

Homer, S. (2013, May 6). White on white. *St. Paul Pioneer Press,* A3.

Janks, H. (2014). *Doing critical literacy: Texts and activities for students and teachers.* New York: Routledge.

Leander, K., & Rowe, D. (2006). Mapping literacy spaces in motion: A rhizomatic analysis of a classroom literacy performance. *Reading Research Quarterly, 41*(4), 428–460.

Lewis, C., & Tierney, J. D. (2011). Mobilizing emotion in an urban English classroom. *Changing English: Studies in Culture and Education, 18*(3), 319–329.

Lewis, C., & Tierney, J. D. (2013). Mobilizing emotion in an urban classroom: Producing identities and transforming signs in a race-related discussion. *Linguistics and Education, 24,* 289–304. http://dx.doi.org/10.1016/j.linged.2013.03.003

Mandell, J., & Wolf, J. (2003). *Acting, learning, and change: Creating original plays with adolescents.* Portsmouth, NH: Heinemann Drama.

Micciche, L. (2007). *Doing emotion: Rhetoric, writing, teaching.* Portsmouth, NH: Heinemann.

Morrell, E. (2004). *Becoming critical researchers: Literacy and empowerment for urban youth.* New York: Peter Lang Publishing.

Morrison, T. (1998, January 19). Interview by C. Rose [web based recording]. An hour with Nobel Prize winner Toni Morrison. Retrieved from http://www.charlierose.com/view/interview/5135

Pyscher, T., & Crampton, A. (2013). *Traumatic histories & traumatic narratives: Transformation in the literary transaction.* Paper presented at the meeting of the Literacy Research Association, Dallas.

Rymes, B. (2001). *Conversational borderlands: Language and identity in an alternative suburban high school.* New York: Teachers College Press.

Sanchez, R. (2006). On critical realist theory of identity. In L. M. Alcoff, M. Hames-Garcia, S. P. Mohanty, & P.M.L. Moya (Eds.), *Identity politics reconsidered* (pp. 31–52). New York: Palgrave MacMillan.

Sawyer, R. K. (2003). *Improvised dialogues: Emergence and creativity in conversation.* Westport, CT: Ablex Publishing.

Soja, E. W. (1998). *Thirdspace: Journeys to Los Angeles and other real-and-imagined places.* Malden, MA: Blackwell.

Tanner, S. (2014). *A youth participatory action research (YPAR), theatrical inquiry into Whiteness.* Doctoral dissertation, University of Minnesota.

Taylor, S. G. (2013). Social action and the status quo: Bravery in first year composition. *Hybrid Pedagogy.* Retrieved from http://tinyurl.com/myox766

Thein, A. H., Guise, M., & Sloan, D. L. (2015). Examining the circulation of emotional rules in the English classroom: A critical discourse analysis of one student's literary responses in two academic contexts. *Research in the Teaching of English, 49*(3), 200–223.

VanDerPloeg, L. (2012). *Literacy for a better world: The promise of teaching in diverse classrooms.* New York: Teachers College Press.

Wetherell, M. (2012). *Affect and emotion: A new social science understanding.* Los Angeles: Sage.

Zembylas, M. (2002). "Structures of feeling" in curriculum and teaching: Theorizing the emotional rules. *Educational Theory, 52*(2), 187–208.

7

REFLECTING ON IDENTITY DEVELOPMENT OVER TIME

High school is this dramatic transition period full of cliques and you pick what road you want to go down—do you pick the college road, the military road, or go work at McDonald's road? It's how high school sort of defines you; you can let it define you, but I'm not defined by any group. I just hate seeing these popular girls; they think that winning homecoming queen is the most amazing thing in the world, but I'm sitting in the marching band watching you and you look stupid and I don't understand that you spent three hundred dollars on a dress and you are going to wear that once. What are you going to do when you get out of high school—there's going to be nothing for you after that. Those are the people I get worried about, because I have a future that people will never get that I've been working on for two years out of my life, and I've had a huge history of the Navy in my family, so I have full family support on this. We're graduating in a month, people, you have to grow up and realize that your homecoming crown ain't crap in college. Nobody cares who you are in college; nobody is going to know who you are in college.

Ellie, JHS student

In Chapter 5, we described how students learn to negotiate identity difference as they move *horizontally* across different social worlds, leading them to learn to critique those worlds, as described in Chapter 6. In this chapter, we focus on how students develop their identities through moving *vertically* from past to present and future worlds. As they move through these different worlds, they recognize the need to revise or develop new identity practices to adjust to the norms and expectations of those different worlds. Kari describes this movement across time during four years of high school as

a roller coaster. You kind of find your place in the first two years and then stuff kind of flips; you're in the lower portion and then you switch to upperclassman. There's a big divide between freshman and sophomore years. Once you're an upperclassman you're looked up to because you've already done some of these classes. The first two years determines the rest of high school if you're going to finish high school. Your freshman year it's kind of like school and then your sophomore year, there's more work, and then, by the way, when you're a junior it's going to get a whole lot worse . . . everyone is trying to prepare for the next step.

Moving Beyond Deficit Conceptions of Adolescent Development

There are a wide range of different notions on how students do or should develop over time, notions that often frame adolescent development that defines adolescents in deficit ways. As Nancy Lesko (2013) notes:

> Young people become shared objects of feeling in that we read them as needy, as not knowing any better, and as needing help if disaster is to be avoided. There is also a sense of danger in the portrayal of youth and children, for they may subvert social order through crime, by perpetuating the status quo, or by growing up too fast.

This deficit framing of adolescents is evident in references identifying low-income students of color as "culturally disadvantaged/deprived" or "at risk," references based on the "achievement gap" notion derived from standardized test score disparities between White students and students of color (Baldridge, 2014). The "achievement gap" notion leads to defining adolescent development in terms of improving their test scores given their presumed lack of certain abilities or knowledge as measured by standardized tests as opposed to recognizing disparities in adolescent development given differences in the quality and kinds of historical and economic opportunities available for students that would assist in their development (Baldridge, 2014; Ladson-Billings, 2006).

This suggests the need to reframe the "achievement gap" as an "opportunity gap" associated with disparities in district per-pupil spending between low-income, urban versus middle-income, suburban schools, resulting in differences in class size, teacher salaries/experience, extracurricular opportunities, and technology support. Increases in school funding for low-income urban schools over a twelve-year period as documented in one study found an increase in school completion, higher earning for graduating adults, and a reduction in poverty for low-income students (Jackson, Johnson, & Persico 2014, p. 1).

Given the assumption that low-income students lack certain competencies, there is also a need to provide them with activities to display competence in ways that enhance their agency fostering their further development, as opposed to focusing on remedial "skill-drill" instruction that can limit rather than enhance their sense of agency.

A related framing of student development focuses on the importance of students' dispositions as serving to motivate them to develop academically over time. For example, Paul Tough (2012) identifies four dispositions—grit, resilience, perseverance, and optimism—critical to students' academic success. He points to how adults assume the role of fostering these dispositions through the quality of their attachment to their children.

When children confront difficult challenges, they need to know how to be resilient enough to persevere in coping with those challenges. A parent or teacher can help students acquire the grit or resilience through verbal support or by modeling their own demonstration of these dispositions. One study that tracked children of first-time low-income mothers over forty years found that the extent to which these children received this support from parents was a strong predictor as to whether a child would graduate from high school (Kristof, 2012).

However, one problem with focusing on differences in individual students' dispositions such as grit or perseverance shaping their motivation is that it can shift attention away from focusing on the quality of classroom activities fostering engagement, interest, and display of competence to enhance agency (Sparks, 2014a), as well as blaming parents for not employing certain parenting methods.

Moreover, while some research suggests that grit and perseverance predict completion of well-structured tasks, other research finds that there is no relationship between grit and perseverance and success in creative activity such as writing, art, or problem solving, which are more likely to be influenced by openness to new experiences and alternative perspectives (Sparks, 2014b).

Given the need to not label students based on assumed dispositions, within a successful afterschool community-based program for African American students, instructors deliberately avoided use of deficit categories for describing students as "at risk" by moving to descriptors that emphasized the students' assets (Baldridge, 2014). Within this program, students took courses related to exploration of identities in terms of race, ethnicity, class, gender, sexuality, and cultural differences, and these were particularly popular with students. A course instructor noted the value of these courses in helping prepare students to succeed when they attend colleges that are often predominantly White:

> We need to be able to send them off with a firm grounding and understanding of who they are. And, where they come from so that once they go into these settings, they can thrive.
>
> *(p. 456)*

It is also the case that schools and teachers perpetuate deficit perceptions of students by presupposing that they will engage in deviant ways, leading to an emphasis on monitoring and control of students' actions. Rather than adopt a stance of control, Elizabeth focuses on establishing positive relationships with her JHS students given their need for positive emotional support:

> Here's the thing about high school students—they really just want to be liked. If they act bossy or rude, they are just trying to get attention. Sometimes, they just want one person to smile at them. It's nice for them to have one grown-up person treat them like they are a person. People don't listen to them. They don't validate them, and I try to do that because I actually care about them; I like them.

Defining Identity Development as Multiple Paths

In contrast to these deficit models of development that focus on individual students' lack of certain abilities or dispositions, implying that they need remediation to foster development based on singular, predetermined pathways, Nasir and Hand (2006) present a model of identity using the metaphor of the paths one has taken, the path one is currently on, and the potential paths to take in the future.

> The activities that people seek out are generally embedded in broader constellations of activity framed by particular social, cultural, and political spaces. These constellations maintain well-worn paths of development that are more easily traversed because of overlaps in practices. This is not to imply that these paths are fixed and isolated, but rather that they afford and constrain particular trajectories of activity. The identities and practices that an individual is exposed to and negotiates along a trajectory of activity support an array of imagined trajectories of becoming. A more constrained trajectory results in less variety in imagined identities.
>
> *(p. 468)*

Thus, while the process of selecting activities and shaping behavior to motivate one's own development is flexible to some degree, the perceived choices of what can be done and how one should do it are necessarily *constrained* by a history of participation. These constraints speak to the importance of considering how students have experienced schooling and examining how engagements in an ELA classroom can serve as vehicles for experimentation with new or alternative "paths."

Exploring different paths entails being open to exploring new experiences and ways of thinking as opposed to foreclosing any of these possibilities. Fostering different paths for students recognizes that students may not know who or what may happen to them in the future as opposed to assuming that I'll never be an x, because I'm not good at y—as in "I'll never go into science, because I don't do well in my science classes."

Based on her notion of mindfulness as a "psychology of possibility" (p. 15), Ellen Langer (2009) posits the need for people to consider what they would like to be without assuming that they can't do certain things. This includes the ability to not let perceptions of unsuccessful actions lead to negative self-perceptions—that because a student made certain decisions resulting in a problematic or failed relationship, that he has certain negative attributes—that "I can't seem to get along with others."

Learning New Practices Versus Long-Term Development of Identity Practices

For the purposes of this chapter, we define *development* as going beyond simply learning new practices. The process of *learning* or acquiring new practices differs from *development* in that development involves long-term change in the ability to consistently employ practices as recognized within and by their social world or institution (Grimmett, 2014). *Development* therefore occurs when students have acquired new, established use of a practice in a way that represents a *change* in their identity. Grimmett (2014) quotes Hedegaard's (2011) distinction between learning and development:

> People *learn* when their activities change their social relations in a practice and thereby give them possibilities for new activities. *Development* occurs when a person's learning takes place across institutional practices and changes the person's relation qualitatively across all the practices in which the person participates.
>
> *(Hedegaard, p. 12, italics added) (p. 9)*

For example, students may learn to adopt a critical stance as a new practice. Then, over time, learning to adopt that critical stance leads students to acquire that practice constituting their identity as someone who is critical of the status quo.

Students may be aware of learning a new practice but they may not be aware of development of their practices over time. In responding to Marjane Satrapi's memoir, *Persepolis: The Story of a Childhood* (Satrapi, 2004), Jenna notes that Marjane is aware that she is *changing* but less aware of the nature of her *development*:

> She's telling you her experience of how everything changes; you can kind of relate to that. Her struggle. When you're younger, it's hard to understand; that's how she came across in the book, she didn't understand but she thought she knew about all of the changes she's going through.

In their interviews with Richard, when asked how they have changed over time, JHS students were able to describe their development as well as those experiences fostering their development. As previously noted, for Ruby, learning to engage in effective debate on the JHS debate team resulted in her long-term development as someone who is widely recognized in her school and by statewide debate judges as an effective debater. She notes that without her participation in debate:

> I would be a totally different person. Speech made me be able to talk in front of people. Debate increased my knowledge bank. I think I learned more from debate than from what I learned in school. . . . I learned other ways of thinking and how to critically think about anything. I don't have an opinion anymore because I've had to defend both sides on everything.

Fostering students' development therefore involves students' metacognitive recognition that they have acquired the ability to employ certain identity practices in ways that represent change or development in their identities; for example, Ruby recognizes that through learning to think critically that she is a "totally different person."

Bridging Past and Current Identity Practices

Given the need to go beyond deficit framing of students' identities, you can foster students' identity development by helping them build on their strengths, interests, and abilities to display competence and agency in ways that lead to development. Often referred to as "bridging," an important instructional strategy is to have students build on their past and current strengths, interests, and abilities to acquire new strengths, interests, and abilities, leading to development.

Building on this notion of bridging, we argue that helping students to recognize their competencies associated with their strengths, interests, and abilities, even those that may seem out of place in a school setting, can be a resource for developing new competencies. During the Touchstone Text final project on *The Absolutely True Diary of a Part-Time Indian* (Alexie, 2007), Andrea wrote a thoughtful, stream-of-consciousness essay about love and the capacity for teens to be in love. Taking seriously the instruction for students to select for their final a topic that was of authentic interest, Andrea used the assignment as a way to channel her rage toward people in her family or peer group who were critical of her relationship with her boyfriend.

Andrea, who had a history of fighting and allowing her temper to get the best of her, began producing the essay as an answer "to the haters," and she then revised and improved the essay for her final project. Andrea's capacity to have a strong emotional response had been demonstrated a number of times in heated classroom discussions about the book and other issues, but this was the first time she took the risk of using this competency of being passionate to create an academic piece of writing. It is important for our purposes to note that she was reflexive about this choice, and in her final interview about two months after presenting the piece, she talked about how writing the essay helped her heal from anger she was feeling at the time and that she was proud of the essay itself as an academic achievement. Reflecting the importance of emotions leading to critique as described in Chapter 6, Andrea learned to channel her emotions over time in ways that enhanced her development as a writer.

Recognizing the Need for Change in Status Quo Perspectives

Fostering students' identity development includes helping them recognize the limitations of their status quo perspectives in ways that lead to change. Students are more apt to recognize the need for change leading to development when they experience challenges to their status quo identity practices and beliefs. In their analysis of an online, cross-cultural interaction between a group of adolescents in India and a group of adolescents in New York, Hull and Stornaiuolo (2014) describe how each group had difficulty understanding each other's videos on the topic of violence. The students from India created a video about violence toward women while the students from New York created a video about gang violence toward new gang members who did not conform to a gang's dictates. The students from India could not understand why adolescents would even want to engage in self-destructive activity by participating in gangs, reflecting a lack of understanding of the role of gangs in low-income, urban worlds. In response to the videos from India, the students from New York assumed that they could share their own experience of gender discrimination with the females' plight in India without understanding the abject poverty and cultural attitudes operating in India limiting females' agency.

However, in creating his own video as a reaction to the interaction between the two groups' responses to each other's video, one of the New York students, Emilio, began to recognize the limitation of his presuppositions about the plight of females in India. While his plans for his own video focused on the economic aspects of his neighborhood, after viewing a female's video from India about her coping with abject poverty, he changed his focus to addressing issues of poverty in his neighborhood by recognizing the influence of poverty operating in both India and New York. To represent his recognition of the value of considering alternative cultural perspectives, Emilio included clips of his own body moving across the ocean from New York to India as well as clips from the videos created by the two groups. As a result, he was physically and metaphorically positioning himself as someone who is attempting to understand the two different cultural perspectives associated with these different worlds. Through adopting a different perspective, Emilio developed what Hull and Stornaiuolo (2014) define as a "cosmopolitan identity" as the kind of person who is open to entertaining alternative perspectives, resulting in identity development.

This suggests the value of exposing students to experiences and texts that challenge their status quo identity practices, giving rise to their reflection on and sharing of encounters with alternative perspectives leading to development. In reflecting on his experience of being a relatively dark-skinned Caucasian, Joshua notes that when he's then perceived as not Caucasian, he also develops a sense of the need to recognize the limitations of existing in an all-White culture. As he notes in an interview, experiencing a sense of racial/ethnic difference serves as a "learning experience":

> When I walk into a room, one of the things I notice is that everybody in the room is White. I'm Caucasian ethnically, but my skin will get as dark if not darker than some of the Latinos in this school so sometimes I'm actually considered to be a minority, which kind of is funny. [Other students] are subconsciously aware [that it's an all-White context], but it's not as consciously as it is for me. I've always felt it's a learning situation when you're learning from people who are not just like you. There's a diverse student population in the school, but you can also branch out and experience a different standpoint.

Activity: Reflecting on Experiences in New Contexts Leading to Identity Development

Students recognize the limitations of their status quo perspectives and practices when they recognize challenges to those perspectives and practices to acquire new ones. You can therefore have students reflect on their experiences with a new school, organization, activity, or event that challenges their status quo practices and on how these experiences contributed to changes in their use of practices leading to identity development. For example, for many adolescents, the shift from middle school to high school represents a challenge in that they are moving from a middle school culture that generally focuses on early adolescents' development and cross-disciplinary curriculum to a high school culture that focuses on academic socialization in quite different disciplinary areas as well as an increased emphasis on postsecondary options.

In reflecting on their school experiences, many of the JHS students recalled positive experiences from middle school with teachers who expressed a personal interest in them and attempted to help them cope with learning issues. They also noted that in high school, they experienced marked differences in their performances across different subjects, reflecting differences in their attitudes and knowledge of disciplinary literacies. This shift in school cultures required a change in their identities as "students" through acquiring discipline-specific ways of knowing and thinking, as well as an increasing need to identify postsecondary college or career options.

Engaging in "Identity Projects" Leading to Development

Students also develop through engagement in "identity projects" constituting a focus on certain sustained activities that build on their strengths, interests, and abilities (Young et al., 2011), particularly in terms of identifying postsecondary college or career options. Knowing that they want to be a pilot, doctor, social worker, teacher, or so forth helps students identify certain competencies associated with adopting these roles (McLeod & Yates, 2006), as was the case with Benjamin and Ellie, preparing to enter the military.

While these projected identities may be premature, ephemeral, or idealistic, they can provide a sense of purpose for students by not only deciding on future education or career options, but also on potential civic or community contributions; their roles as supportive family members; and development of their artistic, musical, religious, literary, media, or political interests.

To foster students' identification of these "identity projects," you can have students discuss or write about their particular strengths, interests, and abilities that serve to foster such a project. JHS student Linnea wrote about her strong interest in observing and assisting species who live along a creek in her neighborhood, leading to her concern about the need to protect and preserve certain species threatened by water pollution and human activity, an interest that served to define her future academic interest in studying marine biology at the University of California, Santa Barbara.

Defining Goals or Outcomes for Identity Projects

By identifying the goals or outcomes they hope to achieve through their participation in these projects, students are then acquiring their sense of *intentionality* based on planned, goal-oriented actions reflected in statements such as "'I intend to go to university,' or 'I am planning to get married by the time I am 30 years old,'" or I'm learning to be "'responsible for myself,' 'having less parental supervision'" (Young et al., 2011, p. 15).

Having a sense of intentionality serves to drive selection of those actions designed to achieve certain goals or outcomes. To help students recognize the relationships between actions and goal outcomes, you can have them respond to characters' formulation of their goals as shaping goal-oriented actions. For example, in responding to *Death of a Salesman* (Miller, 1996), Linda is encouraging her son Happy to define some goal or purpose to "take hold of some kind of life" (Young et al., 2011, p. 13) as part of her own lifelong parenting career as a mother

> in which they are discussing his future . . . this process takes place over a longer period of time than once was the case, often a decade or more, well after 18 years of age. Third, what constitutes a successful transition to adulthood is less clear than it once was. Marriage, full-time employment, and leaving the family home are not the decisive markers of adulthood that they were even 50 years ago, the kind of markers that Linda Loman sought for her son.

(p. 11)

The fact that Happy Loman is reluctant to commit himself to a specific career path reflects his inability to identify goals and actions to achieve those goals, just as Linda's attempt to encourage him to make a commitment reflects her goals as a concerned mother to attempt to support her son's development. So, the ability to define certain identity paths itself serves to constitute identities—as is the case with Happy as "lost son" and Linda as "supportive mother."

To achieve their goals, students or characters need to have confidence in their ability to select and successfully employ those actions to achieve those goals, self-confidence defined by Richard Petty as "the stuff that turns thoughts into action" (Kay & Shipman, 2014, p. 66).

Taking action and self-confidence are therefore intertwined; having the confidence that one can achieve certain goals leads to successful fulfillment of those actions, which, in turn, leads to bolstering one's confidence that one has the ability to succeed. In *Death of a Salesman* (Miller, 1996), Happy struggles because he lacks the self-confidence needed to take those actions required to establish a career, actions associated with his long-term identity development.

Having the self-confidence to achieve certain goals stems from an *internal* desire or need the student wants to fulfill, as opposed to achieving a certain *external* reward or recognition (Wrzesniewski & Schwartz, 2014). For example, JHS student Ellie, who was quoted in the beginning of this chapter, describes how her goal of joining the Navy as a future medic led her to engage in certain actions to achieve that goal, for example, losing 75 pounds so that she could qualify to apply to the Navy. She was motivated to achieve this goal given her desire to prove to herself that she had the self-discipline to lose the 75 pounds, self-discipline associated with her potential identity as a member of the military:

> Being in the Navy had shaped me in terms of my needing discipline. It has given me structure and a backbone that I never had. It has given me the ability to say no and not being gullible . . . you're going to have a backbone and have discipline and get through all of the problems you have. You can't be a coward; I have to have courage in everything I do. That's part of my oath that I took when I stepped into the Navy.

Students could also then recall instances when they successfully engaged in certain actions in ways that bolstered their self-confidence, particularly when they faced setbacks in achieving their goals. Coping with these setbacks required that they develop a resiliency constituting their identity. For example, JHS student Hannah, an avid skier, was training for the Junior Olympics when she injured her knee in a skiing accident, requiring her to shift her goals to address that injury:

> I'm a goal setter. I had a goal to go to the Junior Olympics in Park City, Utah, and that's my goal, and it's still my goal, but I can't go anymore,

so and I just really focused on that one thing and then everything just fell into place—rehab, exercising, and being careful about what I do so I found something I really wanted to do so I focused on that so I made little goals, but I also kept a positive attitude because I didn't get down on myself because I was mad at myself because it was a ski accident. I was mad that it happened and I hated the situation but then I had to have a positive attitude because I wasn't going to get healthy or better. If I was in a state of anger nothing was going to come from that, so I put all of my energy into getting better and finding things in life that aren't skiing. So I had to distract myself. I started working more. I focused more on spending time with friends. I focused more on art; I love art. So I found other interests that don't require knee strength.

Activity: Reflecting on How Goals Shape Actions

To have students reflect on how their own or characters' goals shape their actions, students could address questions such as:

What is this action all about?

What action or activity, related to your or the characters' monitoring project, did you do?

What were you or the character hoping to accomplish through this action/activity?

What were your or the character's thoughts and feelings as you or they participated in this activity?

How did the activity turn out, and what (if anything) got in the way of you or the character achieving certain goals? (Young et al., 2011, p. 25)

By having students write about characters' goals, students could then determine reasons for characters succeeding in achieving or failing to achieve their goals. In responding to *Catcher in the Rye* (Salinger, 1991), Elizabeth's students wrote about Holden's setbacks in attempting to achieve his goal of establishing positive relationships with others. They posited that, given his lack of self-confidence and negative self-perceptions, he assumed that he would have difficulty establishing positive relationships, perceptions that they compared to their own perceptions. Abby noted that because Holden adopts a negative self-image, he lacks a sense of purpose for his life: "He doesn't see the point because no one ever made him feel like he could do something great." She recognizes that she adopts similar negative perceptions, but

that only results in depression, so I think about the people who actually care and the genuine things people do . . . not for what they display to society but the good they are capable of.

Tara noted that Holden has difficulty not reacting impulsively to others' rejection of him as well as denying that he needs help in addressing his problems. She noted that she herself

> was in denial of every single problem and obligation I had. I'd skip school and leave the house anytime my mom was home, but obviously that got me nowhere. I've grown up a lot since then and now I'm committed to my school work, my job, and people I care about.

Hannah wrote about Holden's initiation into adulthood as problematic given his reluctance to recognize that

> nobody stays innocent and when people do become an adult, things that are bad or immoral happen. . . . Holden needs to learn that adulthood is inevitable whether he completes these initiations or not.

She does agree with Holden's critique of the adult world as corrupt, but she also notes that

> one point of adulthood is accepting the things you cannot change. . . . I have learned that focusing on the evils and corruption in life will get me nowhere and I wish Holden would have learned that earlier.

Resource for Long-Term Identity Work: The Theme Study Project

Based on your reflection on your own learning experiences in school, you may recall certain activities or assignments that have tended to stay with you, informing your view of yourself as a learner, providing skills and content that proved essential in new learning contexts. Often, it is the larger projects that engender such memories. It may have been an exciting project that combined math and science skills, or a mock trial that brought your history class to life, or a reenactment of a scene from a particularly dramatic work of literature. Rarely is it a vocabulary quiz or other test-prep assignment.

When Anthony was a teacher at SBH, he taught AP English and wanted students to not only do well on the AP exam but also develop a new and exciting relationship with literature. One major project that supported this was the Theme Study project. In addition to the usual work done in AP English lit (test prep, reading multiple novels, in-class essay writing), students selected a theme that was rooted in genuine interests or enduring questions they carried.

Anthony then supported students in finding three works of literature (works that could later be applied when writing essays on the AP exam) that addressed the theme or questions they hoped to learn more about. Students spent the year balancing the assigned whole-class reading with the reading of their three separate books.

Later in the year, once the books were read, students wrote a fifteen- to twenty-page essay that placed the books, and their own viewpoints, in a conversation about the particular theme. Given the skill sets that students entered AP English with at SBH, about 25% of all students passed the AP exam (compared to roughly 50% nationwide). As former student Einar describes below, the Theme Study project helped soften the blow of not passing the AP exam while also preparing them with the skills and experience that would support writing essays in college.

Students' Response to the Theme Study Project's Long-Term Identity Work

For this book, Anthony reached out to former students, all recent college graduates, to discuss their memories of the Theme Study project and the ways it impacted their long-term identity development. One former student, Einar, did his theme study on the theme of *God Vs. Humans.* Einar had struggled with the high expectations and sheer workload in an AP English class. He eventually passed the class but not the exam, and he valued the project for giving him an opportunity to find success in ways that fostered needed confidence for college. Einar, who recently graduated college with a BA in journalism and political science, shared:

> I struggled a lot in AP English, because I was not as good at writing academic essays as I thought I was. In my grade, I was considered one of the best writers amongst my peers. However, this did not translate into AP English. This assignment reassured me that I was a good writer by receiving the co-highest grade in the class for the project.

Einar also noted that, unlike many of the experiences of high school learning, this project was an authentic preparation for college because it was both relevant to his interests and accompanied by higher expectations. He recalls,

> I truly enjoyed this experience, because I was given the freedom I had never gotten in school. I was reluctant to do most assignments in high school, because I wasn't interested in them or felt they wouldn't help me learn anything. In this instance, I got to choose my own topic and which books to read. I enjoyed the books I read and enjoyed writing about them in depth. The theme study allowed me to gain a better understanding of how to write at a college level.

Angie, who was in the same class as Einar and is currently earning a master's toward becoming an English teacher herself, also had fond memories for the project and spoke about the importance of self-selecting her theme for study:

> I really wanted to work on a theme that was relevant to what was going on in my life at the time. I had recently gone on a pretty scary but rewarding

journey (it was my first time leaving the state and the country, and for the first leg, I traveled alone), and I was applying to colleges far from home. I was hoping the project could help me both process and prepare.

Angie, who would be the first in her family to attend college, learned early on while attending Barnard that, "even the nicest Barnard girls can also be much more educated than you and much more competitive, too." However, her memories of completing this project fueled her:

> I already had a pretty positive identity as a student, but the hard work I put in and the fact that it was rewarded not only with seeing my own finished product, but also with the praise of my teacher, lifted my confidence up just when I needed it the most—right as I was entering a new academic setting.

Zoe, a former student now working with a nonprofit that supports young people who have an incarcerated parent, elected to select one author, Alice Walker, and then read her works to trace her development as a writer. The project helped her consider the ways that art can be used to explore political and topical issues. "I remember thoroughly analyzing Alice Walker's perspective on female genital mutilation after reading *Possessing the Secret of Joy*. That analysis helped inform my thinking of how political issues can come up in literature in meaningful ways." She spoke of the value of spending time really studying one author:

> What I learned the most from the project was how you can see an author develop their ideas over multiple works. It was amazing to see connections in books that were so different. I also felt a real connection to Alice Walker after the project and continued to read more of her literature, including *The Temple of My Familiar* and *You Can't Keep a Good Woman Down*. It was like I got a taste of who she was as a person through the assignment and I wanted to know more.

All students noted that the project served them well in college, not only because of the skills they developed and the rigor of the project, but also due to the identities they developed having completed the project. Angie pointed out the memory steeled her for more difficult projects in college: "When I was writing my first of two senior thesis papers, about *One Hundred Years of Solitude*, I drew on my feelings of success on the theme project to get me through challenging portions. 'If I could write 20 pages in high school, I can do 30 pages now.'" Zoe shared, "There were a couple moments in college where I recalled the author study project. Mostly when doing research or writing papers where I chose a similar approach. I read multiple books by Manning Marable to do an analysis for a course I took called *Black Intellectuals*." Einar noted the sense of empowerment and shifting academic identity the project supported: "This assignment also allows for young adults to make self-discoveries that they otherwise may not have. Reading a book that a teacher assigns one is not the same as reading a book that one chooses themselves."

Historical Events Influencing Identity Development

People's identity development is also shaped by their participation in historical events that foster or limit their development as shaped by "history in person" (Holland & Lave, 2001). Students could interview parents, grandparents, or other adults about their recollections of their experience with certain historical events—for example, their experience of the civil rights movement of the late 1960s and 1970s—related to shifting racial and gender attitudes, to explore whether and why their current beliefs and attitudes may have changed over time in terms of experience with more current historical events or shifts in cultural attitudes. Based on their interviews, students could then write short biographical portraits of their parents, grandparents, or other adults in terms of how their past identities were shaped by these historical events.

Students could also examine how people's cultural attitudes influenced their interpretations of events. For example, Johnson and Cowles (2009) interviewed an African American female, Orlonia Phillips (a pseudonym), who was born in 1960 and who grew up in a segregated town where she was rejected from attending all-White schools. Phillips noted that in a newspaper account of a protest at a store that refused to hire African Americans, the reporter had described the fact that one of the protesters, an older woman, was drinking a cold drink and eating a package of crackers from the store, which the reporter had interpreted as a contradiction, in that someone who is picketing a store would not also purchase something from that store (Fivush et al., 2011). Phillips challenged the reporter's interpretation by noting that the woman was probably given the drink and crackers by the store so that she could be framed as crossing the picket line, an interpretation that challenges how a discourse of White history and racism was shaping the reporter's interpretation of that event.

Identifying the role of attitudes helps students infer how categories for defining identities were in vogue during certain historical periods or cultural contexts, for example, what it meant to be a "woman" or "man" during certain periods or in certain contexts as portrayed in autobiographical or historical fiction. For example, at SBH, in the AP English Literature class, students read Kate Chopin's (1899/2014) novella, *The Awakening*, in which the main character, Edna, deals with the extremely oppressed and limited world that women faced in the turn-of-the-century South. Her feminist views on motherhood and the role of a wife were unorthodox for the time, as well as for some contexts today.

By discussing her dilemma, students gained an appreciation of the changing realities for women, as well as questioning some of their own held views. During class discussions on the book, a key topic was the dismissive way in which she treated her children, prompting a rich discussion about whether or not a mother has the right to put her own life and needs above those of her children. Given the makeup of the class, largely Latino and Catholic, some expressed anger toward Edna and others defended her actions, reflecting awareness of gender identity.

Activity: Reflecting on Identity Development Through Autobiographical Narratives or Memoirs

Through examining their identity development over time, students reflect on autobiographical narratives or memoir writing about specific turning-point events that served to foster identity development. These turning-point events lead to shifts in students' beliefs about themselves and the world that result in their identity development. For example, in an interview, Brady described changes in his identity associated with a key turning-point event when he left his church:

> In 8th grade, I stopped going to church—that might be a changing point. I started to feel more happy because I was more happy with whom I am so I don't get angry with people. I don't feel pressured to feel a certain way about aspects of life; I feel more comfortable to feel the way that I do on my own basis; I don't feel like I'm wrong necessarily. I never really followed their belief system so when I got out of it I was able to formulate my own beliefs and it made me more comfortable.

To gain an understanding of effective strategies for describing past events, students could read examples of autobiographical narratives/memoirs, for instance, examples on the Narratively (http://narrative.ly) site that portray people coping with challenges and difficulties in their lives. Or they can read literacy narratives housed on the Digital Archive of Literacy Narratives (http://daln.osu.edu), in which contributors describe their past literacy development, for example, learning to acquire certain reading or writing practices in ways that changed their identities.

In addition to the previously mentioned *The Things They Carried* (O'Brien, 2009), students could also read autobiographical books such as Anne Frank, *Anne Frank: Diary of a Young Girl*; Francisco Jiménez, *Breaking Through*; Gary Soto, *A Summer Life*; or Walter Dean Myers, *Bad Boy* (for other examples on the website, see http://tinyurl.com/nldavau).

Rather than create what are often superficial, laundry list descriptions of a series of past events leading up to the present, it is often more productive if students focus on one or two specific past turning-point events so that they can portray events through descriptions of the setting, participants, actions, and dialogue.

In preparing to write their autobiographical narratives or memoirs, students could reflect on or discuss responses to the following questions:

In this turning-point event in your life, what specifically happened?

What about that event represented that it was a turning-point event?

During the time of that event, how would you describe how you perceived yourself as a certain kind of person?

How do you perceive yourself now, and how is that different from how you perceived yourself in the past during that event?

During that past event, what were your beliefs or attitudes or ways of thinking about the world?

How have your beliefs or attitudes or ways of thinking changed from then to now in the present?

What things have influenced how you've changed in how you now think about the world?

What did you learn about yourself from that event?

In writing about past events, it is critical that students describe events through their past perspective to portray how that past perspective influenced their perceptions of the event, as contrasted with their present perspective. By adopting their past perspective on an event, they reconstruct how they were perceiving events in terms of their past ways of thinking and believing. Readers infer students' past identities through *how* students describe their past experiences. For example, in responding to Maya Angelou's (1997) *I Know Why the Caged Bird Sings* and reading about Angelou's perceptions of witnessing racist treatment of her grandmother, students gain a sense of how, as a child, Angelou is gaining an understanding of how racism operates in society.

At the same time, readers experience tensions between writers' present and past perspectives associated with knowing about the writers' current versus past identity. Readers know that Angelou later developed into a prolific writer with strong views about racism, knowledge that informs their recognition that as a child, she was beginning to form her attitudes at an early age.

To capture their past perspective, students could find examples of writing from the period of the event about which they are writing. They could also interview parents or friends who knew them during that period to ask them to recall their perceptions of the student's ways of thinking and knowing associated with that time period. Students could then employ language or dialogue consistent with their particular identity development.

In planning personal autobiographical narrative assignments, it's important to recognize that when students from immigrant, single-parent, adopted, or low-income families are given specific assignments to write about certain experiences they never had—for example, what they did on a "family vacation"—students may be concerned about not being perceived or positioned as "normal" or about being marginalized in the class, so they may resent such assignments or create fictional versions (Laidlaw & So-Har Wong, 2013). The alternative is to let students choose how to portray their past identities, for example, letting them write about a certain time frame, their favorite activities, or someone who was special to them in their lives (Laidlaw & So-Har Wong, 2013).

It is also important to recognize that in writing autobiographical narratives, students may experience vulnerability associated with the emotions of fear, loss, discomfort, shame, and confusion related to coping with writing about difficult experiences with drug use, domestic violence, or pregnancy. Rather than position students as vulnerable, for example, to control by adults based on a protectionist discourse, students can be positioned as having expertise in coping with difficult issues.

Activity: Creating Multimodal Autobiographies

You can also have students create their autobiographies using multimodal productions using images, videos, comics, or digital storytelling. Based on their reading of *Night* (Wiesel, 2006) and *Persepolis* (Satrapi, 2004), Elizabeth asked her students to create memoirs about past events as "defining moments" in their lives using the Comic Life comics creation tool (http://plasq.com) to create a comic-like narrative that included photos and/or drawings along with text bubbles that convey both dialogue and thoughts about a specific event in their life. In her assignment, she describes how the memoir genre portrays identity:

> A memoir does not only recount an episode or a memory (like we often see in personal narrative), but also the memoir reveals the person. For example, a personal narrative may recount a first bike ride, or a trip to the beach. For the memoirist, the purpose of the story is to reveal something enduring about oneself. As the writer, you are searching for the truth and significance of the story. Think about the two memoirs, *Night* and *Persepolis*, we have we read this term.
>
> - External Events move the story forward: What do the pictures show the reader?
> - External Responses: What does the main character (you) and minor characters say?
> - Internal Responses create a journey of feelings: What do the characters think?
> - As the external events of the story move along, the main character will begin to feel, see, and think differently.

In describing this assignment, Elizabeth noted that she wanted students to consider how certain events or institutional forces were impacting their lives:

> It's easy to see how things affect characters—in *Night*, it's the Holocaust; in *Persepolis*, it's the Islamic revolution. So, what are things that are going on outside in the world that are affecting me as a person? And some of the kids are really good at that—poverty, homelessness, or whatever. It helps them address things they've dealt with. A couple years ago, there were a lot of them who wrote about families struggling with money.

In her Comic Life memoir, "Neutral Party," Deborah uses her own drawings of people to portray the past experience of the death of her older brother when she was 3, and of needing her "'other half' back," something she found in the friendship with her best friend over an extended time period. When another friend asked her who she "liked," she was concerned that rather than a male, she most liked her female friend, but that did not mean that she was gay. She then experienced an email critique of her statement interpreted by her friend that she was anti-gay, which was not the case. At the end of the comic, she adds that she has "chosen to remain neutral in this time of change and opinion because of this night that happened two years ago. I refuse to let differing political beliefs come between me and my family and friends."

Activity: Responding to and Creating Biographies of Others' Identity Development

Students could also respond to print or documentary biographies to discuss the identity development of people portrayed in these biographies. Students could read biographies for young adults such as Joseph Bruchac, *Pocahontas*; Deborah Ohrn (Ed.), *Herstory: Women Who Changed the World*; Kerry Madden, *Harper Lee, Up Close*; Walter Dean Myers, *The Greatest: Muhammad Ali*; or Jon Krakauer, *Into the Wild* and discuss how changes in persons' goal-oriented actions resulted in development over time, as well as what factors influenced those changes (for examples of other biographies on the website, see http://tinyurl.com/o5ay2n9). In doing so, they could track changes in or goals driving a person's development, noting reasons for those changes over time. Students could also discuss the documentaries listed below portraying people's development.

For recent films portraying identity development over time, student may watch *Boyhood* (Linklater, 2014), a fictional film with an actual male actor from ages 6 to 18 shot over a twelve-year period, or the *7-14-21-28-35-42-49-56 UP* series (Apted, 1964–2012) that tracks British people from ages 7 to 56 every seven years. In responding to the movie *Boyhood* (Linklater, 2014), portraying challenges of identity development from childhood to early and then late adolescence, students could discuss how changes over the twelve-year period represent his development in his identity practices, for example, his ability to navigate between his biological father's and his other family worlds.

Or, in responding to the *7-14-21-28-35-42-49-56 UP* documentary series (Apted, 1964–2012) portraying changes in British people from different class backgrounds over a forty-nine-year period, students could discuss how factors of class, gender, and race influenced their identity development. In that series, some of the upper-class participants followed a set, predetermined path defined by their class status through attendance at private schools and elite universities to acquire their professional role, while low-income participants struggled in facing challenges of gender bias and mental illness.

Based on reading or viewing these biographical texts, students could then create their own abbreviated biographies of family members, familiar adults, or peers based on interviews and collection of documents. In doing so, they can track changes leading to their development as well as factors that serve to foster or impede that development.

Imagining the Development of Future Identities

In addition to reflecting on their past and current identities, students are also imagining their development of future identities by identifying those literacy practices and resources that will be needed to achieve these future identities. Pat Enciso (2012) perceives this process of moving from the past into the future that "'brings the end into the beginning' and entails a projection of a probable future, based on an idealized past, into a present moment of interaction" (p. 6).

She cites the example of a dramatic inquiry project that involved bringing "an imagined future forward" in which, in responding to a book portraying anti-immigration bigotry, she had a class of immigrant and a class of nonimmigrant students create a video-based news program in which they interviewed each other about the experience of bigotry and their responses to the book and then shared their video interviews with each other across the two classes. She also assumed the role of the neo-Nazi bigot portrayed in the book and asked students how they would respond to her telling them "This is MY America" or "Go back to your country!" Through participation in this activity, the students were drawing on their past experiences with bigotry "while imagining and enacting a future in which they could identify the 'feeling and form' of bigotry and resist its harsh intent in their lives" (p. 11).

Activity: Reflecting on Development of "Prospective Identities"

As previously noted, during high school, students are focusing on their future postsecondary "prospective identities" (Williamson, 2013, p. 103). To do so, they could reflect on the following questions:

What are some of your plans, hopes, and dreams for the future?

What do you hope to accomplish in your life: what are some of your goals for the future?

In what ways do you perceive yourself changing if at all in the future?

What may be some factors that may influence how or why you might change?

If you plan to eventually attend college, what do you believe will be some of the academic or social challenges you may face in terms of being successful in college?

How would you cope with those challenges—what things do you believe would contribute to your being successful in college?

Imagining their future identity development involves reflecting on their lives in the future, which includes coping with challenges such as globalism, climate change, economic inequality, lack of employment opportunities, and so forth. To do so, students can read science fiction novels portraying future worlds and compare characters' coping strategies with these future challenges with how they themselves might cope with these challenges. For example, in reading the novel *The Collapse of Western Civilization: A View from the Future* (Oreskes & Conway, 2014), which portrays a Chinese historian's recollections in the 24th century as to how and why people failed to address climate change, students could discuss how they envision their future in a world affected by climate change (Beach, in press).

Or students could participate in games or virtual world sites portraying life in the future to adopt certain roles associated with coping with future challenges. In the Quest to Learn high schools in New York and Chicago, students assume the "identities and behaviors of explorers, mathematicians, historians, writers, and evolutionary biologists as they work through a dynamic, challenge-based curriculum (http://www.chicagoquest.org) (Williamson, 2013, p. 106).

Activity: Drawing on Role Models to Define Future Identity Careers

Students can also write about certain people whom they perceive as role models for their own identity development. JHS student Jacob has a strong interest in politics: "I have a love for politics; it's one of my things. If I felt confident enough in my ability to be speaking in front of a bunch of people, I would for sure be going into politics." For a scholarship essay contest, he wrote about one of his role models, the late Senator Paul Wellstone from Minnesota, who "appealed to me in how people could trust him and how he got people going; he was really intriguing." The essay prompt required applicants to focus on

a political figure who risked his career by doing something courageous. It specifies John F. Kennedy's *Profiles in Courage* book he wrote in the 1950s, so I read a large chunk of the book; in his eyes he doesn't see anything more courageous than someone going against the people that put him where he is now. So, going against opinion of the country, so for Wellstone, at the time, the majority of Minnesota was in favor of going into the Iraq War, but the fact that he went against that and that fact that Minnesota had voted him in, just him sticking to his ideals in that situation showed him as courageous.

In writing about others' identity development, students are making predictions about how and why they may develop in certain ways based on their past and current interests, needs, aspirations, and goals.

Providing Students With Support in Determining Future Academic and Career Identities

When JHS students were asked to envision their future identities in terms of academic and career options, their descriptions reflected a disconnect between their aspirations versus the realities of student success in completing high school and college, the costs of college related to accumulating potential debt, as well as obtaining the requisite academic training or degrees necessary for certain careers. While high school graduates in the 1960s to 1980s could obtain well-paying jobs without a college degree, given the shift toward a "knowledge economy," requiring more advanced education and training for employment, Americans in 2013 with four-year college degrees made 98% more an hour on average than people without a degree, an increase of 85% from a decade earlier, indicating the importance of obtaining a four-year degree (Leonhardt, 2014).

All of this suggests that students, particularly low-income students, need support in making decisions about their future academic and career choices, without necessarily assuming that all students need to obtain a four-year degree. Even low-income students who do well in high school often do not apply to or attend selective colleges (Leonhardt, 2013), with only a third of high-achieving high school seniors in the bottom income bracket attending selective colleges (Hoxby & Avery, 2012). While these students may be reluctant to leave their home communities and therefore attend local colleges, they may not be aware of the fact that, while the tuition at selective colleges is quite high, they can receive scholarships and engage in available work-study programs. This suggests the need for schools as well as these selective college themselves to inform students about these support options (Leonhardt, 2013).

In providing this support to his students, Mr. Weinstein, an English teacher at Da Vinci Science High School in Los Angeles, did follow-up interviews with students who were admitted to college but then later decided not to attend college or switched from consideration of a four-year to a community college given issues of leaving their family or paying out-of-state tuition (Sparks, 2014a). He then revised his activities so that he asks his students to do extensive writing about their specific career and academic goals; discuss realistic financial support options with families; analyze the costs and benefits of attending college. They also collect data to share on spreadsheets regarding college student–faculty ratios, available majors, living and transportation costs, and admissions/testing requirements (Sparks, 2014a).

Those students who are applying to college during their senior year need assistance in analyzing college options, writing application essays, and submitting applications, including information about needed financial aid. Elizabeth has her 12th graders write their application essays in response to a long list of topic assignments employed by college admissions programs and then provides feedback relative to the degree to which she perceived their essays as having a potential positive uptake.

Activity: Using E-Portfolios to Foster Students' Self-Reflection on Identity Development

As we have argued, fostering students' self-reflection on changes leading to development is central to fostering identity development. Students can use e-portfolio collections of their work over time to reflect on their development, reflections they can use for imagining future development or for use in creating college admissions documentation.

One advantage of e-portfolios over paper portfolios is that students can store and organize their work based on certain categories according to chronology by grade level or genres (narratives, argumentative writing, reports, blog posts, etc.), as well as link to digital/media productions (Beach et al., 2014).

To create e-portfolios, rather than using commercial e-portfolio platforms that can be too structured or prescriptive, students can employ blogs, wikis, or website platforms such as Google Sites that may already contain the students' writing. They then just need to add in their reflections about changes over time in that writing in response to specific prompts or criteria. You could use our identity practices to create prompts or criteria for having students collect examples of their work to demonstrate how over time they:

- gained an awareness of alternative cultural perspectives through their literary responses or writing.
- developed the ability to define thematic connections between people and texts.
- acquired practices for productively transferring their experiences across different worlds.

- adopted critical engagement responses to different texts based on their concern with representations of race, class, and/or gender in these texts.
- consistently improved the quality of their literary responses or writing, representing an enhanced sense of agency.

You could also draw on the Common Core standards (Council of Chief State School Officers and National Governors Association, 2010) to generate similar criteria so that, based on the students' self-reflections, you can reflect on the effectiveness of your own instruction in meeting these standards. For example, for the Reading Standard, "analyze how two or more texts address similar themes or topics in order to build knowledge or to compare the approaches the authors take" (p. 31), which parallels defining thematic connections between people and texts, students could reflect on how they improved in their ability to define these connections. Or, for the Writing Standard, "strengthen writing as needed by planning, revising, editing, rewriting, or trying a new approach" (p. 37), they could reflect on how adopting alternative perspectives enhanced the degree to which they revised their writing in ways that improved it.

To foster their reflection on their work over time, Elizabeth asked her college writing students to use some blog posts to reflect on their uses of digital writing in the class in response to some prompts:

What did you learn to do well? How do you know this?

"I learned how to express my opinion. I know this because I was always scared to share my opinion because I was scared of what other people would think, but now I learned that no matter what your opinion there is always information to back up your theory and if people don't think the same way you do then you prove your opinion and come up with things to support you."

(Shannon Saleck in Beach et al., 2014, p. 260)

How did your digital writing change at all over the last two terms? Do you think you will use any of these tools in the future because of these changes?

"My writing changed a lot over the two terms. I became a lot more outgoing in my writing instead of being scared to share my feelings. I became a lot more advanced in my writing skills. I also became more knowledgeable about many different kinds of writing styles. I think I will use a lot of these skills in the future. I plan on making a blog just to talk about things because that really helped me express my feelings instead of not talking about it."

(Shannon Saleck in Beach et al., 2014, p. 262)

In these reflections, Shannon frames her development in terms of how changes in her practices led her to engage in new practices. She noted that, in learning to voice her opinion for audiences with different perspectives, she recognized the need to "prove your opinion and come up with things to support you" (Shannon Saleck in Beach et al., 2014, p. 260). She also recognized how acquiring alternative writing styles resulted in development of her writing identity as someone who is "a lot more outgoing in my writing instead of being scared to share my feelings" (Beach et al., 2014, p. 262).

> What are some things you want to work on in the future in your writing?
>
> "The main thing that I have been deeply thinking about is using my digital skills combined with writing skills I both learned in this class also combined with my passion for film and documentary to create a homelessness-awareness blog through journal entries and a short documentary series that creates awareness and a push for involvement in youth when it comes to homelessness."
>
> *(Josh Hiben in Beach et al., 2014, p. 261)*

In this reflection, Josh is projecting into the future in terms of an "identity project" (Young et al., 2011) related to goal-oriented actions through creating a blog and documentary to address the issue of homelessness.

Summary

In this chapter, we described ways to go beyond acquiring new practices to how doing so results in long-term identity development. Fostering such development involves challenging status quo practices and perspectives, leading students to realize the need for change. Students can also study examples of characters' and people's development in fiction and autobiographies/biographies to describe the nature of and reasons for their development. And, within their school context, students may reflect on development based on acquiring certain disciplinary literacies, as well as participate in cross-disciplinary curriculums focused on identity construction. (For additional resources, activities, and further reading, see http://tinyurl.com/mc99lan.)

References

Alexie, S. (2007). *The absolutely true diary of a part-time Indian.* Boston: Little Brown.

Angelou, M. (1997). *I know why the caged bird sings.* New York: Bantam.

Apted, M. (Director). (1964–2012). *7–14–21–28–35–42–49–56 up.* [Motion picture]. United States: Straight Up Productions.

Baldridge, B. J. (2014). Relocating the deficit: Reimagining Black youth in neoliberal times. *American Educational Research Journal, 51*(3), 440–472.

Beach, R. (in press). Imagining a future for the planet through literature, writing, images, and drama. *Journal of Adolescent and Adult Literacy.*

Beach, R., Anson, C., Kastman-Breuch, L-A., & Reynolds, T. (2014). *Understanding and creating digital texts: An activity-based approach.* Lanham, MD: Rowman & Littlefield.

Chopin, K. (1899/2014). *The awakening.* Seattle: CreateSpace Independent Publishing.

Council of Chief State School Officers and the National Governors Association. (2010). Common Core State Standards from English Language Arts. Authors. Retrieved from http://www.corestandards.org/ELA-Literacy

Enciso, P. (2012, June 23). Bringing the future forward: The critical role of literature and the arts in reading education. The 31st Annual University of Wisconsin Reading Research Symposium, Madison, Wisconsin.

Fivush, R., Habermas, T., Waters, T. E. A., & Zaman, W. (2011). The making of auto-biographical memory: Intersections of culture, narratives and identity. *International Journal of Psychology, 46*(5), 321–345.

Grimmett, H. L. (2014). *The practice of teachers' professional development: A cultural-historical approach.* Rotterdam, Netherlands: Sense Publishers.

Hedegaard, M. (2011). *Learning and child development.* Dulles, VA: David Brown Book Company.

Holland, D., & Lave, J. (2001). *History in person: Enduring struggles, contentious practice, intimate identities.* Albuquerque, NM: School of American Research Publications.

Hoxby, C. M., & Avery, C. (2012). *The missing "one-offs": The hidden supply of high-achieving, low income students.* Cambridge, MA: National Bureau of Economic Research. Retrieved from http://tinyurl.com/ogroa67

Hull, G., & Stornaiuolo, A. (2014). Cosmopolitan literacies, social networks, and "proper distance": Striving to understand in a global world. *Curriculum Inquiry, 44*(1), 15–44.

Jackson, C. K., Johnson, R., & Persico, C. (2014). *The effect of school finance reforms on the distribution of spending, academic achievement, and adult outcomes.* NBER Working Paper No. 20118, Cambridge, MA, National Bureau of Economic Research.

Johnson, A. S., & Cowles, L. (2009). Orlonia's "literacy-in-persons": Expanding notions of literacy through biography and history. *Journal of Adolescent & Adult Literacy, 52*(5), 410–420.

Kay, K., & Shipman, C. (2014). The confidence gap. *The Atlantic, 313*(4), 57–66.

Kristof, N. D. (2012, December 7). Profiting from a child's illiteracy. *The New York Times.* Retrieved from http://tinyurl.com/ar4leb6

Ladson-Billings, G. (2006). From the achievement gap to the education debt: Under-standing achievement in U.S. schools. *Educational Researcher, 35*(7), 3–12.

Laidlaw, L., & So-Har Wong, S. (2013). The trouble with "getting personal": New nar-ratives for new times in classroom writing assignments. *English Teaching: Practice and Critique, 12*(3). Retrieved from http://education.waikato.ac.nz/research/files/etpc/files/2013v12n3art6.pdf

Langer, E. (2009). *Counter-clockwise: Mindful health and the power of possibility.* New York: Ballantine.

Leonhardt, D. (2014, May 27). Is college worth it? Clearly, new data say. *The New York Times.* Retrieved from http://tinyurl.com/lpqxc2s

Leonhardt, D. (2013, March 16). Better colleges failing to lure talented poor. *The New York Times.* Retrieved from http://tinyurl.com/cbtovo4

Lesko, N. (2013) Conceptions of youth and children in the *Theory Into Practice* archive. *Theory Into Practice, 52*(1), 22–30.

Linklater, R. (Director). (2014). *Boyhood* [Motion picture]. United States: ICF Films.

McLeod, J., & Yates, I. (2006). *Making modern lives: Subjectivity, schooling, and social change.* Albany: State University of New York Press.

Miller, A. (1996). *Death of a salesman.* New York: Viking.

Nasir, N. S., & Hand, V. M. (2006) Exploring socio-cultural perspectives of race, culture and learning. *Review of Educational Research, 26*, 449–475.

O'Brien, T. (2009). *The things they carried.* Boston: Mariner Press.

Oreskes, N., & Conway, E. M. (2014). *The collapse of western civilization: A view from the future.* New York: Columbia University Press.

Salinger, J. D. (1991). *Catcher in the rye.* New York: Little Brown and Company.

Satrapi, M. (2004). *Persepolis: The story of a childhood.* New York: Pantheon.

Sparks, S. D. (2014a, June 5). Student motivation: Age-old problem gets new attention. *Education Week, 33*(34), 8–9. Retrieved from http://tinyurl.com/q8ec7rk

Sparks, S. D. (2014b, August 20). "Grit" may not spur creative success, scholars say. *Education Week, 34*(1), 9. Retrieved from http://tinyurl.com/ofn2kly

Tough, P. (2012). *How children succeed: Grit, curiosity, and the hidden power of character.* Boston: Mariner Press.

Wiesel, E. (2006). *Night.* New York: Hill and Wang.

Williamson, B. (2013, June 11). Learning identities in a softwarised society: Making up networkers, self-programmers and algorithmic actors. Paper presented at Graduate School of Education, University of Bristol. Retrieved from http://tinyurl.com/orcrotn

Wrzesniewski, A., & Schwartz, B. (2014, July 4). The secret of effective motivation. *The New York Times.* Retrieved from http://tinyurl.com/qbwbgg2

Young, R. A., Marshall, S. K., Valach, L., Domene, J. F., Graham, M. D., & Zaidman-Zait, A. (2011). *Transition to adulthood: Action, projects, and counseling.* New York: Springer.

8

CHANGING CLASSROOM SPACES AND SCHOOLS TO FOSTER IDENTITY DEVELOPMENT

In previous chapters, we have provided you with illustrative examples of adopting an identity-focused approach that involves refocusing your instruction in ways that draw on students' identity construction for their writing, literary response, drama activities, language study, and digital/media production (Beach et al., 2014). We also recognize that, given individual differences in teachers' identities, your creation of classroom communities may vary based on the social and cultural context of your school and on your own unique identity. We therefore describe how the featured teachers in this book, Rose and Elizabeth, perceived their own instructional methods, recognizing that their approaches may differ from your approaches.

Constructing Teacher Identities to Support Student Identity Construction

As we noted in Chapter 1, *how* and *why* you teach, and how you enact your identity as a teacher, may be just as important in fostering learning as *what* you teach. By *how* you teach, we mean the ways in which you *perceive, learn about, and interact with students in ways that communicate to them that you care about them as people.* This does not mean that you are a peer or a "friend" to your students, but it does mean that you are friendly with your students, that you are interested in their opinions and attitudes, and that you see them as developing human beings with important insights and knowledge to offer in your classroom.

Students enact identities based on their perceptions of your identity as teacher. Students often assume that their teachers act in a certain manner reflecting certain self-perceptions, interests, tastes, attitudes, and desires, that they will be valued by use of similar attributes associated with students' identities. Your relationship with students is therefore reciprocal. How you construct your identity in the classroom influences how students construct their identities.

As a teacher, you are playing a key role in establishing a caring relationship with students. Students know the difference between teachers who "just teach" without caring and teachers who provide support for students because they have an interest in their students (Chhuon & Wallace, 2014). And students resent teachers who apply deficit generalizations and misconceptions about young people onto them. These attitudes lead to resistance, resulting in disruptive behaviors (Chhuon & Wallace, 2014).

Finally, as noted in Chapter 1, it is important to continually reflect upon *why* you choose certain actions for interacting with or judging students. We recommend continually questioning your beliefs and attitudes about particular students—for instance, why are you lenient with a student whom you believe to be dealing with some major family issues while you challenge another underperforming student because you know that she is capable of doing better?

All of this suggests the need for you as teacher to build positive relationships with students based on knowledge of their interests, needs, self-perceptions, and goals—knowledge that helps you focus on their potential for development over time. Teachers who were perceived as creating positive relationships with male students were willing to reach out to those students, identify and respond to their particular needs and interests, share their own interests and characteristics with students, disclose their own personal experiences and vulnerabilities with students, and accommodate some degree of opposition (Reichert & Hawley, 2014). These teachers reported improved behavior by students due to the establishment of supportive relationships.

We would therefore argue that adopting an identity-focused approach benefits students in terms of their classroom behavior and engagement. While some students at SBH reach 12th grade, many of them consider dropping out of school, especially if they had a negative experience in 11th grade. All of the students Anthony worked with, save one, graduated the following year (Cat would complete her requirements over the summer and earn her diploma a bit later).

Rose described how the collective of students was changed by participating in an identity-centered approach to ELA:

> I felt like the project went particularly well with them. And then also this sense of doing something special—I remember feeling like that really carried us through the year. Like that class group got really tight. It engendered some really amazing community building for that really challenging group. I feel like prior to that quarter that class was just generally out of hand. I feel like that really shifted after that semester. It was, especially for a couple kids, a sort of academic turning point that happened at that book [Alexie novel].

Important for the SBH context was the extent to which students who traditionally struggled with school thrived under this identity-focused curriculum. As Rose said about Carlos:

> Carlos, he's the one that, like, sticks out to me the most. Carlos never became an F English student again, and he graduated ON TIME—which is still blowing my mind [laughs]. A little switch got turned on for Carlos that quarter. We still had our moments; he struggled with certain teachers. But he maintained pretty good English grades; he ended the year with a B. Last year, in English 12 he had a B, he did summer school all summer and WENT every day, got like two courses done. Then he did night school as well as cyber high all year his senior year—which just wasn't the Carlos I knew before that. But this was necessary if he wanted to graduate on time—and he did. I think that there was really something, like an "Oh, I can handle this!"—and that really seemed like the place it started.

Rose's Identity

One reason Rose had success fostering a space for students to publicly consider and explore identity was that she modeled this risk taking in sharing her own identity with students. From her perspective, this was an imperative, though scary, prospect:

> Teachers need to be as authentic with students as possible in terms of being themselves. I think anything else the kids sniff out like a bad piece of cheese. It's not possible. Now, I can't say that all oppression is the same, that I would know what it means to be a gay man who is out in a classroom; every context is different. But I had to be "out" as a teacher, and it was something I feared the most about becoming a teacher. It kept me out of teaching for a good six years. Because I just thought, I can't handle that; I worried I'd get fired from some homophobic administrator, it's so vulnerable, I'd have to deal with hateful parents. Yet, it hasn't been like that at all. It may be about the contexts I am working in, but it hasn't been an issue. In part, it is because the schools I work in need my help, they need me to help the kids nobody else can teach. And those are the kids I want to teach, so at this point, this is how I am seen. I'm the squeaky wheel. I'm teaching these kids who are sort of at the bottom of this big school, but then I'm also sort of an intense teacher, I feel like you gotta connect to the family, you gotta connect to the kids, you gotta learn about the kid. I believe that, to teach you I gotta love you but to love you I gotta know you, and I think that the identity-driven curriculum says, "Tell me something about you, as much as you can."

Rose considered why this approach may be a challenge, especially for newer teachers. She explained,

> You're not going to be able to sell it to students unless you're ready to take these risks yourself. If you're not settled in yourself and able to be open about yourself, then I doubt you'll do as well with this approach—and that will be the hard piece. And then you have to be honest about that—it's okay to say you're trying something and you don't know how to do it yet. I'm not good at this but let's try it. Kids appreciate that. If you love them, they'll do anything for you.

As we noted in Chapter 2, Rose adopted roles of friend/parent/therapist, which often made her role as teacher difficult. Students who misbehaved or were disrespectful in her class did so knowing she would never ask them to step outside, would never send them to the principal or tell them to serve detention, so she experienced certain behaviors other teachers would not tolerate. Her lack of consequences and structures for dealing with problems related to discipline was a big reason for why she at times had class sessions where little actual academic work occurred, although this was rare. Rose's ability to create community and make students feel a sense of ownership over the space provided a controlling and soothing influence around behavior and allowed for some of the important risk taking and identity work to occur during her unit on *The Absolutely True Diary of a Part-Time Indian* (Alexie, 2007).

Elizabeth's Identity

In reflecting on her own identity within the context of teaching in a middle-class suburb, Elizabeth positions herself as an "outsider" to that community, as well as someone who relates to students who are disengaged with the high school:

> What I try to do is to let them know that I'm an outsider. I'm not from Bloomington. Where my family comes from, nobody is going to give you anything, and you come to this place and everybody gives you everything and you don't have to earn it, it's totally different. I'm not a mom who has kids. I haven't been teaching that long. So what I try to do is to make sure they know that I'm not your typical high school English teacher; you don't have to be afraid of me.

Elizabeth describes how she varies how she interacts with students based on their unique identities to build relationships with her students:

> I'm lucky that I get to have conversations with students so I know a lot about them. I think that is one thing that I'm good at in my role as a

teacher in a way that makes that person feel like, "She likes me because she teases me" or "She likes me because she never teases me" or "She likes me because she writes a lot of things on my paper" or "She likes me because she tells jokes that only I understand." So I try really hard to be able to be gentle with the people who need that and to be crass with the people who like that, so I do switch how I treat people so that they see that I am trying even though it doesn't work.

She also builds trust with her students through being frank with them about certain realities in their lives:

I work at a school called Jefferson. And we were talking about Thomas Jefferson, and someone said, asking, "What's his wife's name?" and I said, "Which one?" I said, his actual one or the women with whom he fathered children, his slave wife, and they said that what, Jefferson didn't have slaves—he was the founding father. Then we had a long discussion about Sally Hemings and all of the children who actually were his slaves, and that he didn't release his slave wife and this girl just slammed her fist on her desk and said, "Why doesn't anyone ever tell us anything? . . . We're led to believe all of the myths about the place that we live. We go to Thomas Jefferson High School and I never had any idea that he was a slave owner." I really believe in telling people the truth and I'm really blunt about it.

And, because most all of the students in Elizabeth's classes were planning to or did attend college, they noted that, given their experience in her classes, they believed that they were better prepared for college work, particularly given her supportive focus on improving their writing and critical analysis of texts.

Activity: Engaging in Teacher Action Research

In addition to fostering student self-reflection leading to development, your own self-reflection is essential for your development as a teacher. As evident in Rose's and Elizabeth's interview reflections on their teaching, their ability to reflect on how and why they employed certain activities based on an awareness of their students' identities was a critical factor in fostering learning in their classrooms. This points to the value of teacher self-reflection through teacher action research. In such research, you are reflecting on your instruction in a *systematic* manner focusing on how the use of a particular aspect of your instruction serves to foster certain learning (Mills, 2010; Phillips & Carr, 2010).

Teacher action research involves posing a question that intrigues you about your instruction. For example, given the need to foster students' risk taking as described in Chapter 3, you may pose the question as to how praise for students taking risks and even failing leads to students actually engaging in more risk taking. You may then collect data to address this question, for example, by identifying some students who are reluctant to take risks and providing them praise for instances in which they took risks in your classroom. Then, based on their discussion responses and writing, you can determine whether they are engaged in more risk taking over time. You can also interview the students about whether your feedback led them to take more risks.

Assessing Students' Use of Identity Practices Through Descriptive Feedback

How, then, can you assess students' use of identity practices? Effective assessment entails tailoring and varying specific, descriptive feedback according to students' individual needs, abilities, interests, and aspirations which shape their use of practices in a certain task, as opposed to providing global praise about their work or their identities as in "good work on that paper" or "you're an effective writer," feedback that provides little direction for students' future development (Wiliam, 2011). As noted in Chapter 3, it is also useful to describe instances in which students are taking risks, including recognizing their frustrations in doing such, so that you can encourage risk taking.

Rather than relying on rubrics or grades representing global, standardized assessment *of* student learning, we recommend use of face-to-face conferences or audio/written commentary for assessment *for* learning (Wiliam, 2011). You can employ annotation or commenting tools such as Google Docs, Diigo, or iAnnotate for written feedback, and audio recording or screencasting software or apps to provide audio feedback.

By providing descriptive, reader-based feedback to student work (Elbow, 1973), you are describing how you perceive their work "as a reader," making explicit how your beliefs, knowledge, and expectations constituting your identity shape your perceptions of their work. For example, in responding to students' autobiographical narratives, you might describe connections to your own experiences.

In discussing how she responds to students' writing in her college composition classes, Rebecca Fremo (2013) makes explicit how her responses are shaped by her own identity as a White woman, transplanted Southerner, writing instructor, and so forth, what she calls, "the nexus of positions that we occupy by choice and by external categorization" (p. 6). She is therefore modeling how identities shape response—how her beliefs, knowledge, and expectations influence her perceptions. She also has her students reflect on how they construct their perceptions of her and their peers as audiences by asking them the following questions—questions that you could use to determine how your students are constructing your identity as their reader:

1. How did you imagine your audience at the time that you wrote this work? Who, specifically, were you writing to/for?

2. If Rebecca Fremo was a member of that intended audience, what kinds of assumptions did you make about her reading expectations? In other words, what did you imagine she'd like or dislike as a reader?

3. What were your assumptions about Rebecca Fremo's reading preferences based on? In other words, how did you come to "know" her as a reader? What did she say or do in class to give you these impressions? (p. 15)

She finds that students construct her identity in ways that are inconsistent with the identities she constructs for her students. For example, one student assumed that, as an English professor who has taught many writing and literature classes, Fremo has read "'many essays her students must have written in the past and living up to her standard would be near impossible'" (p. 10). This student therefore created an audience identity for Fremo that served to create a high level of anxiety that in turn shaped her own writer identity as someone who could not live up to what she constructed as Fremo's former students' identities as high-quality writers.

Given these misconceptions of her identity, Fremo focuses on the topic of identity in her course, "Stories, Selves, and Communities," by having students read literary texts to discuss how writers position their identities in relationship to their audiences. She also speaks "explicitly about my own values as a reader, my own subject positions, and how those positions affect how I read their work" (p. 9), including how her own use of language and reading practices are shaping her responses.

Consistent with the idea of fostering students' risk taking described in Chapter 3, in giving feedback to encourage her students to keep trying to improve, Elizabeth notes that, "even if they didn't do the best job, you can tell that this is the best job you've done so far; it's like watering a plant so it just starts to grow and they turn like a sunflower to you."

Using Peer Feedback

Given large class sizes, it is often difficult for you to provide face-to-face individual feedback on all of your students' work. You can therefore employ peer feedback as an alternative so that students themselves provide each other with feedback. However, to insure that their feedback is productive, it is essential that students receive training in use of descriptive, reader-based feedback so that their feedback does not consist of negative or vague comments such as "good job" (Beach & Friedrich, 2006). You can provide such training by modeling use of descriptive, reader-based feedback with students so that students then engage in one-to-one or small-group peer feedback sessions with each other.

Students can provide descriptive peer feedback about each other's discussion contributions. Based on the Socratic Circle method, students sit in concentric circles with discussion participants in an inner circle and peers giving feedback in an outer circle. After completion of a discussion, students in the outer circle who are paired with a student in the inner circle take notes about their paired-student's contributions and provide feedback to their designated student. For example, a student may note that he liked the fact that his peer voiced a number of provocative ideas as well as served as a facilitator by asking other peers for their ideas. Students then reverse roles, with students in the inner circle serving as observers in the outer circle.

Finally, students respond to each other's drafts in pairs or small groups by describing their responses as audiences and making explicit how their knowledge, beliefs, attitudes, and interests constituting their identities influence those responses. As did Fremo's students, peers gain an understanding of the need to consider their audiences' identities in making revisions. In writing about her interest in the issue of the loss of bees needed for plant pollination, and learning that her peer audience had little knowledge about the role of bees in plant pollination, a student would then recognize the need to add that information in her revision.

Adopting a School-Wide Identity-Focused Curriculum

Adopting an identity-focused approach needs to go beyond just your classroom to encompass school-wide support for students' identity development throughout their school experience. This suggests the need for more school-wide, interdisciplinary curriculum development involving cross-disciplinary curriculum planning based on fostering identity practices as well as sharing information about how students are doing in all of their classes.

It also suggests the value of having some knowledge of what students are reading or writing about across their different English classes, so that you can make connections between their experiences in these different classes. Elizabeth noted that she made herself aware of the texts other JHS teachers assigned in their classes so that she could have students make connections between these texts:

> I really like it when they make those connections between stories. So if we're reading *1984* in 12th grade I can ask them if they remember reading *Red Scarf Girl* in 9th grade—I don't teach that book—they can relate Winston's experience to the experience of the girl in that book. I read all of the stuff that other teachers teach so that I can bring up texts they read in other classes, so how is it like in that text or how would you like to have a dad that's in *The Glass Castle*, and we'll try to relate characters to characters and try to do some comparison and contrasting.

Given the increased push from the Common Core State Standards related to integrating learning in social studies and science with English instruction, there is an increased focus on reading, writing, and communication across the curriculum. In the past, ELA teachers were trained in "content-area reading instruction," for teaching strategies such as "KWL" (what a student knows [K], wants to know [W], and has learned [L] about a topic) or "SQR3" (survey, question, read, recite, review) for application to reading across the curriculum. However, more recent research indicates differences in how people in different disciplines read, write, or communicate. This research suggests that such generic strategies fail to address these differences in disciplinary literacies involved in learning in different subjects (Shanahan, Shanahan, & Misischia, 2011). For example, in reading interpretations of historical events, historians focus on individual differences in particular historians' ideological orientations shaping their interpretations, while scientists reading science reports are focused more on the empirical methods and evidence.

Knowing about the unique disciplinary literacies students are adopting in their different classes can help you inform students about how they need to vary their literacy practices across different subjects. For example, in writing in their science classes, students learn to adopt the persona or ethos of the science researcher who focuses on reporting empirical data and analysis, a persona or ethos that differs from writing personal, subjective responses to literature in your classes. Or, in their math classes, they employ visual "chalk-talk" representations of numbers and symbols to make explicit their problem solving while the visual display mediates their thinking about solving a problem.

Given the need for school-wide identity-focused curriculum planning, you could work with other subject-matter teachers to create interdisciplinary activities that involve making thematic or topical connections across different subjects. If you are having your students write about historical and cultural construction of identities in American literature of the 1930s and 1940s, you can team up with a social studies teacher who could have students engage in historical analysis of related events portrayed in the literature. For example, having an understanding of the historical and cultural shifts occurring in the 1930s and 1940s helps students understand characters' identities in *The Grapes of Wrath* (Steinbeck, 2002), *The Heart Is a Lonely Hunter* (McCullers, 2000), or *Native Son* (Wright, 2009), in which characters are coping with the Great Depression and changes in gender and racial attitudes.

Based on a focus on identity construction across different social worlds, you could create cross-disciplinary units with social studies teachers on the influence of neighborhood/community, regional/national, or historical events on identity construction. One useful resource site for social studies teachers is the Facing History and Ourselves (http://www.facinghistory.org) site with extensive units and resources associated with the influence of events such as the Holocaust, genocide, poverty, war, and so forth on people's identity.

For example, the ten lessons of the Identity and Community curriculum unit (http://tinyurl.com/ljo7p37) designed for use with 6th graders in the Memphis Public Schools focus on the influence of community membership on identity construction. Students begin with an understanding of how members of a community learn about, perceive, and judge each other. They create identity charts for describing how members of Esperanza's community in *The House on Mango Street* (Cisneros, 1991) perceive her based on race, nationality, gender, family role, religion, and so forth, leading to creating identity charts about themselves as shaped by these factors. Students then use these charts to create an eleven-line "biopoem" describing themselves or historical figures as shaped by their community allegiances.

Students then consider how others perceive and label people, with references to how Japanese Americans during and after World War II in California were perceived as enemies, as portrayed in *Farewell to Manzanar* (Houston & Wakatsuki, 1995). Students also consider how they present themselves to others through responding to the poem "We Wear the Mask" (Dunbar, 2000), in terms of how African Americans in history had to adopt certain masks. Students then create their own masks and engage in an exhibit of the students' biopoems and masks in their classroom to make inferences about how their identities are shaped by their class as a group and/or community.

Students then reflect on what factors contribute to creating a sense of community in terms of members' sense of being responsible for each other based on a sense of shared purpose for achieving certain goals. Students apply these conceptions of community to analyze the historical development of Memphis as a community, for example, focusing on the role of blues and rock music as providing a shared sense of community. Students consider how members of communities distinguish between who is "in" versus "outside" or "other" based on assumptions about normality and difference. They apply these concepts in responding to "The In Group" reading based on Eve Shalen's experience as an 8th-grade "outsider" girl who is invited to join an "in" group only to find that members of that group taunt other students (http://tinyurl.com/q3xk3qs), perceptions that are then applied to historical events in which people such as Joan of Arc were persecuted for being "outsiders." Students then discuss how communities create customs, rules, contracts, or laws that serve to define members based on discrimination or positive support of members, leading to creating a class contract based on norms constituting a positive classroom community. The fact that this unit draws heavily on literary texts represents an effective integration of social studies and English language arts instruction.

Central to the success of such cross-disciplinary curricula is a focus on producing texts in ways that allow for display of competence, as is the case with creating "biopoems" or masks. At the High School for the Digital Arts in Cleveland, students engage in art/digital production activities revolving around cross-disciplinary units such as "Get In Character" that focus on identifying the nature and character of people through analysis of characters in films, voice in music, or people's role in science, leading up to generating their own videos, a game design, and a recording on the topic of character (O'Donnell, 2014).

Based on this cross-disciplinary planning, you and your colleagues could collect examples of lesson plans, resources, and related students' work to house in a central digital repository for access by teachers in your school (Beach, 2012). By analyzing student work, you and your colleagues could then determine the influence of your curriculum based on the extent or degree to which students are effectively engaging in certain identity practices related to their identity development.

For students facing certain challenges, your school can create supportive peer groups or clubs that provide them with a sense of collective identity in that they are not alone in coping with these challenges. For example, students at JHS could participate as members of a number of different organizations focusing on diversity and change, such as the "Diversity Committee," "Gay-Straight Alliance," "Positive Forces for Change," and "Topple" (Teaching Our Peers Peace, Love, and Encouragement). Through participating in these organizations, students experience support from peers and adults for coping with their sense of being "different."

Wrapping Up: Adopting an Identity-Focused Approach to ELA Instruction

In conclusion, we perceive an identity-focused approach for teaching ELA as emphasizing:

- students' unique experiences, interests, talents, and goals for planning activities building on those experiences, interests, talents, and goals.
- building positive social relationships between yourself and students as well as between students to create a sense of community to support students' adopting alternative identities.
- being open to having students adopt alternative perspectives through discussions and writing.
- encouraging students to make connections between their experiences and texts and across texts based on certain aspects of identity construction.
- reflecting on how movement across different worlds involves adopting alternative identities constituted by different social and cultural norms composing those worlds.
- adopting a critical stance on those institutional forces shaping students' identity construction.
- fostering identity development across time through reflection on changes leading to development.
- providing feedback to students related to their ability to reflect on past, current, and future identities.

Summary

In this final chapter, we posit the influence of your identity as teacher on fostering student identity construction given how students perceive you in terms of building relationships with their teachers. In giving feedback to students, you reference how your identities influence responses to that work. To reflect on how your identity is shaping your instruction or students' perceptions, you can conduct action research projects examining how specific instructional strategies are influencing students' use of certain practices. We also argued that adopting an identity-focused approach entails a school-wide curriculum focus on cross-disciplinary curriculum planning around themes or topics related to identity construction, as illustrated by the Memphis Public School's "Identity and Community" curriculum. (For additional resources, activities, and further reading related to this chapter, as well as professional development resources for teaching English, see http://tinyurl.com/lgxwcdc.)

Contributions to the Book's Resource Wiki

In closing, we hope that the ideas and activities in this book help you in reframing your instruction around an identity-focused approach. If you have developed lesson plans or activities based on this approach, we invite you to share those plans or activities on the book's wiki resource site at http://identities.pbworks.com or send those plans or activities to Richard at rbeach@umn.edu who will add them to the wiki.

References

Alexie, S. (2007). *The absolutely true diary of a part-time Indian.* Boston: Little Brown.

Beach, R. (2012). Can online learning foster professional development? *Language Arts, 89*(4), 256–262.

Beach, R., Anson, C., Kastman-Breuch, L-A., & Reynolds, T. (2014). *Understanding and creating digital texts: An activity-based approach.* Lanham, MD: Rowman & Littlefield.

Beach, R., & Friedrich, T. (2006). Response to writing. In C. A. MacArthur, S. Graham, & J. Fitzgerald (Eds.), *Handbook of writing research* (pp. 222–234). New York: Guilford Press.

Chhuon, V., & Wallace, T. L. (2014). Creating connectedness through being known: Fulfilling the need to belong in U.S. high schools. *Youth & Society, 46*(3), 379–401.

Cisneros, S. (1991). *The house on Mango Street.* New York: Vintage.

Dunbar, P. L. (2000). We wear the mask. In P. L. Dunbar, *The lyrics of lowly life.* New York: Citadel Press.

Elbow, P. (1973). *Writing without teachers.* New York: Oxford University Press.

Fremo, R. (2013). Assumptions, theories, and best guesses: Rethinking the teacher as audience. *Minnesota English Journal, 48,* 5–13.

Houston, J. D., & Wakatsuki, J. (1995). *Farewell to Manzanar.* New York: Laurel Leaf.

McCullers, C. (2000). *The heart is a lonely hunter.* New York: Mariner.

Mills, G. R. (2010). *Action research: A guide for the teacher researcher* (4th ed.). London: Pearson.

O'Donnell, P. (2014, July 30). Lights. Camera. Action! Cleveland high school with film, recording and video games opens on Monday. *The Cleveland Plain Dealer.* Retrieved from http://tinyurl.com/m34vajh

Phillips, D. K., & Carr, K. (2010). *Becoming a teacher through action research: Process, context, and self-study.* New York: Routledge.

Reichert, M., & Hawley, R. (2014). Successfully teaching boys: Findings from a new international study [web log post]. Retrieved from http://tinyurl.com/32xg8w6

Shanahan, C., Shanahan, T., & Misischia, C. (2011). Analysis of expert readers in three disciplines: History, mathematics, and chemistry. *Journal of Literacy Research, 43*(4), 393–429.

Steinbeck, J. (2002). *The grapes of wrath*. New York: Penguin.

Wiliam, D. (2011). *Embedded formative assessment*. Bloomington, IN: Solution Tree Press.

Wright, R. (2009). *Native son*. New York: HarperCollins.

INDEX